A STREET PHOTOGRAPHY MANIFESTO

Brian Lloyd Duckett

A Street Photography Manifesto

Brian Lloyd Duckett

brianduckett.com

Project editor: Maggie Yates
Project manager: Lisa Brazieal
Marketing manager: Koryn Olage
Copyeditor: Maggie Yates
Layout: Kim Scott, Bumpy Design
Cover design: Max Marcil

ISBN: 979-8-88814-334-6

1st Edition (1st printing)

© 2025 Brian Lloyd Duckett

Rocky Nook Inc.
1010 B Street, Suite
San Rafael, CA 94901
USA53227
www.rockynook.com
info@rockynook.com
(415) 747-8756

Represented in the E.U. by:
350 Rheinwerk Verlag GmbH
Rheinwerkallee 4
Bonn
Germany
service@rheinwerk-verlag.de

Distributed in the UK and Europe by Publishers Group UK
Distributed in the U.S. and all other territories by Publishers Group West

Library of Congress Control Number: 2024947696

Printed in Korea

This book is dedicated to my family, who are a constant source of inspiration and encouragement—thank you Johannah, Alex, Maisie, Jenny, and Laura for keeping me on track!

I'm also eternally grateful to the members of the StreetSnappers Collective, whose work continues to inspire me and who provide me with the motivation to continue to shoot, publish, and teach street photography.

You all had your part to play in this book!

CONTENTS

1   Introduction   2

2   Find Your Street Photography Voice   16

3   Inspiration and Motivation   38

4   Choosing the Right Gear—and Mastering It   56

5   Develop a Street Photographer's Mindset   80

6   Build Your Confidence and Beat the Fear!   102

7   Avoid These 20 Street Photography Mistakes   122

8   The Recipe for a Strong Image   140

9   Projects   160

10   Promoting You and Your Work   178

Assignments   203

Index   224

1

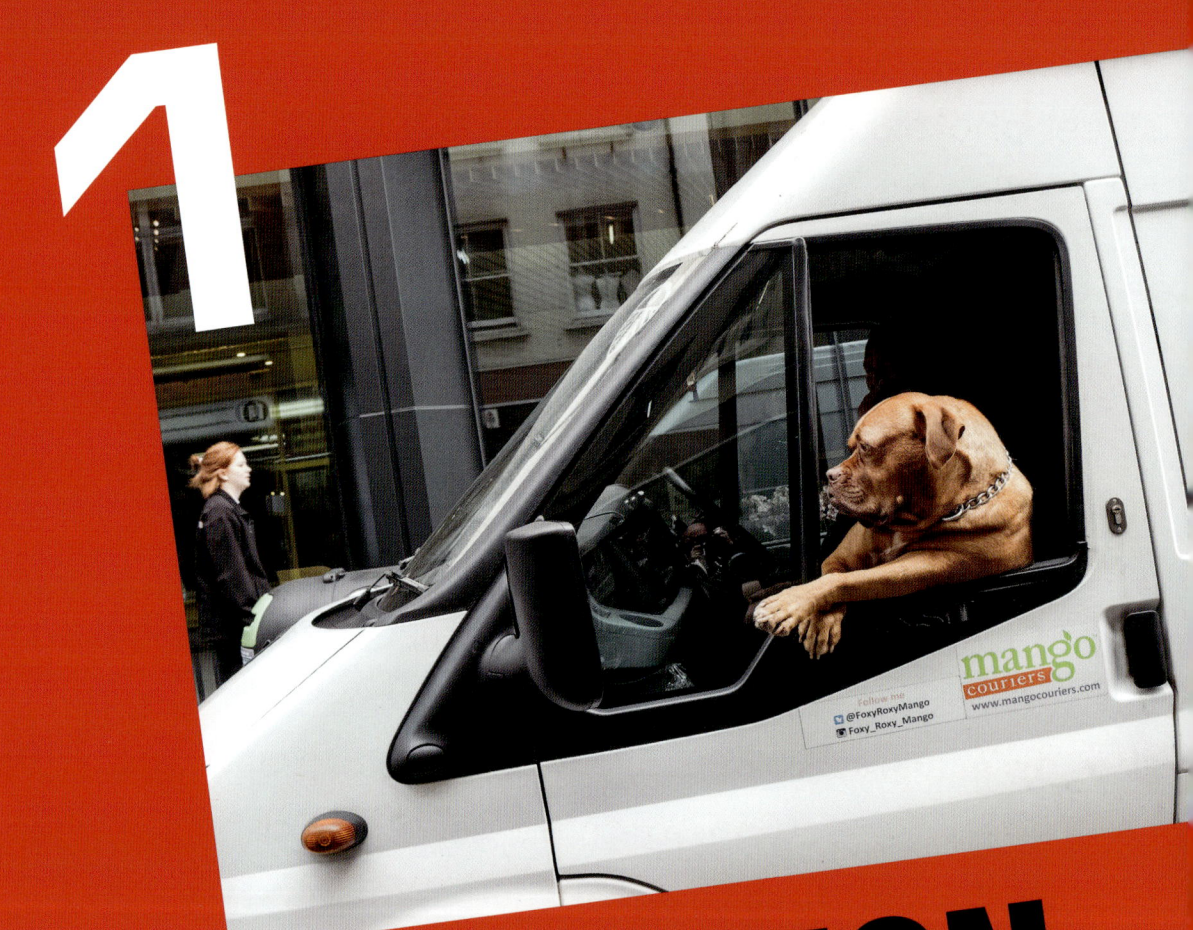

INTRODUCTION

You can find lots of great guidance and tuition for street photographers available out there, whether by reading books and on/offline articles, watching YouTube videos, joining groups, or attending workshops. I'm heavily involved in all of these educational channels . . .

The problem is, everyone wants to tell you something different. The "educators" in the world of street photography (actually, few of them actually *are* educators) each have their own view of what constitutes street photography, which lens to use, the correct camera settings, what you can and can't shoot, and so on. All this often-conflicting information can lead to confusion. Which way to turn? Whom or what should we believe? They can't all be right, surely.

The main subject isn't a human being, so is it really street photography?

Let's backpedal a little. Perhaps we shouldn't try to distinguish "right or wrong" or follow the common pathways to success. Instead, focus more on what works for you. Let's face it: If it works for you, then it works.

I know that for some of you, your motivation for reading this book will be born out of this confusion. Others of you may have reached a plateau with your street photography—you have come so far, but you're finding it difficult to breach the seemingly unscalable wall, beyond which is "the next stage." Perhaps you're just starting out on this incredible journey and want to make sure that you set off on the right foot.

This book, therefore, isn't a technical manual. Let's face it: Street photography doesn't require the technical precision of, say, landscape or studio photography; it's much more free-flowing, serendipitous, and instinctive, and it's something you can be good at with only a very basic theoretical grounding.

So what *is* this book? My mission here is to provide you with a clear pathway to make street photography a more enjoyable, productive, and fulfilling endeavour where you see success (however you are to define it) as achievable.

Over the years I've seen so many people flounder: either falling at the first hurdle or getting to a certain point and being unable to progress. Perhaps they're unable to get beyond shooting images of people walking past walls or silhouettes; maybe they're shooting everything from the hip or from too far away. We've all done it, but we need to stop doing it. Far too many people give up on street photography at an early stage because they think they have failed. The chances are they're not *failing*, they're either expecting too much too soon or they're hearing too much white noise from people offering them bad (and some good) advice.

I make no apologies if this last statement sounds brutal. The truth is sometimes painful, and this book addresses the *realities* of street photography.

No holds are barred, no punches are pulled, and I tell it to you as it is. It's an opinionated, direct, and occasionally blunt set of ideas, philosophies, approaches, and directions. I'll give you a framework to make street photography work for you.

More to the point, the following chapters offer you a way forward, a blueprint for success, a street photographer's charter, the street photographer's bible, even. Let it be your manifesto.

STREET PHOTOGRAPHY: DO WE NEED DEFINITIONS?

Do we really need definitions? Who makes these definitions, and what right do they have to do so? Who cares about any of this stuff?

Well, *I* care, and so should you. Please don't listen to anyone who tells you we don't need definitions. We do, and without at least a basic framework, we will end up with an unfiltered free-for-all world in which very average images flourish and anything goes. We're all better than this!

One could argue that street photography today is swimming in a sea of mediocrity. In this environment where content trumps originality, a world where trends, plagiarism, and derivative works dominate, "likes" are the real hard currency and Instagram leads us into creative voids. There, originality is buried in the morass of pictures of people (often their backs) walking through a shaft of light; yet another picture of a person shot through a bus window; someone walking past street art; or a guy in a suit silhouetted against some offices. And then there are the latest crazes: Let's, for example, make our pictures green and orange and call them "cinematic"; or, let's buy some Adobe Lightroom presets to make our work look just like someone else's.

A controversial view? Perhaps so, but because of the sheer volume of street images in our orbit, it's too easy to get the (wrong) impression that street photography is a very dull and unimaginative form of photography. We all know it isn't (at least it shouldn't be), but that's how it could appear to the uninitiated.

Many of the images we see on a daily basis, particularly those posted on Instagram, lack purpose, intent, or much in the way of artistic vision, and are in no way memorable. They will not stand the test of time. What happens next is they get a thousand "likes" (presumably because they're very "Instagrammable") and the photographer thinks they've created something really special. Then others mimic the style, and the myth of success is perpetuated even more deeply. It's a case of "the emperor's new clothes" where dullness inevitably begets dullness.

A new style of street photography does seem to be emerging—if we can call it street photography. Enter the YouTubers with pictures of buses, lone figures in bright sunlight, and random people doing nothing in particular. Judging by all the positive comments ("awesome pics!" and so on), they are doing something which

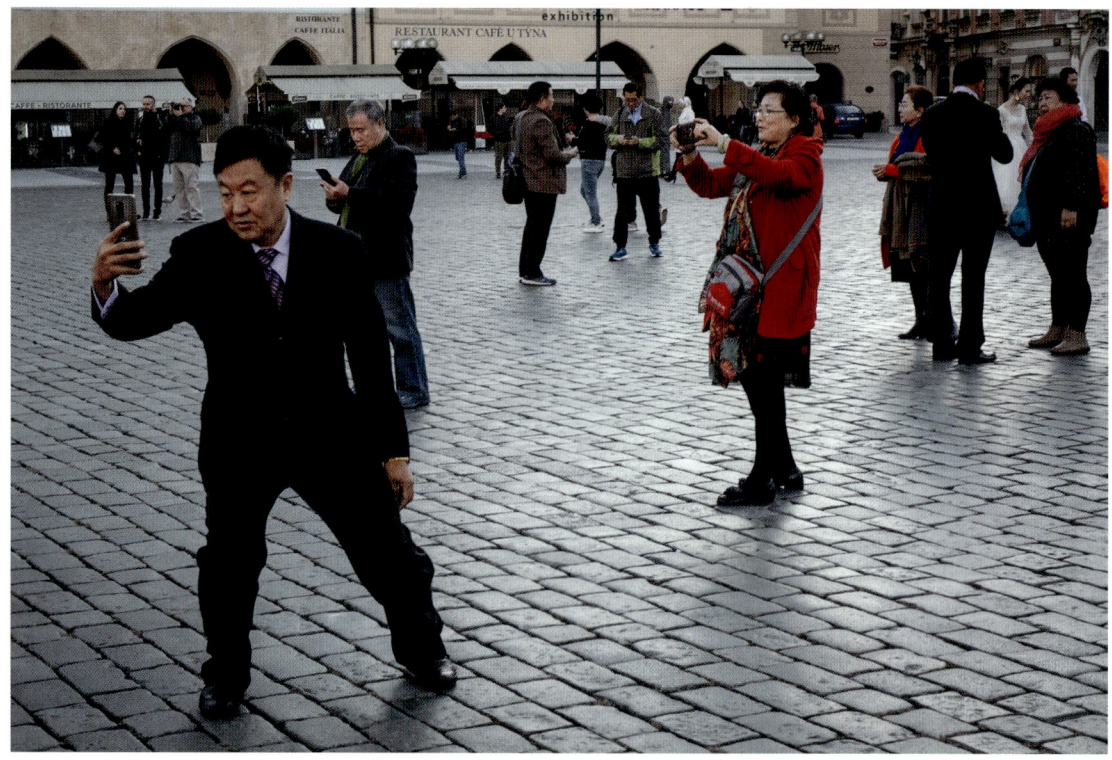

We need to find something to lift an image beyond the ordinary. It could be something as simple as an awkward pose or gesture.

clearly appeals to a certain market—perhaps a market that doesn't have much idea about the true concept of street photography and its place as a distinct approach and a considered art form (as opposed to simply "pictures taken on a street").

But, like it or not, that market exists; perhaps it satisfies a less discerning artistic palate. Maybe this represents the future for street photography. But is it street photography just because it was shot on the street? If a cat was born in a kipper box, does that make it a kipper?

You can see where I'm going with this. I think YouTubers have a lot to answer for (and yes, I know, I'm one too). People who are perhaps exploring the genre for the first time are being fed the misconception that a picture of a guy sitting on a bench reading the paper is street photography, perpetuating the myth that anything will do as long as it was shot on a street. Perhaps this stuff is street photography—but is it *good* street photography? Will it stand the test of time? Maybe, but most likely not. There's little curation and, disappointingly, little originality of concept.

We all have different views on this and I'm not saying that I'm right and everyone else is wrong. I'm an observational street photographer, but sometimes I feel I'm in the minority and something has been lost in translation. Has something happened to the art of observation? Is the true *flâneur* becoming an extinct species, making way for those who make videos of normal, everyday street scenes with a GoPro, out-of-tune Muzak playing in the background? But who wants normal?

Should we attempt to define street photography in such a way that puts clear blue water between the good and the uninteresting? I'm not attempting to be a gatekeeper of the term, and I don't want to narrowly define street photography, but we do need a descriptive framework. In a world where anything goes, the genre is in danger of losing its identity and anything and everything shot on a street will be deemed street photography. The edge, the spark, the fluidity, the serendipitous excitement of the moment—it's all in danger of being replaced by quantity over quality, otherwise known as "content."

HOW IT ALL BEGAN . . .

It all started with the Parisian photographer, Eugène Atget, who documented the streets of Paris with a large format camera in the late 19th and early 20th centuries before the city was demolished and rebuilt by Haussmann. Atget's street scenes were often devoid of people, but it was a start. This early material was so highly thought of that artists and architects would buy his prints to use as reference material for their own work. Atget's evocative images caused some excitement: Street photography was born and was starting to be recognized as an art form.

Hot on Atget's heels (and also shooting in Paris) was the Hungarian photojournalist, André Kertész, who was one of the early adopters of what we could call a modern camera: a handheld Leica, which offered both maneuverability and anonymity. Capturing life at close range with a small, handheld camera had started something new and exciting, and street photography as we know it today had truly begun to take shape.

"I just walk around, observing the subject from various angles until the picture elements arrange themselves into a composition that pleases my eye." **—André Kertész**

Another Hungarian, Brassaï, continued with the Paris theme, creating the atmospheric and evocative "Paris After Dark" series (1933). Brassaï achieved international recognition with exhibitions at the Museum of Modern Art (MoMA) in New York City in 1948, 1953, 1956, and 1968.

A more familiar name was Henri Cartier-Bresson, who was influenced by Kertész and was another Leica aficionado. Cartier-Bresson made a name for himself by reacting to moments as they happened around him, coining the phrase "the decisive moment"—a term which most of us are familiar with today. The term refers to the need to respond instantly to that split second when all the elements in the frame fall into place. There is little doubt that street photography as we know it today can be attributed to Cartier-Bresson.

THE POST-WAR YEARS

This was an influential period, with the end of the Second World War seeing the dawn of another new breed of street photographers: William Klein, Helen Levitt, W. Eugene Smith, and Robert Frank all documented what they saw as real life America. Their approach was edgier than anything seen previously, with images that frequently attracted labels such as ugly and vulgar. Klein, whose images were suffused with energy and movement, had an unconventional style that was chaotic and confrontational.

Robert Frank combined street with documentary photography to produce an influential body of work in his seminal project, *The Americans* (1958). He was a humanist at heart, and he needed to tell a story. *The Americans* was a dark and critical take on humanity, paving the way for a grittier and more subjective approach to the developing genre of street photography.

Other influential street photographers who helped shape the genre during this period include Josef Koudelka, Diane Arbus, and Vivian Maier, whose stylish depiction of life in Chicago and New York during the 1950s and '60s remained largely a secret until after her death in 2009.

This influential post-war period was characterized by **humanism** (with a focus on human connections, struggles, and everyday life), **urbanization** (rapidly changing cityscapes and urban cultures), and **experimentation** (lots of rule-breaking and experimenting with techniques).

"I like to photograph people before they know I'm there." —Vivian Maier

THE NEW YORK SCHOOL

By the early 1960s, street photography had truly come of age; small cameras (usually 35mm Leicas) were now the norm, and the use of colour film had taken centre stage. Luminaries such as Joel Meyerowitz, Garry Winogrand, and Lee Friedlander were the early "hunters" who introduced wit and irony into their work. A key moment for the genre came in 1967 when John Szarkowski, the curator and academic, organised the New Documents exhibition at New York's Museum of Modern Art. This featured the work of Winogrand, Arbus, and Friedlander, whose snapshot approach took Frank's foundations in an entirely new direction. The exhibition had its critics: The move from objective documentary toward "voyeurism and exploitation" didn't go down well in some circles and it took time for these new directions to sink in.

Garry Winogrand was particularly important in shaping the future of street photography. The streets of New York were his theatre, and his approach was nothing short of theatrical. To preserve integrity of the scene in front of him, he presented not like a photographer but instead as a confused tourist, fumbling with his camera as an unsophisticated but effective distraction tactic. When he died in 1984, he left a legacy of over one million images, over 300,000 unedited frames, over 4,000 rolls of undeveloped film, and 6,600 rolls of developed but un-proofed film.

Joel Meyerowitz was also instrumental in bringing street photography to a wider, more mainstream audience. He was one of the earliest advocates of the use of colour in street photography, permanently embracing that medium from around 1972. Meyerowitz had plenty to say on the colour versus black and white debate: "*When I began, in all my innocence, the first roll of film I ever put in a camera was a colour film, because it seemed to me the world was in colour and you'd take pictures of the world as it looked. I didn't understand at that point that black-and-white was considered high art and colour was considered amateurish, commercial, and journalistic. There was a real built-in prejudice and my generation had to fight that fight.*"

THE NEXT 50 YEARS

The last 40 to 50 years have seen an explosive in popularity and have bred a rich diversity in style and approach. The earlier underpinnings served us well and have given contemporary street photographers a solid foundation upon which to build.

As each of the previous five decades have brought us something quite different, let's summarize them in turn.

1980s: Embracing modernity

The 1980s brought a cultural context to street photography, marked by urban expansion, consumerism, and social/political unrest, influencing street photographers to document everyday life, subcultures, and the dynamics of urban life.

Everything got a little edgier, with photographers like Bruce Davidson, Nan Goldin, Bruce Gilden, and Martin Parr exploring more personal, candid, and often provocative subject matter. Small 35mm cameras (particularly the Leica M-series) dominated, allowing photographers to capture fleeting moments discreetly.

1990s: Globalization and diversification

The genre's cultural scope was broadened as the focus expanded beyond the traditional Western urban centres such as New York, London, and Paris; diverse global cities such as Tokyo, Hong Kong, and Bombay (Mumbai) joined the game.

By the 1990s, colour photography was starting to dominate. Previously seen as less serious and artistic than black-and-white, colour allowed for more vibrant storytelling.

The Magnum effect started to bear down on the street photography world, with photographers like Trent Parke and Alex Webb bringing a more aesthetic approach, using layered compositions and striking use of high contrast.

2000s: The digital revolution

The rise of small and affordable digital cameras democratized street photography; people could now experiment and easily share their work. Platforms like Flickr and early blogs fostered communities of amateur and professional photographers, making street photography more accessible.

2010s: The age of smartphones and social media

The ubiquity of smartphone cameras and apps such as Instagram transformed how street photography was practiced and shared. Everyone could now be involved, and photography became instantaneous, enabling photographers to document and upload moments in real time.

Collectives such as iN-PUBLiC and Burn My Eye became influential, curating works and showcasing the genre's diversity.

A more abstract approach emerged, with the use of geometry, reflections, shadows and light to create more interpretive works.

2020s: Where are we now?

The COVID-19 pandemic changed urban life and inspired introspective works focusing on isolation, resilience, and the changing fabric of cities. Was street photography becoming more "touchy-feely" and less brash than in earlier decades? Perhaps so.

And then there is the elephant in the room, AI, which is now influencing composition and post-production. Naturally, AI raises questions about authenticity, but it also offers creative opportunities.

Ethics are now much more of a consideration, with the increasing profile of street photography raising conversations about consent, privacy, and representation.

SO WHAT *IS* STREET PHOTOGRAPHY?

Let's attempt to answer the million-dollar question. For context, we'll start with a widely used and accepted definition, taken from Wikipedia:

> *"Street photography is photography conducted for art or enquiry that features unmediated chance encounters and random incidents within public places, usually with the aim of capturing images at a decisive or poignant moment by careful framing and timing."*

So, street photography is very likely to be candid, unstaged, unmediated—a situation encountered and photographed spontaneously as it evolves.

Street photography came of age in the post-war years, reaching a crescendo in the mid-60s in New York, consisting largely of black-and-white images shot with a 35mm Leica. Colour eventually came along, popularized in no small way by the great Joel Meyerowitz.

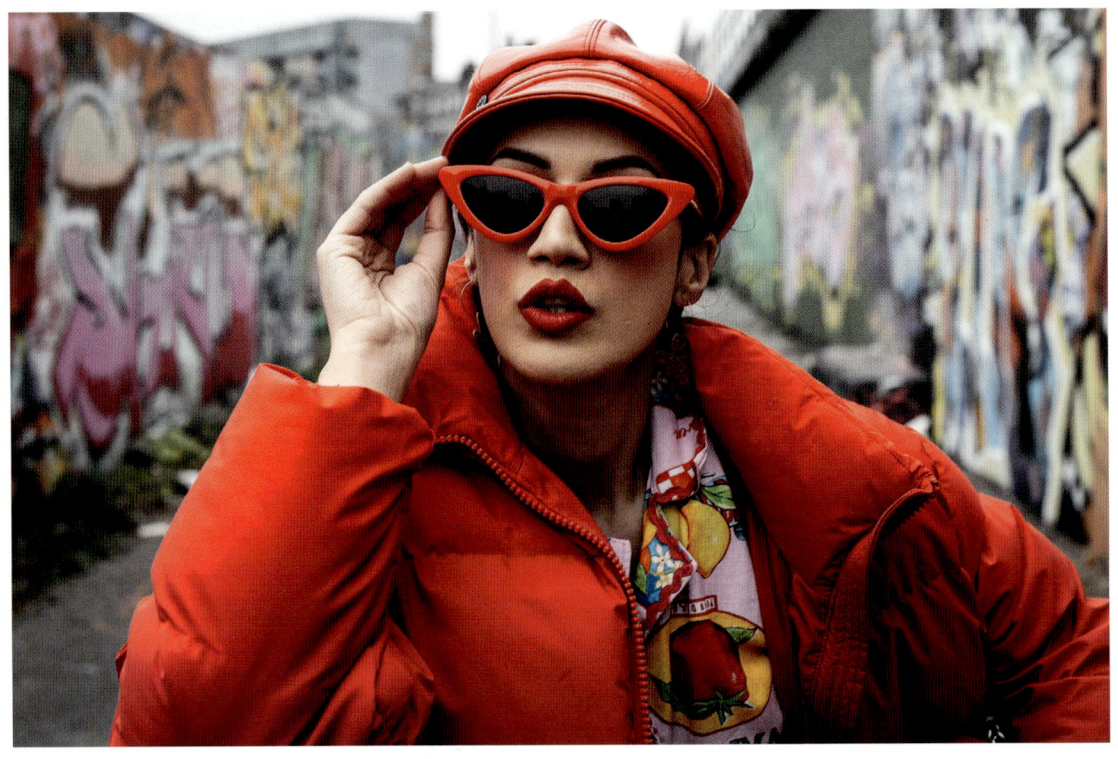

Street portraits tend to polarize opinion. They're shot on the street, but are they street photography? Purists would argue that they're not; I would suggest they are, albeit in the margins of the genre.

There was (and in many ways there still is) a strong brotherhood between street photography and documentary photography. However, as the years went by definitions broadened, as did the boundaries of acceptability. Whether the purists like it or not, we now have a very broad church in which widely differing styles and approaches can comfortably coexist.

There are so many questions to answer: Does street photography need to include people? Should it always be candid? Does it have to be shot on a street? This book will help answer some of these questions, but perhaps you need to work out the answers for yourself. As a starting point, street photography should contain most of the following elements:

- **Candid:** The subjects are usually unaware of the photographer, ensuring naturalness, spontaneity, and authenticity.

- **Shot in a public place:** Street photographers typically shoot in streets, squares, parks, markets, stations—any area the public has easy access to.

- **Contains a human element:** Whilst people are often (but not always) the focal point of the image, we can also focus our attention on objects, architecture, or patterns that catch our eye (in this case, some evidence of humanity is usually required).

- **Conveys some emotion and/or storytelling:** A good street photo often elicits an emotional response or tells a story.

- **Captures normal everyday moments:** The photo highlights the beauty and complexity, and often the mundanity, of ordinary life.

- **Unplanned:** Unlike photography that is set up, street photography thrives on unpredictability and serendipity.

WHERE DO YOU FIT IN?

Finding your place in this confusing world is by no means easy. Looking back to my own humble beginnings, there was no doubt that I was attracted to the humorous elements of street photography. Maybe I was a comedian in a previous life, always needing to entertain and be the funny guy.

Fast-forward to today, and I still enjoy a mischievous and playful style of street photography. This has always been a common thread through my work, certainly during the past 20 years or so. However, as I get older, I'm feeling slightly more magnetized to a more aesthetic style of street photography, inspired by photographers such as Harry Gruyaert, Ernst Haas, and Saul Leiter. Even so, I don't think that the inner joker will ever leave me.

But let's get back to you. A lot has been written about the importance of finding your voice. On the one hand, having a distinctive voice, assuming it's a strong one, is more likely to bring you success, whether one measures success by notoriety, personal fulfilment, or some other factor. On the other hand, I would not suggest being too hasty or impatient about finding your voice, particularly if you're fairly new to street photography. If you become too fixated with a particular style at an early stage, then you probably haven't given yourself the time and space to experiment, explore, and think.

So don't rush in headfirst, proclaiming to be the next Saul Leiter or Daido Moriyama; spend time exploring what you're good at, what you enjoy shooting, what sort of pictures you enjoy looking at, how you want to be perceived, and even what your photographic legacy might look like. This up-front cognitive investment will be time well spent.

WHY BE A STREET PHOTOGRAPHER?

To be a street photographer is to capture authentic moments, to document real life, to tell stories, to make beautiful art, to connect with the world, and to be constantly challenged without knowing what is around that next corner.

If you're the sort of photographer who likes people, is curious, is creative, and is a free thinker who doesn't always want to follow the rules, you've probably found the right photographic genre!

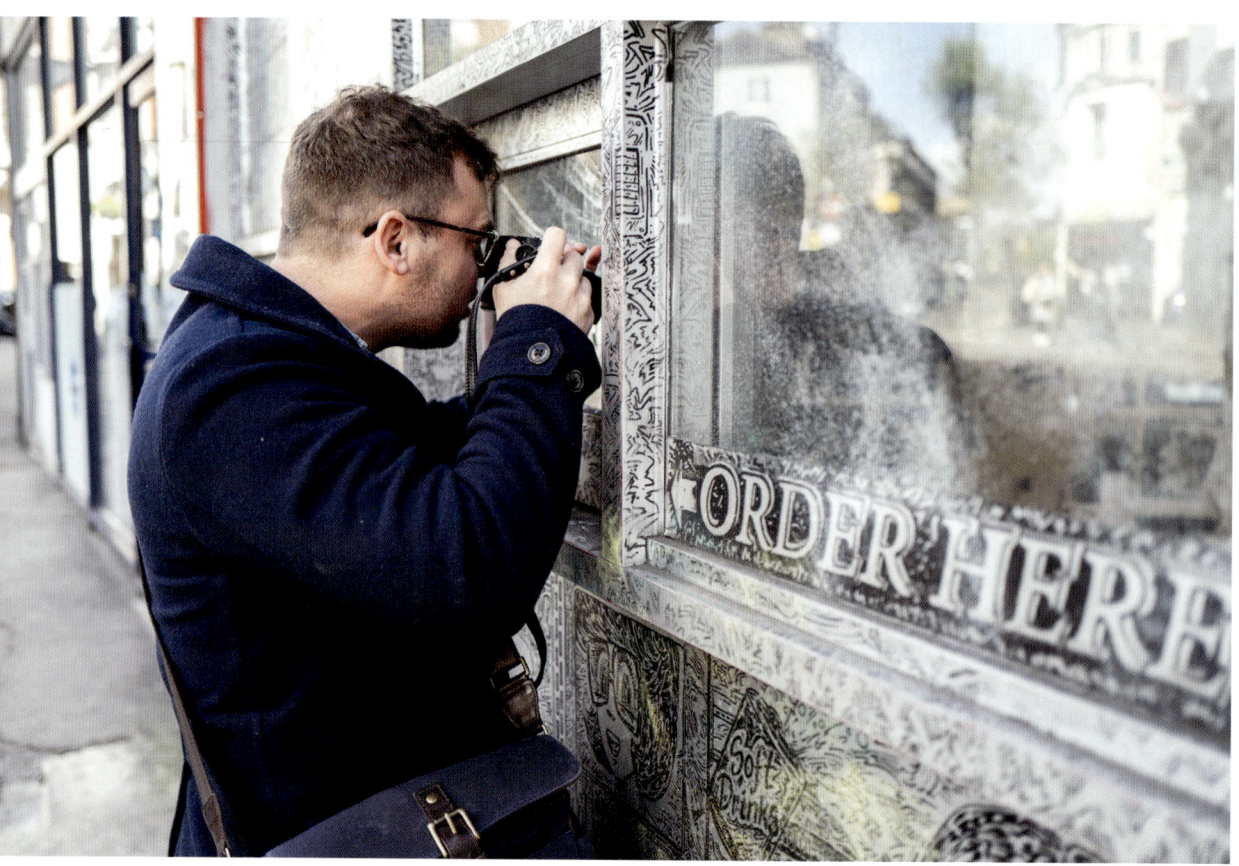

Be prepared for solitude, potential confrontation, and walking many miles in all kinds of weather. Is it worth it? Of course it is!

IS STREET PHOTOGRAPHY FOR YOU?

As you are investing time in reading this book, I sincerely hope so! For some people it's a natural choice. Others take a while to really get into it, but eventually everything starts to fall into place. Some try it and then decide it's not for them. Many wouldn't even try. Assuming you fall into one of the first two categories, it's worth spending a little time analyzing the qualities you need to be a *good* street photographer (see Chapter 3). Think about these qualities and try to work out where any skill gaps are: This should help you put together a rudimentary self-development plan.

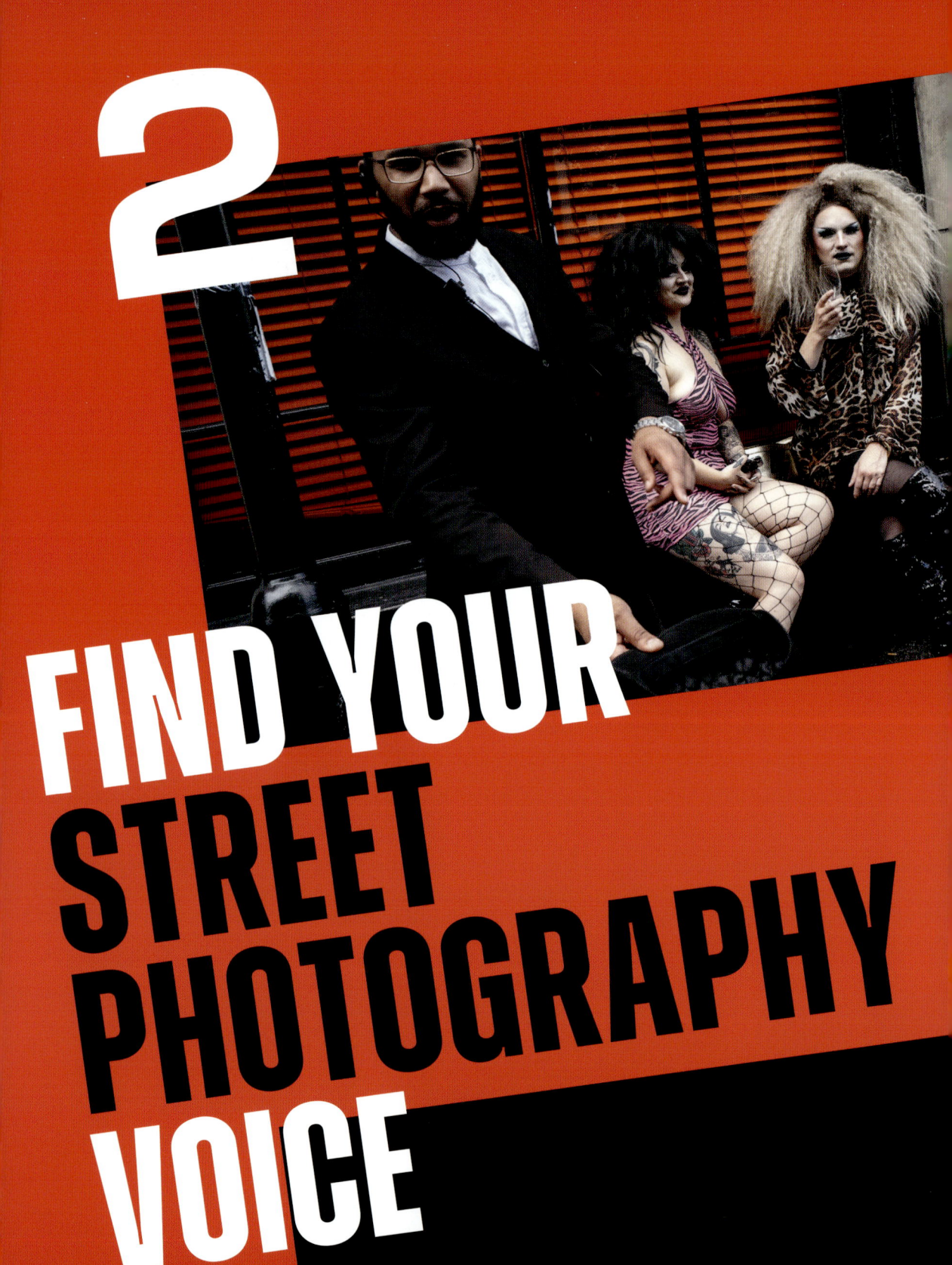

2

FIND YOUR STREET PHOTOGRAPHY VOICE

Let's clarify one thing: Whatever you do, it's probably been done before. Note the use of "probably." Not many of us have a truly *unique* voice, and that's fine. You have probably heard a lot about how photographers should develop their voice; I think this is something we should always keep in mind, but I do think it is easier said than done. Being pragmatic, it's perhaps more about *tone of voice*.

Notwithstanding the above, one of the questions I am frequently asked is: "*How can I find my voice as a street photographer?*" Whilst there is no easy answer to this question, there's plenty you can do to help develop your voice.

There are many ways a photographer can express his or her voice. I think my own voice originated from a desire to make people smile—though today there are, of course, several sub-strands to this voice.

WHAT IS YOUR "VOICE?"

This refers to your unique personal style, artistic vision, interpretation, perspective, and creative expression, which set your work apart from someone else's. Your photographic voice will usually contain several components:

- **Choice of subject:** The consistent themes or types of subjects you gravitate toward. For example: candid observations, street portraits, low-light photography, urban landscapes, or abstract street photography.

- **Interpretation:** Your perspective, point of view, or angle from which images are captured (sometimes determined by your choice of lens). For example: wide scenes, images shot from the hip, or close-ups.

- **Composition:** How you organize elements in a frame. For example: Dutch tilt, leading lines, square compositions, geometric compositions (such as Harry Gruyaert's), rule of thirds, vertical compositions (a big part of Saul Leiter's voice), or even breaking the conventional rules (like William Klein).

- **Lighting:** Natural light, low light, shadows, silhouettes, or dramatic contrast (a major component in Alex Webb's voice).

- **Colour:** Choice of colour tones and shades, such as vibrant hues, complementary colours (like Saul Leiter, whose colour palette was often based on reds, oranges, and yellows), or monochrome (like Trent Parke or Daido Moriyama).

- **Mood, atmosphere, or emotion:** The feeling conveyed by the images. For example: playful (Elliott Erwitt), melancholic (Bruce Davidson), shocking (Weegee), or confrontational (Bruce Gilden).

- **Post-production:** A distinctive editing style. For example: based on color grading, contrast, or grain.

- **Intent:** The messages or the deeper purpose behind the work. For example: to document, inspire, or provoke thought.

Your voice as a photographer evolves over time as you experiment, refine your style, and explore what resonates with you most. As a street photographer, your voice might emerge from the unique way you observe and capture everyday life, from fleeting moments to unspoken stories on the streets.

WHY DOES THIS MATTER?

"*I knew that was one of your pictures as soon as I saw it.*" What a great phrase to hear. In fact, there's no better compliment. For someone to say that about my work, it means I have a distinctive voice: a voice that's unique to me. *My* voice.

No matter how much of a technical wizard you are, how many megapixels your camera has, or how amazing your photographs are, it's your voice that sets your work apart from everyone else's. It's part of your photographic DNA, and it's what defines you.

Finding your voice using the spoken word is relatively straightforward. You can create a tone of voice by the use of the words themselves, their tone, volume, inflection, accent, pitch, and clarity; even the shape of your mouth can affect the outcome.

Language is an integral part of our everyday life, and we don't usually give it a second thought. When communicating with others verbally, we are often on autopilot. Spoken verbal communication relies on shared dictionaries, where meaning can be cross-referenced or explained when there is uncertainty. There is always room for miscommunication, but broadly words and written text, such as you are reading now, are a very effective and efficient way to translate meaning.

BASE YOUR VOICE ON THE RIGHT APPROACH

Without revisiting the conversation about definitions, let's explore the three main approaches to street photography (of course, one could argue that there are more than three approaches, but let's keep things simple).

Whilst it's perfectly possible to practice all three, most street photographers will set themselves toward one dominant style of shooting. If you're at the beginning of your street photography journey, you'll almost certainly be experimenting, figuring out what works and what doesn't, discovering what you enjoy and what you prefer to avoid, and thus finding a direction that suits your artistic taste, your preferred way of shooting, and your personality.

There is no right or wrong approach, and what works for me may not work for you. If we asked Bruce Gilden to shoot in the style of Saul Leiter, I'm sure he would be quite lost—and vice versa. Both photographers have carved out their own approach and have rarely deviated from it, right from their distant beginnings.

THE OBSERVATIONAL APPROACH

This approach really started with Henri Cartier-Bresson back in 1952 with his seminal book, *Images à la Sauvette*. The book was later titled *The Decisive Moment* for its English-language audience, though the original title actually translates to something like "images on the sly" or "hastily taken images."

We can attribute the genesis of this approach to Cartier-Bresson, who said: *"To me, photography is the simultaneous recognition, in a fraction of a second, of the significance of an event as well as of a precise organization of forms which give that event its proper expression."*

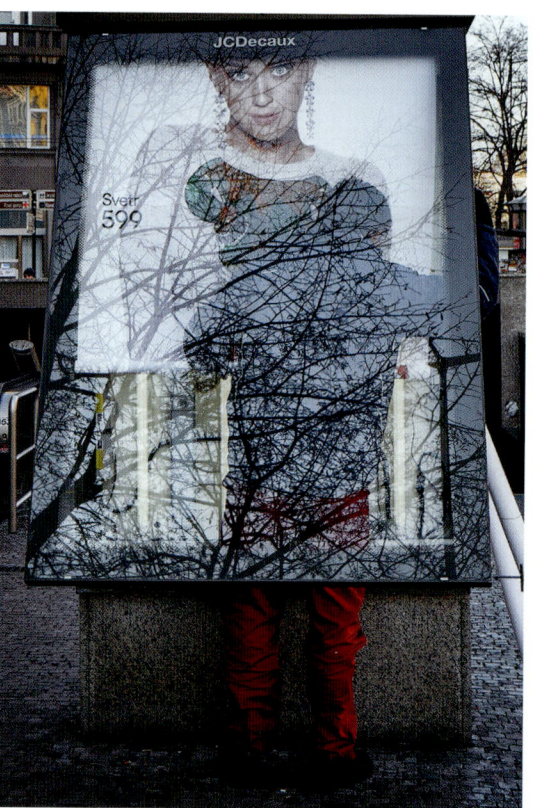

Left: We all need powers of observation that go way beyond those of "normal" people. If you're walking along the street with non-photographer friends and you point out something unusual, they'll probably say something like: *"Wow, how did you see that?"*

Opposite: Many people will automatically associate street photography with humour. It's by no means and essential ingredient, but it's difficult to ignore opportunities like this photo, which was shot in Prague.

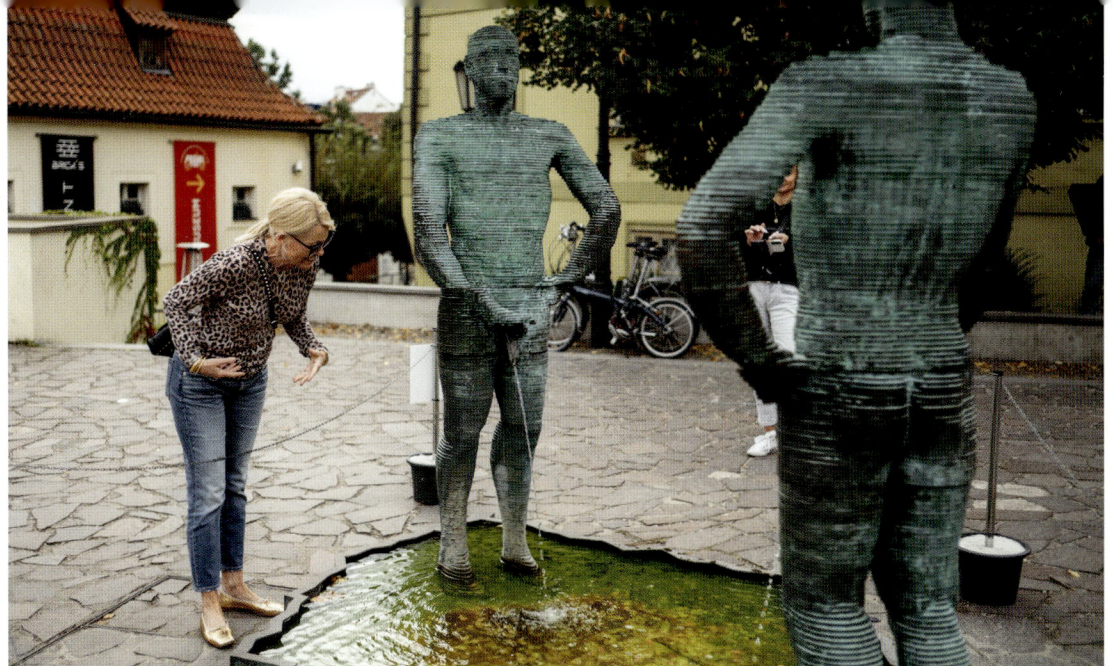

He went on to add: *"Photography is not like painting. There is a creative fraction of a second when you are taking a picture. Your eye must see a composition or an expression that life itself offers you, and you must know with intuition when to click the camera. That is the moment the photographer is creative. Oop! The Moment! Once you miss it, it is gone forever."*

We could call this the traditional or the classical approach to street photography, and it is as popular today as it has always been. Following in Cartier-Bresson's footsteps were others, like Klein, Erwitt, Meyerowitz, and Winogrand, who helped cement this solid foundation for the future direction of street photography. By the mid to late 1960s, street photography had truly come of age and a candid, observational style was gaining momentum.

The role of humour

This approach often relies on an element of humour. At a fundamental level, humour in street photography is created by an interplay between an image's visual elements and the viewer's cognitive processes, often when there is a deviation from established expectations or norms. This is commonly expressed in the form of visual juxtapositions or contrasting elements, such as photographing a person outside of their normal context.

Those who bring humour into their street photography look for absurdities, contrasts, ironies, whimsy, or sarcasm; there's often an element of the unusual in the usual, or the extraordinary in the ordinary.

Juxtaposition

Juxtaposition in street photography refers to the placement of contrasting elements within a frame to create an amusing or visually compelling image. These contrasts could be evocative or provocative or they could highlight a particular narrative, whether personal, cultural, or social.

A note of caution: It's easy to fall into cliché territory with juxtapositions. We see these easy win shots all the time: a homeless person walking past a Rolls-Royce, an obese person walking past a health food shop, and so on. These tropes have been done to death, and we need to try harder to find something more interesting or funny to shoot.

Essentially, your juxtaposition should make a statement through difference or contrast. This is how, through our ability to observe and make connections, we can bring order to an otherwise chaotic street scene.

Then we have signs to play with. Urban streets are dominated by the written word: posters, street signs, banners, graphics in shop windows, advertising on buses and metros, and public information notices. Street photographers have always used this raw material to make witty connections between the words (or objects) and the people or things close to them; with a bit of luck, these connections can be playful, whimsical, mildly witty, or hilarious. Look at every single sign you see, then think about the creative possibilities and about what other element you need to make the sign work for you. Sometimes, the sign on its own is enough to make a smile-inducing image!

The in-your-face style

This is a close-up, bold, and confrontational approach that is pretty raw. This approach is intrusive (if not invasive), often heightened by the use of a wide-angle lens (usually 24mm or 28mm) and very often a burst of flash. Whilst the thought of doing this makes some photographers uncomfortable, it does seem to get a lot of us revved up. Is it ethical? That's questionable, but on balance, I would say yes, why not? If you're out in public, then you have no expectation of privacy and are therefore fair game for photographers. For inspiration, look no further than Bruce Gilden, Mark Cohen, or Garry Winogrand.

Street still life

Street photography doesn't always require the presence of human beings. Street still life can be great fun to shoot, and it just needs a good observational eye to spot the opportunities.

Look for abandoned items, things out of place, funny signs, objects out of context, or small details that just make you smile.

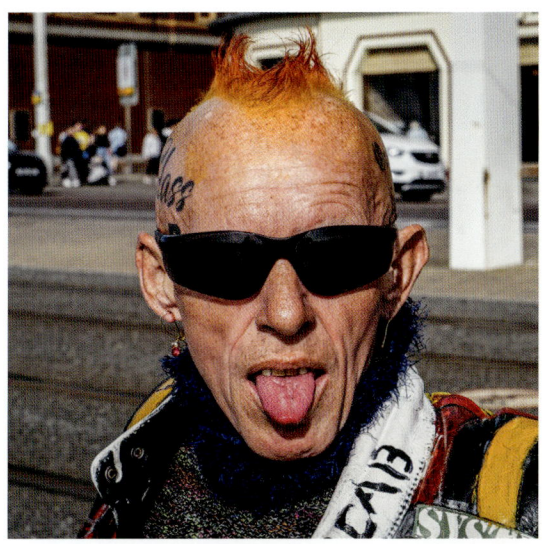

Left: The "up close and personal" style is not for the faint-hearted and it takes a fair bit of courage. This is best done as part of a project—who wants to see random close-ups of strangers?

Below: If you're at all nervous about shooting people, this is a great way to ease yourself into street photography: an abandoned toilet is never going to pick an argument with you!

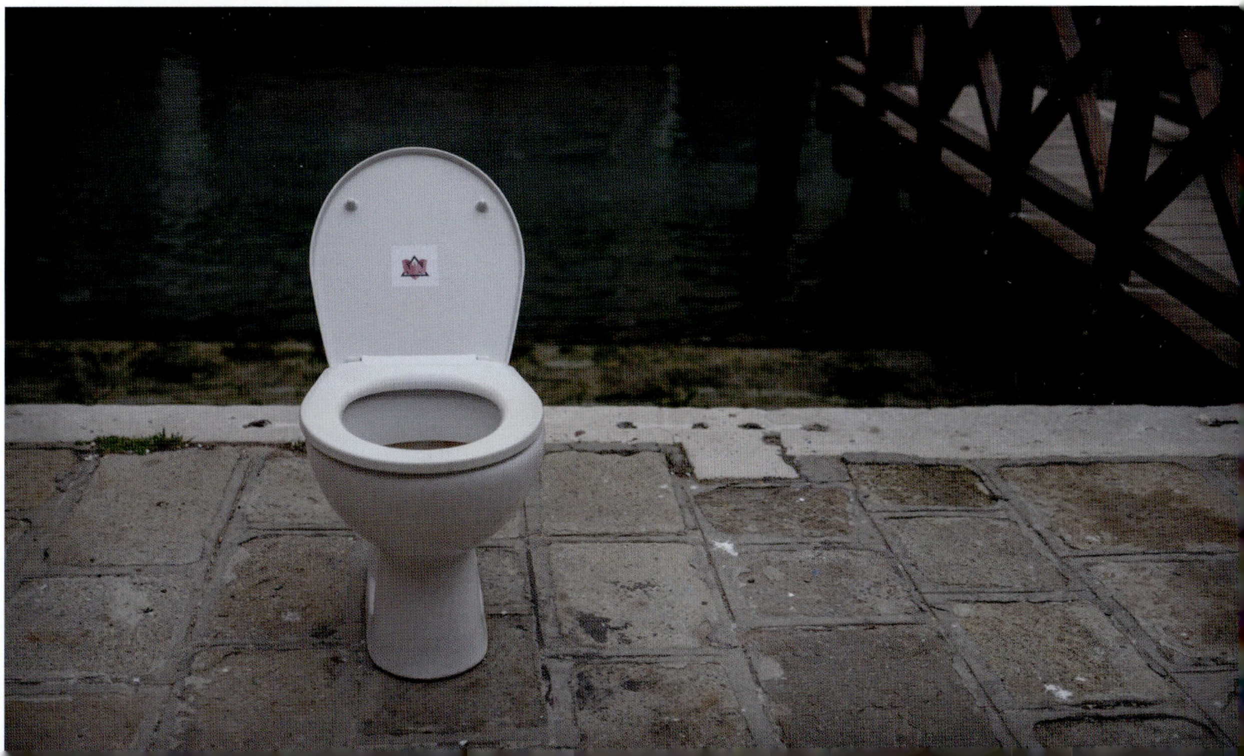

THE NARRATIVE APPROACH

Whilst storytelling is often associated more with documentary than street photography, it has always had a part to play in our genre, and this is perfectly illustrated by Robert Frank in his book, *The Americans*. In this seminal work, Frank travelled across the USA in the 1950s, shooting what we would now refer to as social documentary footage.

If you like to convey messages or make a point with your street photography, then this is perhaps the approach for you. Convention dictates that with the observational approach to street photography our images should be unstaged and unmediated. With this approach, the starting point is usually knowing what the story is—and how you plan to tell it.

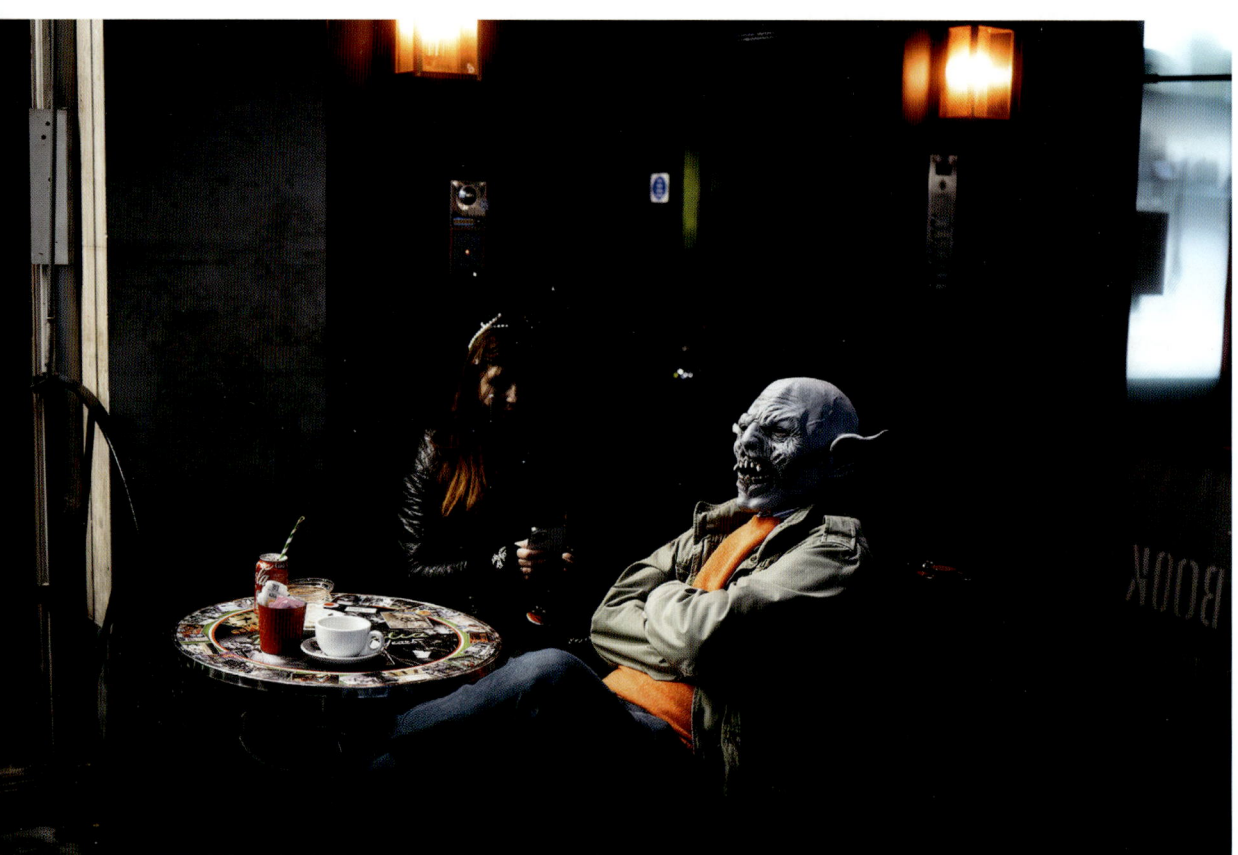

When working on a narrative-based project, I always have a clear idea of what the story is about and I try to build a mental story-board of what the images will look like and how they will work together.

It is useful here to make a distinction between documentary street photography and photojournalism; the latter is often free from bias and the story is usually told as it is. With street photography, however, we have more artistic freedom to express a point of view.

"I have been frequently accused of deliberately twisting subject matter to my point of view. Above all, I know that life for a photographer cannot be a matter of indifference. Opinion often consists of a kind of criticism. But criticism can come out of love." **—Robert Frank**

However, it's not necessarily easy to convey a narrative using a single image—hence the use of projects to help tell our stories (see Chapter 9). The starting point should be a strong concept—a central idea or theme—that you should be able to articulate in a sentence, for example: "In my ongoing project, Darkside, I'm aiming to portray a more sinister side to London's Soho neighbourhood."

Themes may not always be immediately obvious across your work, and they may evolve over time as a bank of pictures develops. I periodically look through my archive for patterns, grouping together images with a similar theme and considering whether I can bring them together as part of a story.

Humanist street photography

It is worth mentioning humanist street photography, which is closely related to this narrative approach. This branch of street photography is concerned more broadly with everyday human experience—"the human condition." Think of it as the sociology of street photography. The genre has been in decline since the 1970s, but there does seem to be a resurgence.

When we think of humanism, photographers such as Henri Cartier-Bresson, Brassaï, Robert Doisneau, and Elliott Erwitt come to mind. They were interested in recording the shared experiences that connect people, regardless of their backgrounds, encouraging empathy and understanding while documenting the subtleties of human life that might otherwise go unnoticed.

Humanist street photography usually has these key components:

- **Emotion and human connection:** Images that evoke emotional responses by portraying universal themes such as love, joy, loneliness, poverty, or struggle.

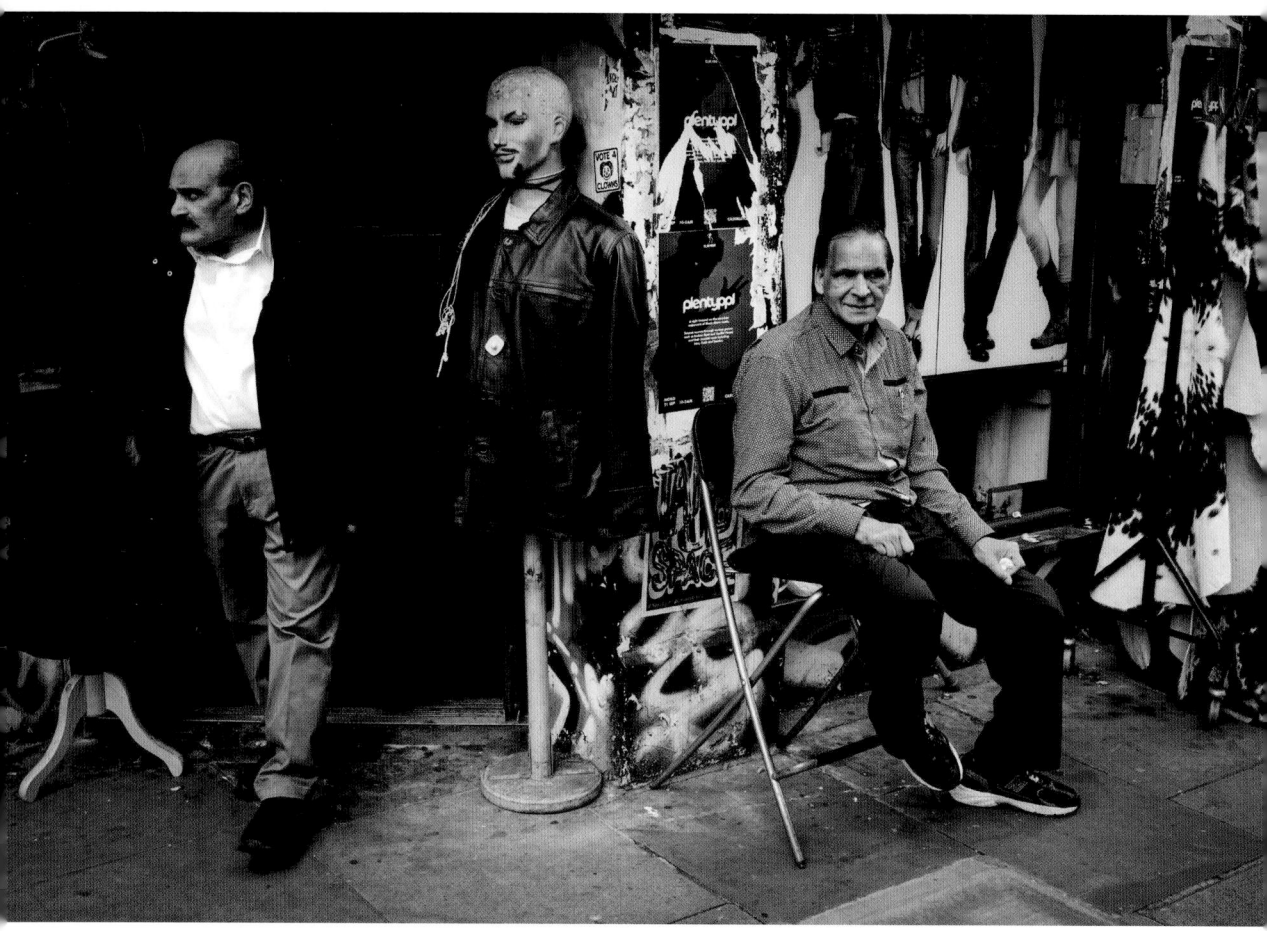

The humanist approach often focuses on local communities and can form an important part of social history, particularly in an age of increasing regeneration and renewal.

- **Cultural and social commentary:** The photographer provides a glimpse into societal norms, traditions, and everyday experiences, offering insights into cultures and communities.

- **Candidness:** Images are typically unstaged, relying on the photographer's ability to observe and capture fleeting moments.

- **People focused:** People are the central subject, with less emphasis on factors such as architecture and light.

- **Simplicity:** Compositions are often strikingly minimalist, drawing attention to the subject and the story rather than technical perfection.

THE AESTHETIC APPROACH

Sometimes street photography is purely about the art. There may be no moment, no playful observation, no meaningful narrative—just a visually compelling image.

This aesthetic style of street photography is very on-trend. Just search the hashtag #streetphotography on Instagram, and you'll discover a constant stream of bold images with strong form and colour, pictures shot through misted-up windows, and striking street abstracts.

The popularity of this style is due, in part, to the influence of Saul Leiter, whose work has experienced a resurgence. There are some purists who would argue that this is not street photography, but I would argue that it is—it's just not traditional street photography.

This style suits the fisher rather than the hunter, being slower paced and more reflective; you are far more likely to find a potential subject, and then spend time figuring out the light and the composition. It's also an approach that is suited to the cautious or introverted street photographer.

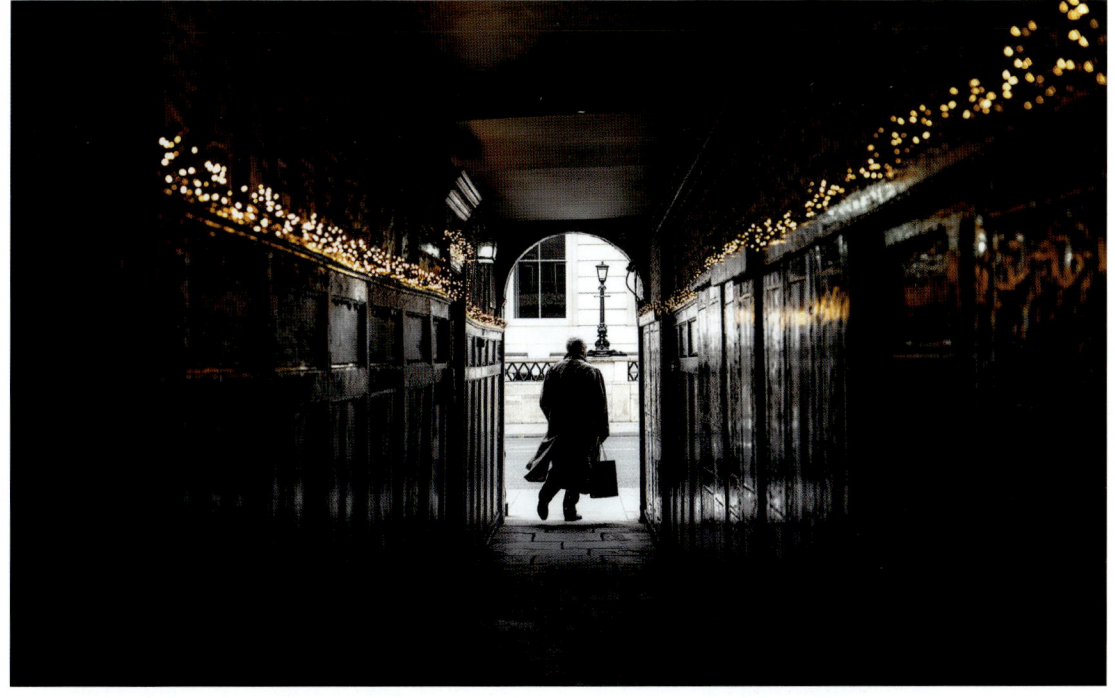

The aesthetic approach is more about a look and a feel rather than a moment or a story.

The high-contrast style

A currently popular approach, the high-contrast style can be seen in the work of Alex Webb, Daido Moriyama, and Constantine Minos, as well as in some of Harry Gruyaert's work. Images in this camp tend to be multilayered and feature bold, saturated colours. They are often complex, engaging your eye and your brain. Don't be fooled by the apparent chaos on the first look. Dig deeper to find multiple subjects, moments, and layers of interest.

If this is an approach you would like to explore, follow these tips:

- **Shoot on bright sunny days:** Seek out harsh lighting. Shoot in the morning or late afternoon for long, dramatic shadows.

- **Incorporate silhouettes:** Position subjects against bright backgrounds to create bold silhouettes (see Alex Webb's work for great examples of this).

- **Underexpose:** This will intensify shadows, saturate colours, and preserve highlights.

- **Increase contrast in post-production:** We can't always get it right in-camera! Also try dodging and burning to direct the viewer's eye to the important parts of the frame.

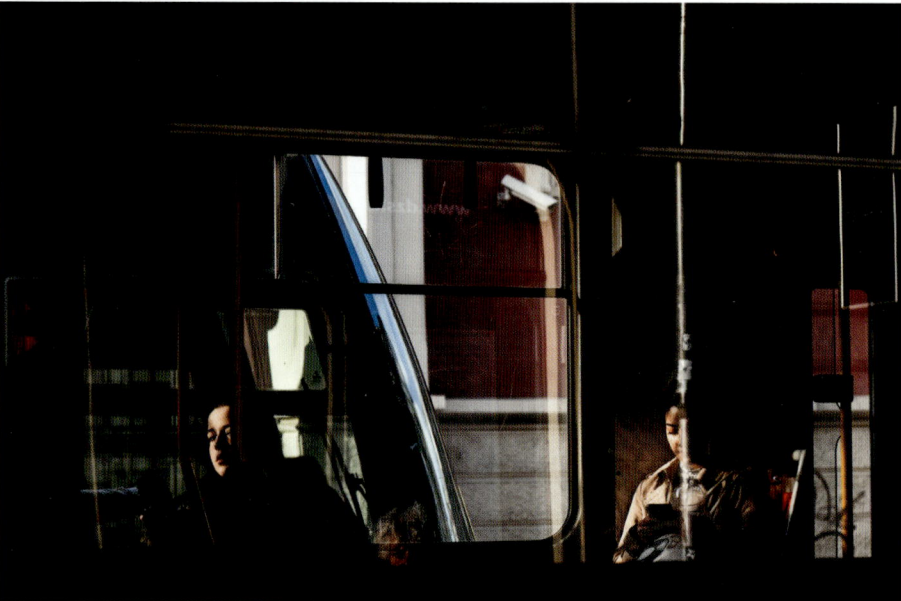

In this shot, I was aiming to shoot in the style of Harry Gruyaert, the Belgian street photographer who was a great proponent of the high-contrast approach. This look was achieved in-camera, simply by underexposing by two stops.

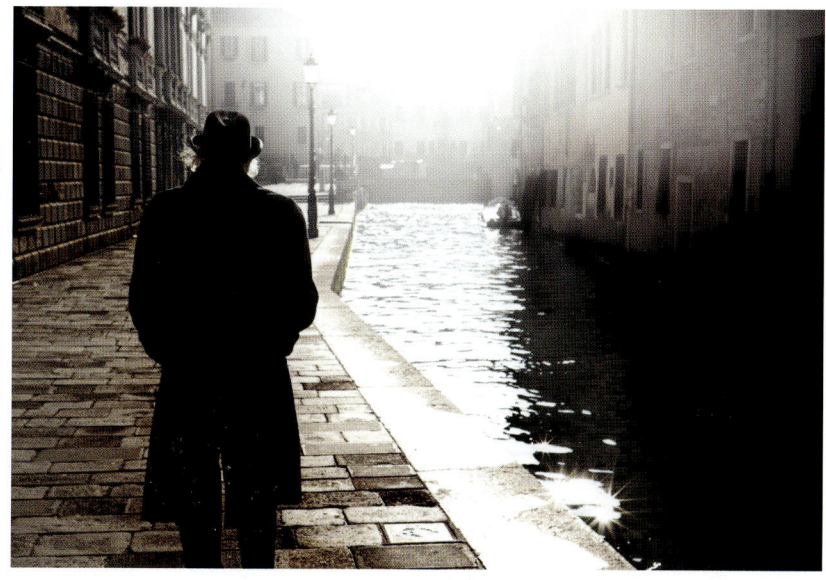

The light is a key factor in poetic street photography, and this scene, shot in Venice, is characterized by beautiful contre-jour early morning sunshine.

The poetic style

It all started with Saul Leiter. Poetic street photography is a highly popular artistic approach to capturing the heart and soul of everyday life. It's a painterly approach, all about finding the rhythm and emotion in everyday life, beauty in the mundane, and creating calm images that feel like visual poetry.

Here are some tips to help you find poetry on the streets:

- **Focus on the mood:** Find dramatic lighting, like golden light, mist, or shadows. Look for fleeting moments that evoke emotions like solitude or mystery. Make the most of weather elements like rain, snow, or mist to enhance the mood.

- **Find layers of meaning:** Look for symbolism or metaphors in everyday situations or objects. Include reflections or silhouettes to create depth.

- **Experiment with composition:** Use leading lines, negative space, or symmetry for balance and harmony.

- **Find human connection:** Look for gestures, expressions, or interactions that can help tell the bigger story; even without people, you can hint at the presence of people with empty chairs, footsteps, or shadows.

- **Embrace silence and stillness:** Seek out calm moments amid the chaos of the city and give emptiness the space to speak just as loudly as action.

The geometric style

Look around the streets of any town or city and you'll see geometric shapes, lines, patterns, and structures all around you. Whilst this is another popular approach today, images that rely on geometry can sometimes feel a little cold and sterile (some people may argue that they are not truly street photographs).

By focusing on architectural details, shadows, reflections, and repetitive forms, this style creates dynamic and abstract compositions. For inspiration, look at the work of Fan Ho and André Kertész.

Look for strong lines and shadow areas in city structures. In this case, the angularity of the scene is broken up by the human form.

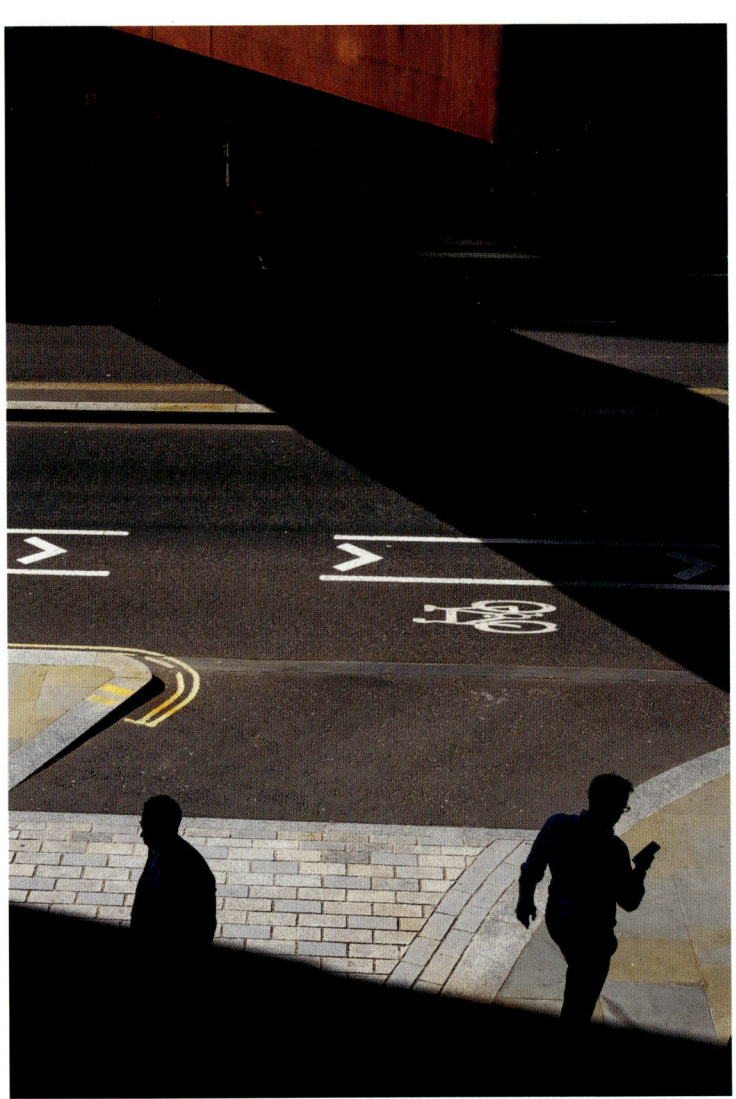

Here are some tips to create compelling geometric street photography:

- **Look for lines:** Capture intersecting, converging, or leading lines that direct the viewer's eye.

- **Use light and shadow:** Use the long shadows early or late in the day to create striking contrasts.

- **Find shapes:** Look for triangles, circles, rectangles, squares, or other forms created by architecture, shadows, or urban structures.

- **Recognize patterns:** Be alert for repetitive shapes or textures that could add rhythm to the image.

- **Layer with reflections:** Look at windows, puddles, or shiny surfaces to add layered geometry.

- **Use perspective:** Shoot from a low angle to exaggerate the lines and curves of buildings, or shoot from a high viewpoint to flatten the perspective.

- **Embrace negative space:** Don't be afraid to incorporate large areas of empty space as a design feature or to draw attention to a small, important subject.

- **Always add human interest:** You need people to provide scale or narrative and to soften the rigidity of the geometry.

DEVELOPING YOUR VOICE

A good starting point is to consider the three approaches outlined above and ask yourself: *"Which of these am I drawn to?"* Answering this question could well set you off on the right path. Think about what you enjoy shooting, what sort of images you enjoy looking at, and what's within your comfort zone. Do you like humour? Are you drawn to more serious messages and stories? Is there an inner artist within you, struggling to get out? Think about what you truly gravitate toward, and this should give you a solid baseline.

Here are some tips to help you to develop your voice.

WORK OUT WHAT AND WHO INSPIRES YOU

We all take inspiration from other artists. We buy books, visit exhibitions, watch films, and many of us gorge on YouTube videos. We start off swimming, seemingly helplessly, in a sea of different and often conflicting styles and approaches. It's easy to get confused by the sheer volume of information that comes our way, but eventually we start to cut through the noise and identify with something that may work. It's important, at this stage, not to get so blinkered that you follow too narrow a path. Let these external influences guide you but not define you, at least not at an early stage.

I recommend that all students study the masters: Henri Cartier-Bresson, Robert Frank, Elliott Erwitt, Garry Winogrand, Vivian Maier, Joel Meyerowitz, Saul Leiter, and Fan Ho. Look at and think about their images, and observe their themes, lighting, composition, and intent. Figure out what attracts you to their work.

Shoot regularly

The more you shoot, the faster all this will start to make sense. Once a month is nowhere enough for a serious street photographer! Even if you are on the street without a camera, maybe walking to work, start to think like a street photographer. Look for connections, anticipate behaviours, evaluate the light, and make compositions in your head.

Experiment

Get out of your comfort zone and take some risks. Do what you wouldn't normally do, go to different places, shoot at different times, and use different gear. Do the opposite of what the experts tell you. Experiment with new techniques just to see what happens. Free your mind from convention and break some rules. Breaking away from the norm in this way can only be a good thing, even if all you learn is what you *don't* like. What's the worst that could happen?

Get feedback

Don't be afraid to engage with your local street photography community and ask for feedback on your work. Also, participate in online communities (though beware of idiots who want only to destroy your confidence), and get opinions from a wide pool of talent and experience. Reflect on any feedback and allow it to help refine your vision, whilst staying true to what feels authentic to you.

CASE STUDY: Neil Johannson

Neil Johansson is a UK-based street photographer who makes a very good case for finding and consistently applying a distinctive voice. I asked Neil some questions about how he developed a clear photographer's voice.

How long did it take to realize you had found your voice?

It did take me time, it's hard to say exactly how long, but I can say it has taken years for me to get to where I am now. My voice came from years of trial and error, experimentation, figuring out what I like and what I don't like. If I had to pin it down, it's when I started doing projects, which was around 2016.

How would you describe your voice?

I know exactly what I'm looking for and why. I go out on the streets with several projects in mind, and I'll always find something one way or another. When I see an opportunity, I know how the image should look—I visualize before I press the shutter. I'm interested in particular themes and subject matter, having been heavily influenced by art and cinema.

I would say I am more aesthetically orientated as a street photographer, but I am interested in ideas and concepts. There has to be meaning.

Now that I've found my voice, it's there all the time. Even when I don't have my camera with me, I'm observing and looking at things all the time.

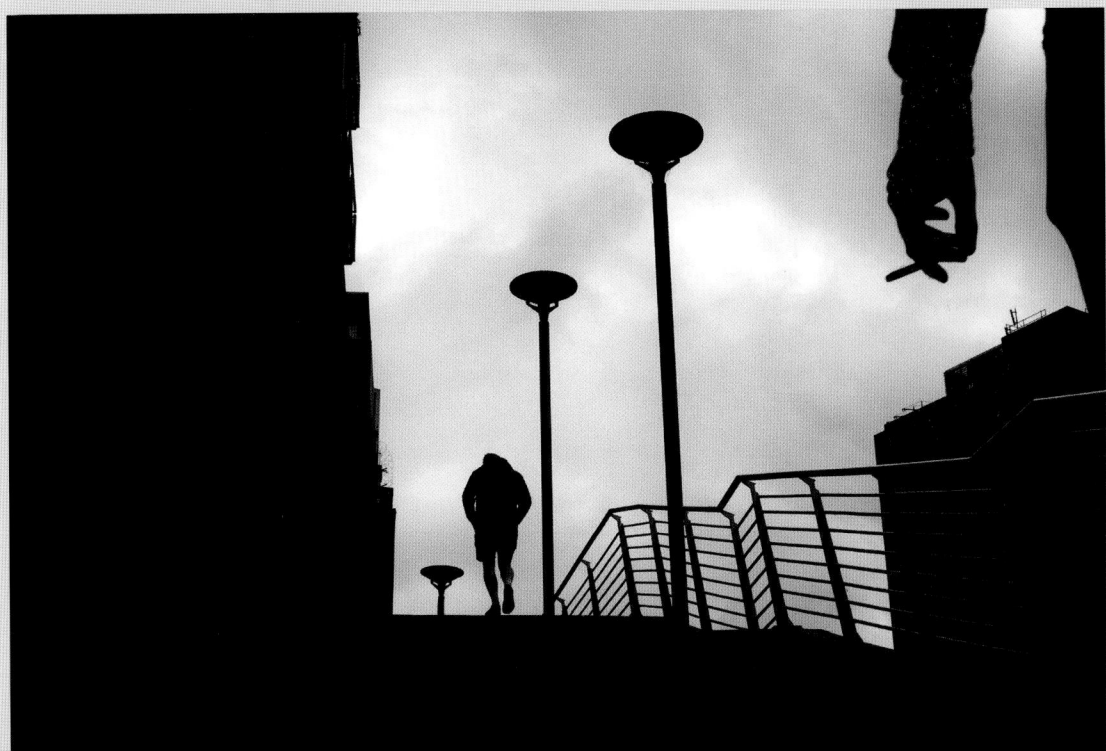

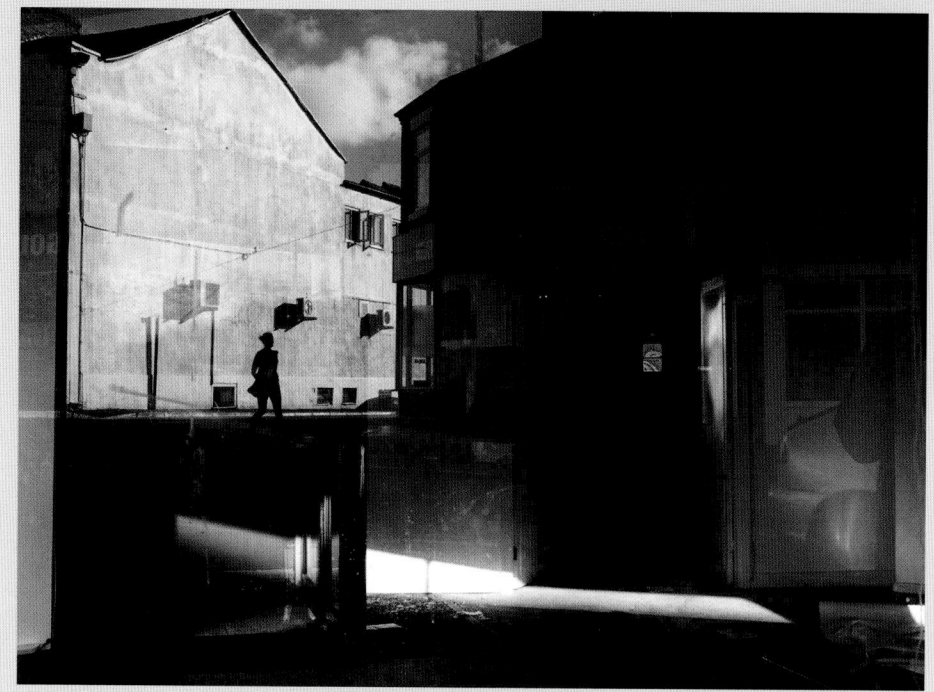

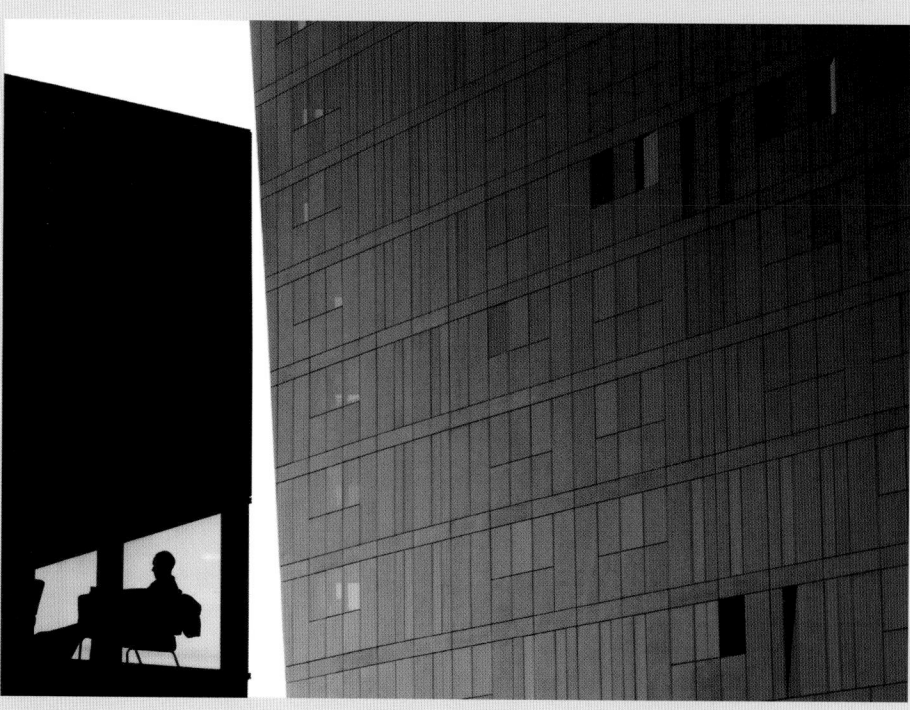

Did you take positive steps to find it, or did it just happen?

To find my voice at first, I just shot as much as I could. I shot first and asked questions later. The more you shoot the more you know what you want or don't want to do.

Ideas for projects eventually developed, and I've been building up my work ever since. However, I do think I always had a predilection for certain things and for viewing the world in a certain way. When I was a young child I observed the world, although I didn't use a camera, I made drawings, which I still have—drawings of roads and lampposts. I've always been fascinated by the urban environment and the ordinary everyday aspects of life.

What advice would you give to others who are struggling to find their voice?

I would say go out there and shoot as much as possible, without having anything particular in mind. Shoot first, and ask questions later is something I've always done and still do now.

Invest in books, not cameras. Look at the works of other photographers as much as possible.

It's also important to do or look at other things outside of photography, such as music, art, and cinema. Ideas can be prompted by the least likely thing.

Perseverance is important; it is important not to give up. By all means take a pause, but never stop completely.

—Neil Johansson (@sven804)

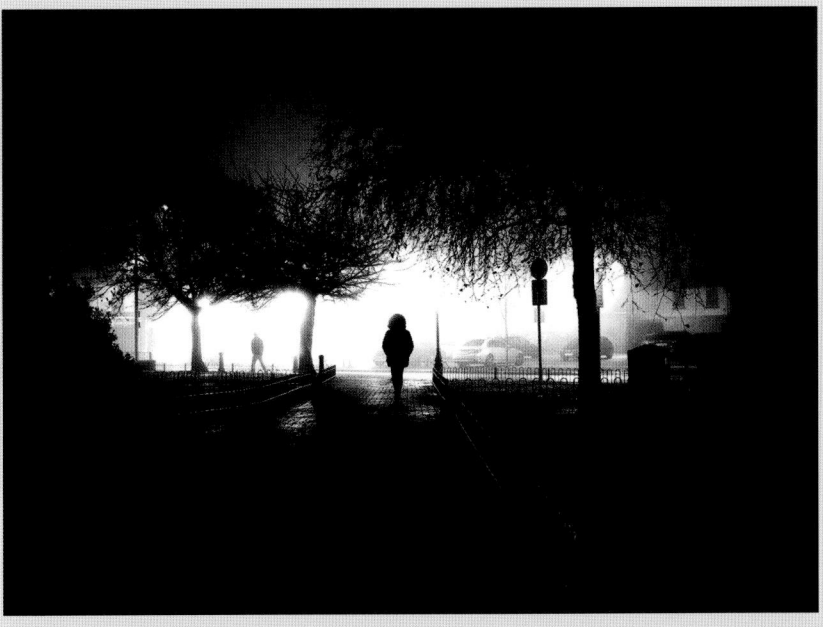

WHAT'S YOUR STREET PHOTOGRAPHY PERSONALITY TYPE?

Part of finding your voice is understanding your street photography personality. We all, of course, have different personalities—not only as people but also as photographers—and the former usually informs the latter.

The first and the most fundamental factor to consider is whether you are an introvert or an extrovert. Before attempting to answer this question it's worth bearing in mind that there is no right or wrong here, but your proclivities one way or the other will help you determine your voice.

INTROVERT OR EXTROVERT?

Introverted and extroverted street photographers are quite different beasts. The introvert usually walks slowly, shoots scenes rather than subjects, walks alone and has a strong preference for fishing over hunting; they will rarely do anything to affect the scene and like to work under a cloak of invisibility. Well-known introverted street photographers include Walker Evans, Diane Arbus, Henri Cartier-Bresson, Vivial Maier, and Lee Friedlander.

When we think of extroverted street photographers, people like Bruce Gilden or Weegee probably come to mind. These guys are always on the move, hunting in search of their prey, and always moving toward their subjects. They are never far from the action and will react instantly to a moment, rarely hesitating. Other extroverts include William Klein, Joel Meyerowitz, Trent Parke, and Dougie Wallace.

KNOWING YOUR TYPE

You probably instinctively already know what your personality type is. Whether you like it or not, it's you, and you should work with it rather than try to change it. Too many potentially good street photographers (just like you) have fallen by the wayside because they have tried to become someone else. I have met countless people who tried street photography, only to proclaim it wasn't for them, usually because they had a preconceived idea of what a street photographer should be like.

Many people have a vision of a street photographer: fearless, outgoing, and cheeky. If this is you, great. If it's not you, equally great. It's vitally important to understand that street photography isn't all about getting in people's faces (though, of course, it can be) and you need to find an approach that chimes with your personality.

The takeaway point here is that it doesn't matter one bit what your personality type is. The important thing is to make the most of what you've got and adapt your shooting style so that it works for you.

3

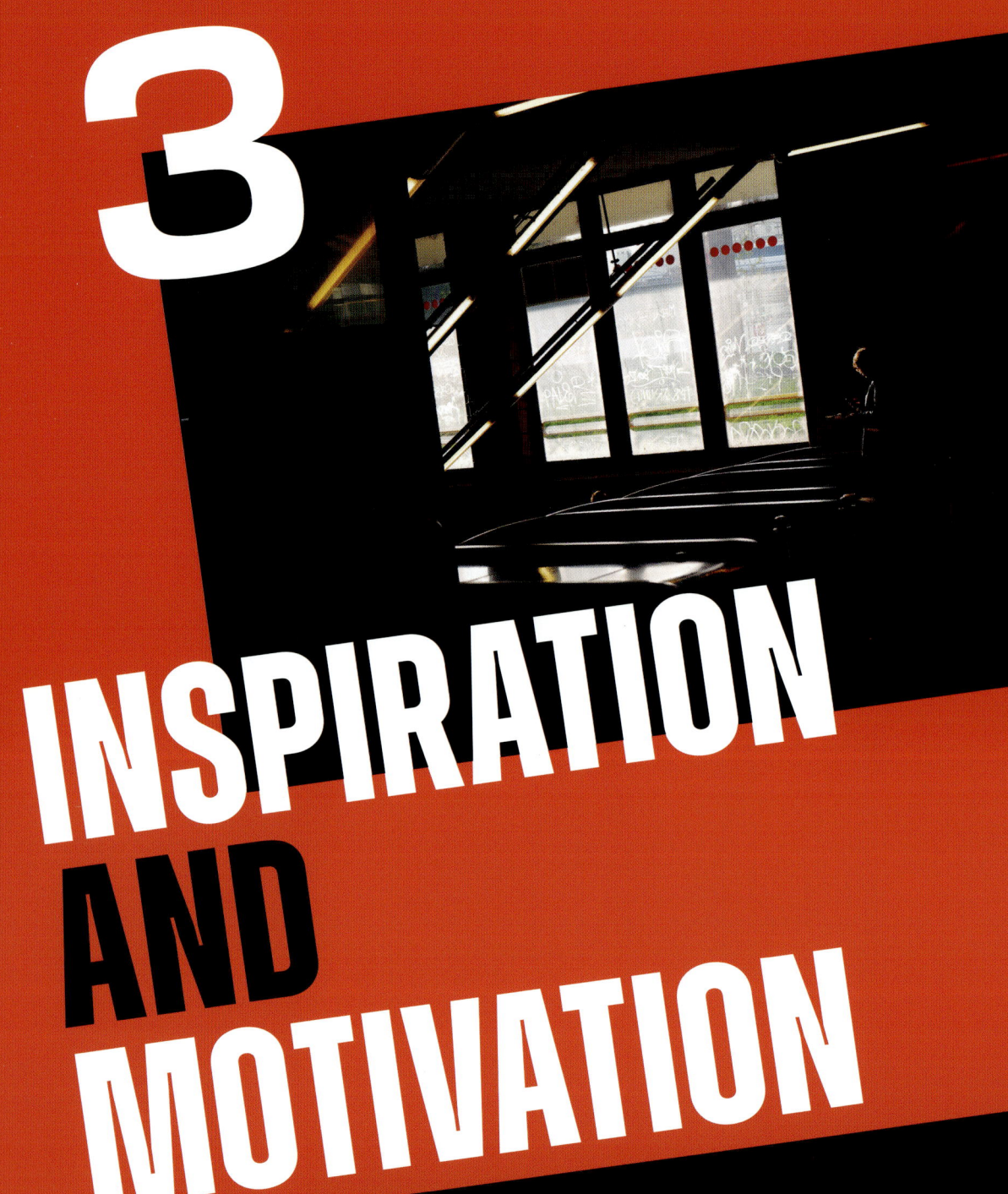

INSPIRATION AND MOTIVATION

I often hear of street photographers losing their mojo and feeling uninspired. It happens to us all to a greater or lesser degree. Lack of inspiration can lead to feelings of unworthiness and self-questioning: *"Am I any good?"*

However, it's too easy to give in to self-doubt. There is plenty we can do to inspire ourselves, whether from internal or from external influences.

Be motivated by the light! Something as simple as lovely light can motivate you to hang around and wait for the right figure to enter the frame.

WHERE TO FIND INSPIRATION

Inspiration could be closer to home than you think and it's easy to overlook the potential in your locality. Explore your neighbourhood with your camera. Try it at different times of day, in different weather conditions, and ideally with a theme or project in mind.

Try areas you've never explored before and observe normal daily life, paying attention to commonplace moments. Look for beauty in the mundane. These fragments of ordinary life can make for compelling images.

Local events like market days, parades, festivals, and public gatherings can offer unique photographic opportunities.

STUDY OTHER STREET PHOTOGRAPHERS

There's no better way to get inspired than to get engrossed in the work of other street photographers. Naturally, you wouldn't want copy what others have done, but we can all take a huge dose of inspiration from the great street photographers, past and present. Explore others' styles and approaches and try to align them to your own aspirations. Interested in fast-paced, hunting-style street photography? Look at Bruce Gilden or Mark Cohen. Attracted to a more poetic style? Explore Saul Leiter and Harry Gruyaert. Dig deep into what was in their mind when they took the picture. How did they compose the frame? What was included or left out? How did they use the light? How did they put together a body of work?

Also study creators in other artistic fields. For example, I know street photographers who are inspired by great film directors such as Stanley Kubrick, Wong Kar-wai, and David Lynch.

Invest in photography books (or at least borrow them from your local library). I find spending time with a new book very inspirational, and it often gives me creative cues for my own work. The same applies to exhibitions.

TRAVEL

Experience new locations. It's easy to get bored with the place you know well, and somewhere new and exciting can provide a big creative nudge. Step into the unknown, and get a taste of different cultures. Even short trips to nearby towns can provide fresh perspectives.

Do some research before you travel. Find out what other street photographers have created at that location, look at what artists have painted, and read what people have written. Get under the skin of the place and try to understand what makes it tick.

Then, make a plan. I always visit a new location with some sort of a project in mind; shooting blind in a new place can be hard work and unproductive.

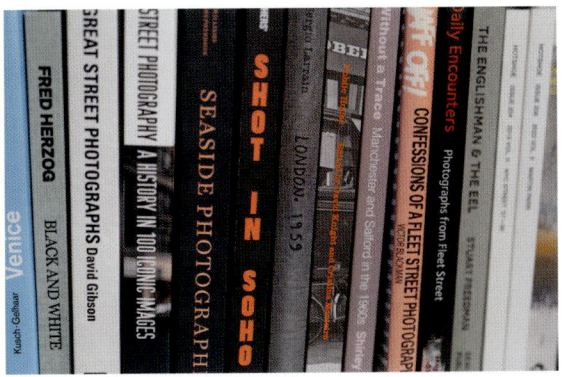

Immerse yourself in as wide a selection of street photography books as possible. This is one of my biggest sources of inspiration.

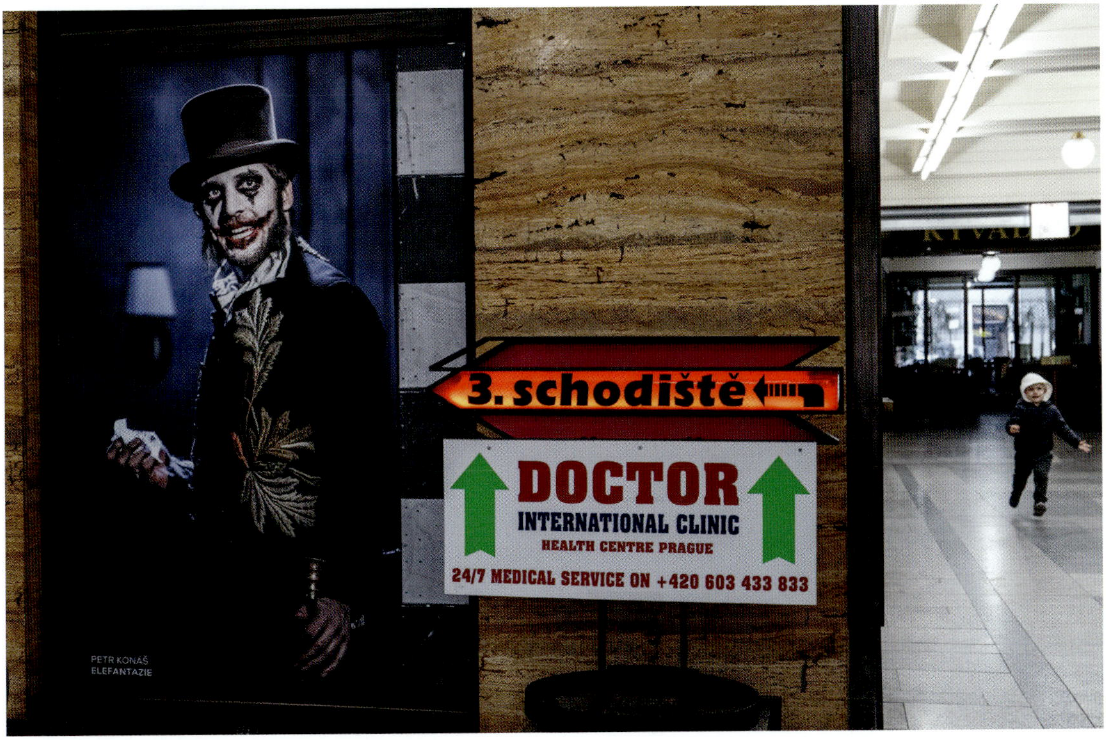

They say that travel broadens the mind. I'm sure that's true. It certainly inspires me as a street photographer! (This image was shot in the city of Prague.)

EXPLORE YOUR ARCHIVE

Look back over previous work to find images you enjoyed taking or enjoy looking at. What makes you fulfilled or happy? Look for patterns or trends—images that have similar qualities that connect with each other in ways you previously overlooked. It's quite common to find positive attributes in images taken months or even years ago; considering them much later with a sense of detachment can be rewarding. I regularly do this, and it sometimes provides me with ideas for new projects. Several of my projects came from finding old images I had forgotten about.

TRY NEW TECHNIQUES

If you shoot mostly in landscape format, try shooting vertically, like Saul Leiter. If you shoot mostly colour, take on a new project in black and white. Someone once said: "If you always do the same, you'll always get the same." Don't worry too much about the results and let your imagination run away with you. Try something new and possibly out of your comfort zone. Think about shooting

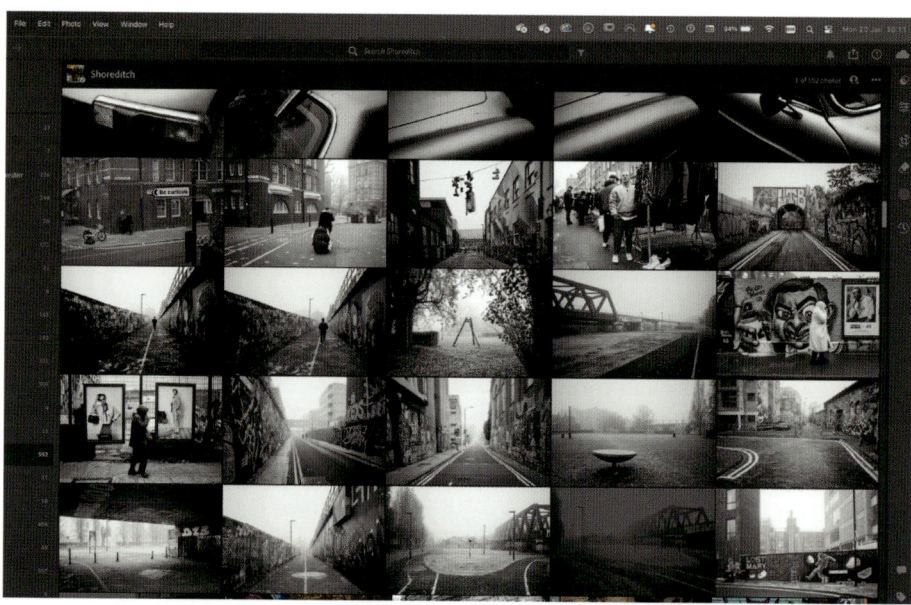

Don't underestimate images you took months or years ago. It's a good exercise to regularly trawl through your archive, looking for ideas to spark interest for new projects.

something that isn't traditional street photography, such as urban landscapes, abstracts, or street portraits. If you normally shoot digitally, maybe buy a cheap analogue camera and experiment with the joys of film. All this could open new inspirational doors for you.

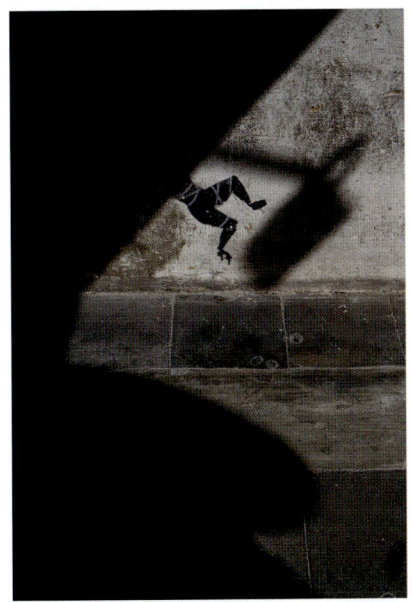

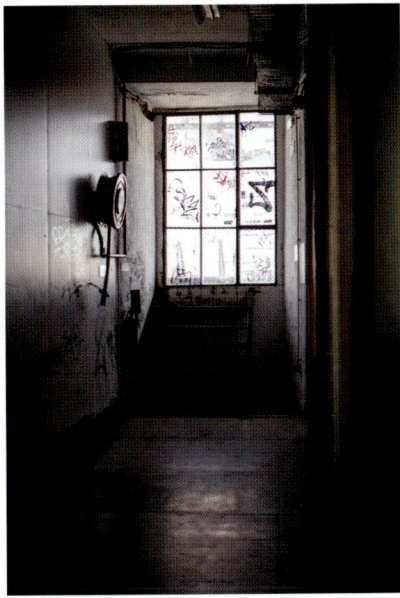

Do something unexpected! I don't normally shoot this type of image, but I was fascinated by the light pouring into Lisbon's LX Factory—so much so that I'm creating a project about it, which will hopefully result in a zine or book.

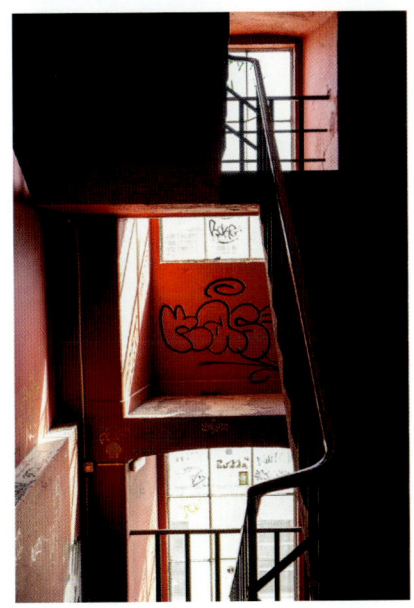

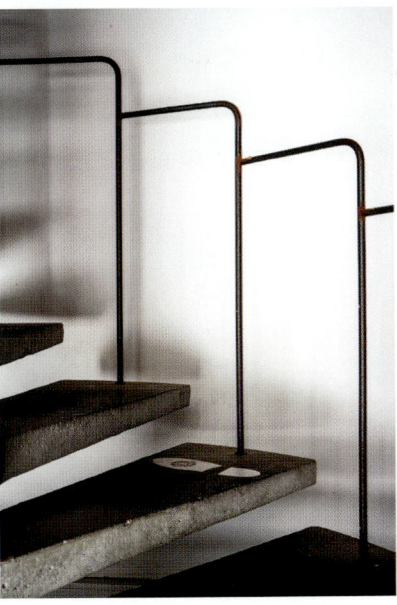

KEEP A JOURNAL

Journaling is a good way to record your daily thoughts and ideas. I always have a notebook in my pocket or in my camera bag and I'm constantly making notes about ideas for new projects, locations, films to watch, books to read, new photographers to explore, and so on. I also record my thoughts, particularly the good and less good things about my street photography at that particular moment. All this provides me with little pinpricks of inspiration, which can often lead to something more substantial. If you don't carry a physical notebook, you can do the same thing using the notebook app on your phone.

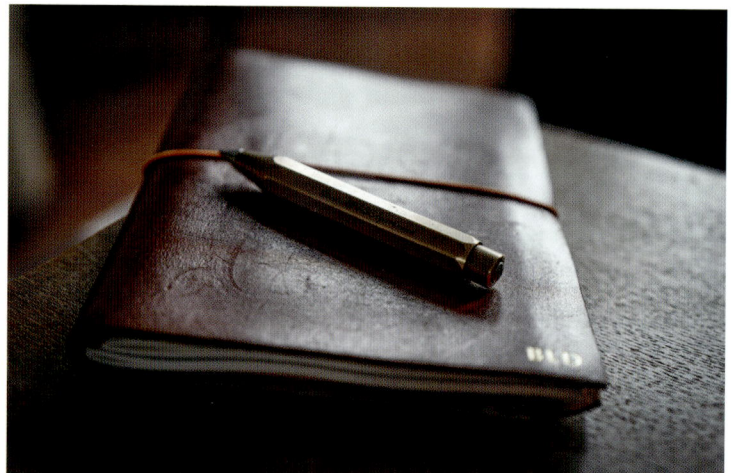

Your journal is your friend! I'm never without this notebook, constantly jotting down thoughts, creative prompts, and, most importantly, ideas for new projects.

ATTEND WORKSHOPS

Street photography workshops can be a great source of inspiration. This is the age of the yearning for learning, and street photography workshops have never been more popular. But how do you find the right workshop for you? Will you be wasting your money or investing it wisely in learning new skills and being inspired by a true professional? Following is a checklist of some of the factors you should consider and questions you should ask to help you make an informed decision.

CHECKLIST: How to choose a street photography workshop

1. How much "me" time will you get?

Workshops are so much more effective, and you will learn more, if you are part of a small group. A small group in this context means single figures; anything more than that and you could be taking part in a photo walk, not a workshop. A good workshop leader will ensure he or she spends a proportionate amount of time with each participant, with plenty of individual coaching and support when and where it's needed.

2. Can the teacher teach?

The answer to this question really must be yes. No matter how good (or famous) they are, a workshop leader who can't get the message across in an inspiring and articulate way is next to useless. A good workshop leader will be enthusiastic, inspiring, professional in approach, committed to the genre, and, of course, be a good teacher. The fact that they know their subject inside out and have been practicing it for quite some years should be a given.

3. Do they specialize?

Whatever you intend to learn, you really should be learning it with a specialist. A business that offers safari shooting in Kenya may not have the expertise to teach street shooting in Istanbul. Take care to ensure that you're getting the focused expertise you believe you are paying for. Would you go to an eye specialist to have your teeth fixed? Would you go to an architectural photographer to learn boudoir? Or a wedding photographer to learn street?

Also think about the gear issue. Some workshop leaders are very committed to one system, so if you're a Fujifilm user, for example, you perhaps wouldn't get as much practical help from a workshop where the Sony system is a key factor in the sales proposition.

4. Does the course leader have a track record as a photographer?

If not, walk away now. Before anything else, look at their work. Do you like and admire it? Do you aspire to their style or particular range of skills? Do you want to shoot the sort of pictures they shoot? Are you impressed by their social media presence, (but maybe not just a presence on Instagram, which can be somewhat misleading)? Are they published in magazines and journals? Do they exhibit their work? Have they published any books? Are they truly a professional photographer? If the workshop leader's personal images are of people walking past walls or just random strangers in the street, it's probably not ideal.

5. How will the workshop meet your objectives?

Before you start looking at what's available, work out what you want to achieve. A workshop is an educational exercise and should be well organized with clearly communicated learning outcomes. Will the workshop deliver those outcomes? Try to work out what you want to achieve before booking.

6. Does the itinerary work for you?

You should have a clear idea of the itinerary before you book. What, exactly, will the workshop cover? I hear about some street photography workshops that are little more than hurried photo walks. The lack of an outline and a vague approach to planning the day may mean a vague workshop.

7. Are you dealing with an established business?

There should be a business-like approach with an informative website, a business email address (rather than something like Gmail), a fair cancellation policy, public liability insurance, and a professional manner in dealing with customers. Also, do you like the way the business communicates with you? Is its approach articulate, helpful, and friendly? The way businesses handle these initial customer interactions is often an indication of how workshops are run.

8. Can you read reviews or testimonials from satisfied customers?

Testimonials on review sites such as TrustPilot tend to be well regulated and, therefore, fair and accurate. Don't be afraid to ask for contact details of satisfied customers and beware of a long list of glowing testimonials which are signed by the likes of "Dave from London."

MOTIVATE YOURSELF

There is perhaps a lot of crossover between motivation and inspiration and many of the points in the previous section will apply here. Finding motivation can be deeply personal, and we sometimes have to dig deep in order to stay engaged. Street photography can be hard work, and it's easy to give up and let it fall by the wayside. But, if you can manage to stay motivated, the rewards will come your way.

9. Do they offer a range of workshops?

In the likely event of you being hooked, can you do a follow-up workshop with them, maybe at an intermediate or advanced level? Can you do workshops in different locations and at different times of the year?

10. Is there any meaningful follow-up from the workshop?

A good workshop provider will follow up after the workshop with additional information, advice, and, ideally, critique. The latter is a crucial part of the learning process and should be a basic component of any workshop.

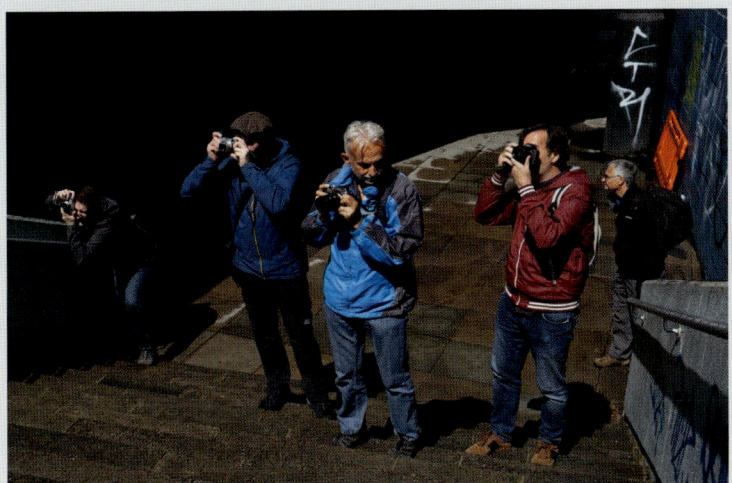

There are plenty of street photography workshops around the world from which to choose, but choose wisely and recognize the difference between "workshop" and "photo walk."

REDISCOVER YOUR "WHY"

Think about why you're doing this: What drew you to street photography in the first place? Was it the thrill and serendipity of candid moments, the interplay of light and shade, the opportunity to create beautiful artworks, or the ability to tell stories? Write down your reasons, and revisit them when you feel unmotivated. It could be that you have lost sight of your original or underlying motivations.

EMBRACE PROJECTS

There is no better way to motivate yourself than to engage in projects (you'll read much more about this in Chapter 9). I come across street photographers all the time who have used the vehicle of a project to bring their flagging motivation back to life, whether it's a 48-hour project or a 48-month project.

Here are three ideas you could try to help give you a sense of purpose:

- **Try setting simple themes.** Focus on a single subject, like gestures, colours, or silhouettes, for a week or month. If you commit to nothing else, at least start a project (read Chapter 9 first!). Even something simple is better than nothing, and it may be just enough to get your mojo working again.

- **Try one of the major initiatives** that many thousands of people contribute to such as a 365 (a photo-a-day) project.

- **Document a different aspect of daily life each day**, maybe on your commute to work, when out walking the dog, or just family life in your home.

Of course, a more enduring, heavyweight project should provide you with ample motivation as you'll have a tangible goal to strive for.

FOCUS MORE ON NARRATIVES

You will probably find that by creating a storyline or narrative with your images, your work will take on a sense of purpose and coherence. You could, for example, document the daily life of a specific community or document an event such as an outdoor show or festival. Alternatively, you could set out to document a topical social issue or something with a political theme.

SHOOT REGULARLY

It's hard to maintain any degree of motivation if you shoot only once a month. You need to keep up the momentum, keeping your skills fresh and your motivation high, which can only be done if you shoot at least weekly—if not more frequently.

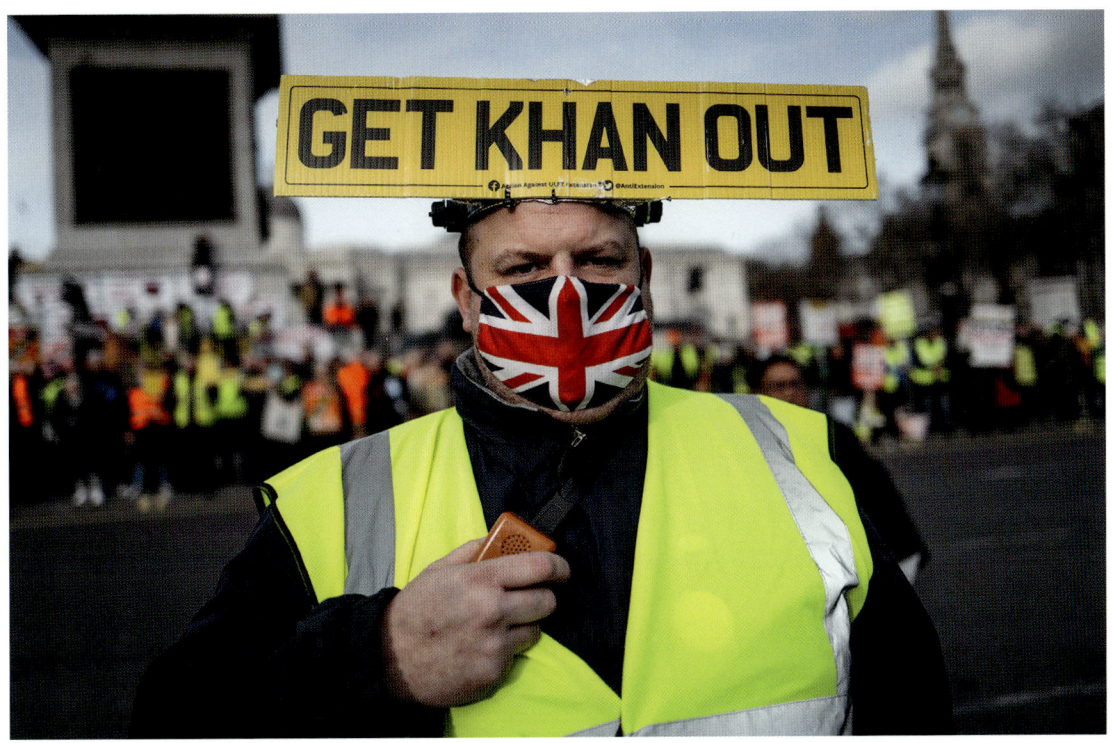

There are often local political events that offer the perfect opportunity to deploy your storytelling skills. You should be able to create a project around a theme like this, and the whole exercise can be highly motivating.

NETWORK WITH OTHER STREET PHOTOGRAPHERS

Street photography is usually a solitary pursuit, and it's too easy to walk the streets on your own, taking a few pictures, and then never discussing either the experience or your images with other street photographers.

In terms of the shooting itself, my personal preference is to shoot alone because I prefer to do it without the distractions of conversation or spending most of the day drinking coffee or beer. The downside of this approach is that it can feel quite isolating. However, I have found a good compromise: start the day with a buddy or a small group in a coffee bar, then split up for a shooting session of three to four hours. Meet up again for a brief lunch break, then split up again for the afternoon session. Reconvene again at the end of the day when you'll share experiences and discuss your images over a drink. Most people find this a good source of motivation and inspiration.

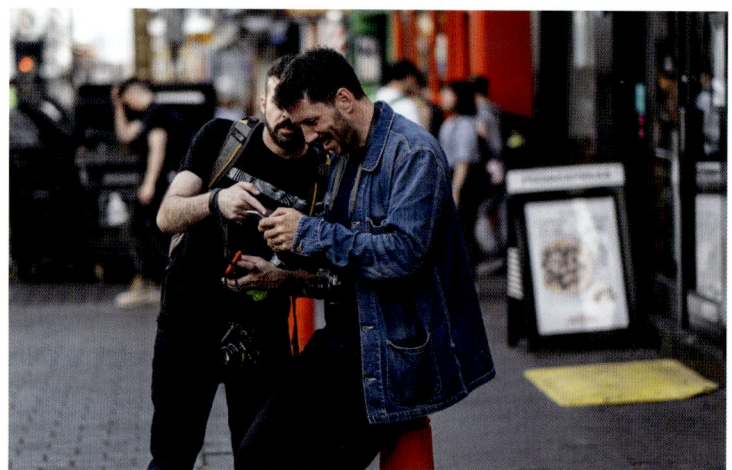

Shooting with a buddy can keep your motivation and your spirits high, but try not to get too distracted by the social aspects of shooting in company.

Where do you find others to shoot with? Wherever you live (certainly in the bigger towns and cities) there are probably photography meet-ups, camera clubs, or groups to share ideas and gain feedback; at the very least there will be groups on social media you can join. Try to surround yourself with positive people who are keen to learn, rather than life's moaners! You'll often find new ideas by seeing how others approach similar subjects.

TAKE A BREAK

Finally, it's sometimes a good idea to step away for a short period to help re-ignite your creativity and passion. Use this downtime to explore other creative pursuits such painting, writing, film making, or music. The influences you get from these can be priceless.

HAVE A STRONG WORK ETHIC

As in life generally, there's a very strong correlation between effort and reward. It is essential to have a strong work ethic if you aim to make real progress with your street photography; it's a long journey that requires dedication, discipline, and real sense of purpose.

Joel Meyerowitz had a strong work ethic, and he put his heart and soul into creating his images. He was quick to identify the correlation between miles walked and the number of "keepers." Of course, sometimes we get lucky (this is one of the true joys of street photography), but you must put the hard work in.

I have analyzed my own style of working and have identified a number of traits which I believe are essential to combining a strong work ethic with the enjoyment of street photography.

SET GOALS

Don't be the aimless street photographer. Know what you want from each day and from each year. Start the day with some goals, and stick to them. Yes, you could go out there and hope for the best, but you'll be more productive if you have some targets to aim for. You could, for example, focus on one or more specific projects. Perhaps you want to work on your storytelling ability or practice or experiment with a certain technique.

Break your goals into actionable steps, and make notes in the journal about your progress.

CREATE ROUTINES

Make space available in your diary and commit to it; dedicate specific shooting times, whether daily or weekly. You could decide to make time for a project on your daily commute, for example. If it's a routine, then it's more likely to happen!

MAKE IT PART OF YOUR LIFESTYLE

It's often said that street photography is a lifestyle choice—a cult, almost. For many, it is indeed a way of life and a key ingredient in their persona. Of course, not everyone wants to take their hobby that far, but there is a probably a happy medium. Whilst some people live, sleep, and breathe street photography, others are happy for it to be nothing more than a weekend hobby.

KEEP FIT!

You need a certain amount of stamina to keep this up. Street photography naturally involves a lot of walking and standing, so maintaining your physical health through exercise and proper nutrition is paramount. Try to ease off the junk food, eat fruit, and drink lots of water to make the day easier on yourself!

Wear comfortable shoes and carry a minimal amount of kit (one camera and one lens) to prevent fatigue.

PRACTICE UNTIL IT HURTS

I find it mildly amusing that whilst musicians practice their art obsessively, photographers don't feel a similar need to do so! What (and how) should you practice as a street photographer?

- **Observation skills:** Practice using your observation skills so that your attention becomes more attuned to subtle details that might otherwise go unnoticed. Train yourself to notice small, meaningful moments around you. Start to notice the unusual in the usual, the unexpected in the expected, or beauty in the mundane. Even when you're walking the streets without a camera, use that time to observe.

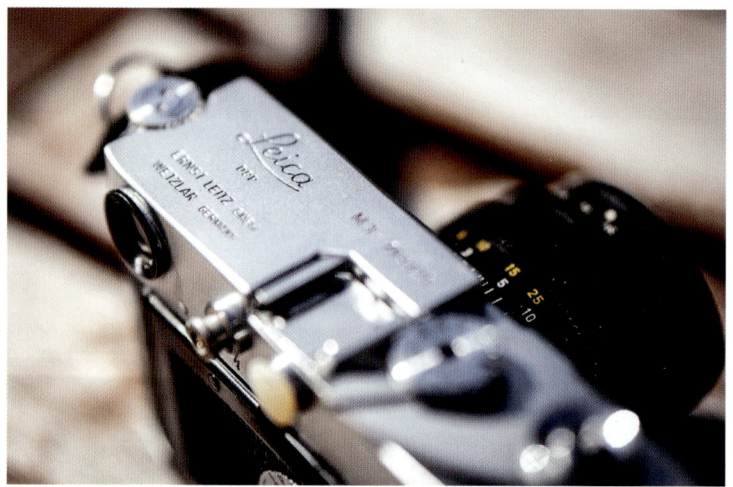

You will often need to shoot quickly, so you need to know your gear inside out. Practice handing your camera and changing the essential settings until you can do it with your eyes closed.

- **Anticipation and timing:** Recording the decisive moment often requires a good sense of anticipation before the moment happens. Whilst Henri Cartier-Bresson identified the concept of the decisive moment, try to think of it as the pregnant moment, whereby you'll be tracking the activity before the key moment arrives. This skill should quickly improve with regular observation and shooting.

- **Framing and composition:** Practicing enhances the ability to frame shots intuitively and compose visually appealing images within unpredictable environments.

- **Confidence:** For many, photographing strangers or candid moments can be awkward or even intimidating. Regular practice helps overcome the fear of photographing people or taking pictures in public spaces.
- **Camera fluency:** Street photography often requires quick reactions to capture fleeting moments, so you need to be totally familiar with your camera and its settings so you can make choices immediately and without thinking. Gary Player, the pro golfer, made a good point: *"The more I practice, the luckier I get."*

NEVER GIVE UP

We all have bad days, and we have good days. Because street photography is largely dependent on external factors outside your control, you can never predict what sort of day you're going to have. Sometimes you spend a long day on the street, walking for miles, but with nothing much to show for it at the end.

But that's fine! It's important to be prepared to take the bad days on the chin and move on from them. Don't see an unproductive day as failure; it happens to the best of us, and please don't lose heart in street photography because the results are not coming fast enough for you. It's the nature of the beast!

MANAGE YOUR EXPECTATIONS

Finally, if you're going to have a relaxing and fulfilling experience on the streets, it is essential to have realistic expectations and not to put pressure on yourself to end your session with a card full of great keepers. It's not going to happen, and you would probably go home disappointed. Street photography is all about patience, serendipity, luck, and being in the right place at the right time. Sometimes it just happens for us, and sometimes it doesn't. I can shoot for weeks without getting one decent image, but that's all part of the game. It doesn't dull my enjoyment of street photography one bit.

My typical day on the street

I think I have a pretty good work ethic when it comes to shooting my own images. My active day starts quite early and finishes late—there's no point in doing this in a half-hearted way! I plan whatever can be planned, though I'm always prepared to be taken off in a completely different direction, depending on what I encounter during the day. I stay well hydrated, and on a typical day walk between 25,000 and 35,000 steps.

You'll see that I wholeheartedly commit the day to street photography; I work extremely hard at it and I don't let anything else get in the way.

Don't leave it to chance! Whilst a lot of what we do is spontaneous and unplanned, at least some degree of preparation will help make your day more productive.

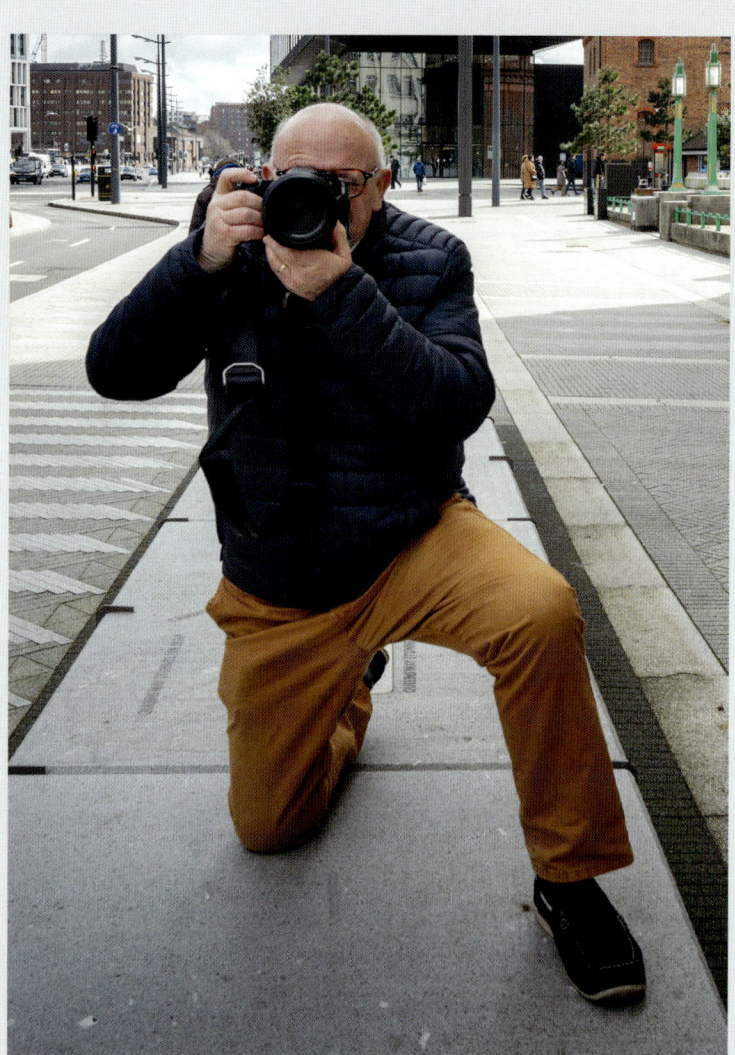

MORNING SESSION

0700-0900: Research, planning, and inspiration

- Look at a photography book or two, catch up with the daily news (noting anything that may be relevant to my day ahead, such as a political event or some sort of gathering).

- Check the weather forecast to see how the conditions may influence my route or activities, paying particular attention to the predicted sunlight.

- Make a plan for the day. This could be focused on specific projects or events. Then I map out a route (which often changes!).

0900-1300: Shooting

- Walk slowly, observing, hunting, fishing. No emails, no social media, and no phone calls!

1300-1400: Lunch break

- Have a coffee or beer, maybe while looking though some pictures on the back of the camera.

- Catch up with social media, and make sure I've uploaded my daily picture to Instagram.

- Recheck my daily plan, and make adjustments as necessary.

AFTERNOON SESSION

1400-1700: Shooting and inspiration

- Shoot as per morning session.

- Visit a gallery and perhaps a bookshop for doses of inspiration.

EVENING SESSION

1700-2200: Break and more shooting

- Stop for some refreshments and a brief rest; catch up on social media and monitor the news channels for any interesting developments (I find X very useful for this).

- Carry on doing normal daylight shooting, or, depending on the time of year, switch to night-shooting mode (wide aperture, 50mm lens, and high ISO; more focused on aesthetics than moments).

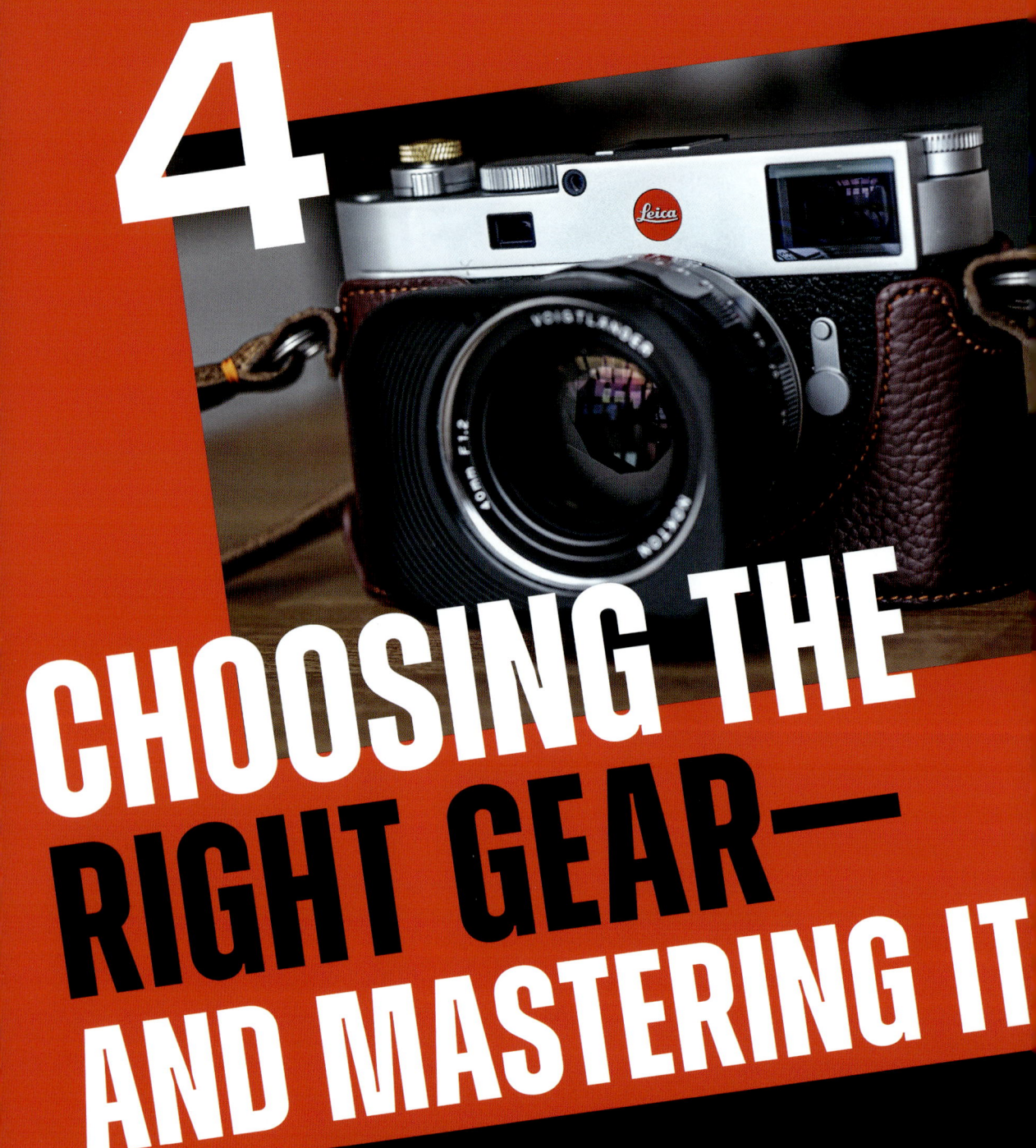

4

CHOOSING THE RIGHT GEAR— AND MASTERING IT

Plenty of people will tell you that gear is irrelevant and that it's perfectly possible to create great street images with very basic gear, a good eye, and a pair of comfy shoes.

In one sense, that's a reasonable proposition. I know plenty of street photographers who consistently produce outstanding work with very rudimentary kit: an old Olympus Trip, a 15-year-old DSLR, a consumer compact camera, even a mobile phone. Sure, the latest mirrorless marvel with 60+ megapixels would ultimately give them a different level of image quality, but would it make them better street photographers? Almost certainly not.

Street photography is much more about *getting the picture* rather than creating the *technically perfect* picture. Just look at all the great street photographers from the past: They often used basic equipment, sometimes with expired film, and they didn't have access to all the great technology we have today. But they still managed to create amazing images. So, in one sense, gear doesn't necessarily matter.

The not unreasonable counter argument is that if the same photographer used both basic gear and sophisticated gear to shoot the same image, then the image created by the latter would inevitably be superior; it may be sharper and have increased dynamic range, better noise levels, more pleasing colours, and so on. However, whilst these factors can be important, as we all want the best possible image, they do not necessarily mean that the picture will be better, if you define "better" in the sense of content or aesthetic.

My advice is, don't let gear hold you back: Buy the best you can afford but don't make the lack of expensive kit be the excuse for not creating good work. And certainly don't assume that by spending pots of money your street photography will automatically improve. It won't.

WHICH CAMERA?

How the camera feels is just as important as what the camera does. A camera is a light-proof box that contains a sensor or film which, when exposed to the light, will record an image. If it does that, you're halfway there. It's too easy to become obsessive about features and tricks, most of which, as street photographers, we'll never use. So don't be tempted by a global shutter that shoots at 120fps or the ability to shoot 8K video or masses of different autofocus modes. If you need these features for genres outside of street photography, fine; but if your camera is mostly for street shooting, then you need only a fairly basic range of features.

MIRRORLESS RANGEFINDER STYLE

There is a clear preference amongst street photographers for the mirrorless rangefinder-style camera. This could be nostalgic or romantic. Perhaps walking the streets with something that looks and feels like Garry Winogrand's Leica from 1966 gives us a warm glow. There's a more apposite reason, however, and that's practicality.

These cameras tend to be smaller, lighter, more discreet, and more maneuverable than DSLRs. This portability is a key factor when spending long days (and nights) out on the street; your wrists, arms, and shoulders will thank you for a small, light camera.

Another great advantage is having the viewfinder eyepiece on the left, allowing the right eye to focus on the scene in the viewfinder while the left eye surveys the surroundings, constantly monitoring evolving scenes and situations.

When considering buying a rangefinder-style camera, lens choice is important. Some come with a fixed lens (such as the Leica Q series with its 28mm lens and the Fujifilm X100 series with a 35mm equivalent lens), and others have interchangeable lenses that allow you to build a true system around the body (Leica M series and Fujifilm X-Pro series, for example).

Another consideration is whether an optical viewfinder (OVF) is important or whether an electronic viewfinder (EVF) will work better for you. Some cameras have both (the Fujifilm range, for example), some have just an EVF (Sony A7C series), and some have only an OVF (Leica M). There's no right or wrong here and your decision will be motivated by personal preference. Many street shooters favour the EVF because it offers true live view whereby the effects of exposure and tonality can be reviewed before taking the picture; others prefer the more organic feel of seeing exactly what the human eye sees through an OVF.

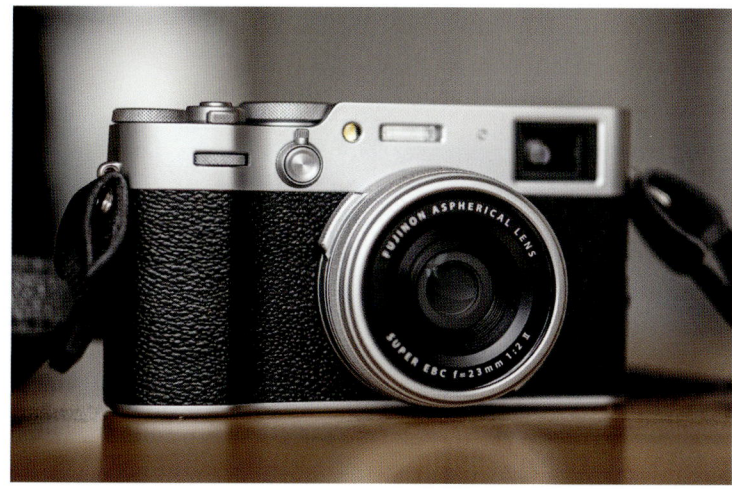

The rangefinder-style camera, initially analogue and now also digital, has been a street photographers' favourite since the days of Cartier-Bresson.

DSLR AND MIRRORLESS DSLR STYLE

The traditional DSLR is becoming a dying breed, being quickly superseded by the more nimble and more technically advanced mirrorless version. This DSLR-style body, with its pentaprism in the middle, takes its styling cues from its older sibling, but with a smaller and lighter form factor.

Most major camera manufacturers make bodies in this style, and they usually allow you to build a system around them. So, if you need the flexibility of having a wide choice of lenses and accessories, then this could well be the camera for you.

Mirrorless DSLR cameras are becoming smaller and lighter and pack a lot of technology into a relatively small body shell.

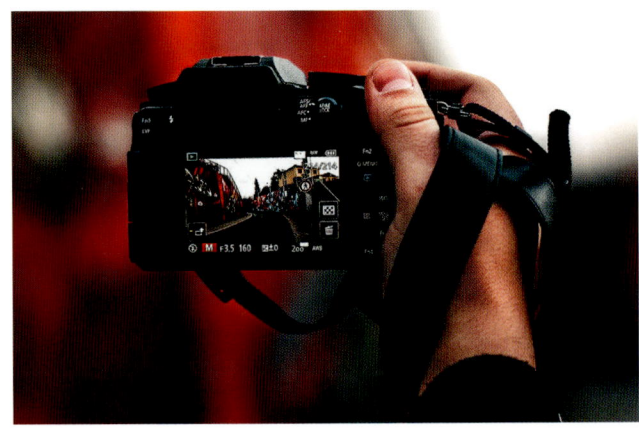

COMPACT

Small compact cameras, often incorporating a zoom lens, are a great entry-point into street photography. They are easy to handle and they're quiet, flexible and discreet. People will pay less attention to you than they would if you were shooting with a big DSLR with zoom lens. You're more likely to look like a tourist rather than a photographer. Choose carefully, as compacts are often slower and clumsier in operation, less responsive, and have smaller sensors than some of the other options. The batteries tend to be quite small, and therefore don't hold as much charge as batteries in bigger cameras.

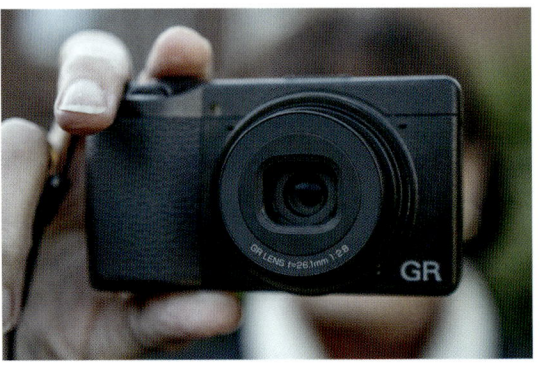

Models such as the Ricoh GR range have brought compact cameras back into the realms of acceptability. If they work for Daido Moriyama, they can work for us!

MEDIUM FORMAT

Digital medium format cameras are much smaller than ever before and can produce images with immense detail and incredible dynamic range. However, they are not natural cameras for street photographers as they're usually bigger, heavier, and considerably slower to operate.

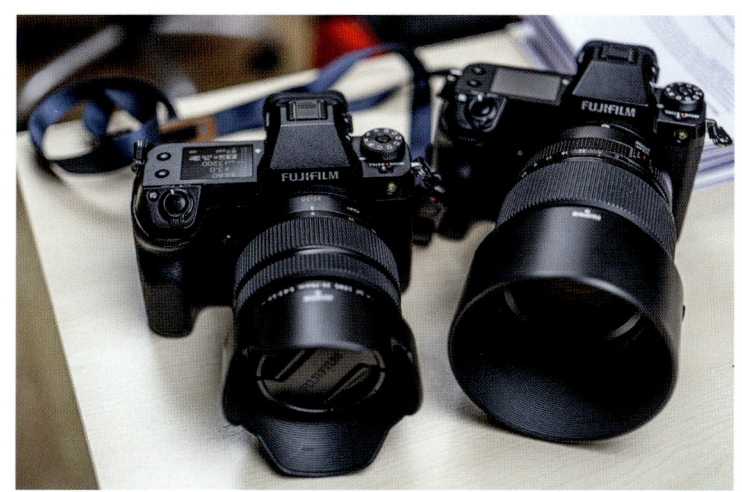

With image quality and dynamic range of full-frame cameras reaching new peaks almost every month, the case for using a medium format camera for street photography isn't particularly strong.

FILM CAMERAS

Analogue street photography is back in style! Just as vinyl has made a comeback on the music scene, we have seen a huge resurgence in the use of film—particularly for street photography.

Film cameras come in all shapes and sizes, from inexpensive compact models like the Olympus Trip to more sophisticated medium format models such as the Pentax 67, Rolleiflex, and Hasselblad. In the middle we have the evergreen SLRs from brands such as Nikon, Olympus, Canon, and Minolta.

There are some clear benefits of shooting film.

Firstly, there's definitely a film look, and it's something you can't easily replicate in Adobe Photoshop. For me, digital is a little too perfect—almost sterile—and it lacks the soft, naturalness of film (some people call it a vintage look). But we should always remember that there are so many variations available with film, with different film stocks producing very different looks.

Secondly, and this is the big deal for me, film slows you down and makes you think more. You think more about timing, light, composition, and framing. Every click costs you money, so you work harder at getting it right. But the main thing is, you don't snap first and think later—you think and *then* you snap. It's a much more satisfying way of doing things.

Thirdly, it's easier to get into the zone and then stay there; you tend to be more focused on your surroundings and what's happening around you than what's going on with your gear. You're not distracted by buttons, menus, or screens. You're there, in the moment, focused on what really matters.

Next, quite simply, the journey is more satisfying. Analogue shooting somehow just feels more *organic*, and I feel much more connected to the world when I'm shooting film.

Finally, when you're spotted on the street using a film camera, everyone will love you! Whereas walking down the street with a huge DSLR around your neck makes you public enemy number one, when people see a film camera, they'll smile and will often want to start up a conversation with you.

One of the downsides is the higher cost attached to film photography. Memory cards are reusable and now very cheap. When shooting analogue, you not only have the cost of the film itself, but also the added cost of processing and printing, which is rarely cheap. Every click of the shutter costs you money, so you won't want to make too many mistakes with a film camera.

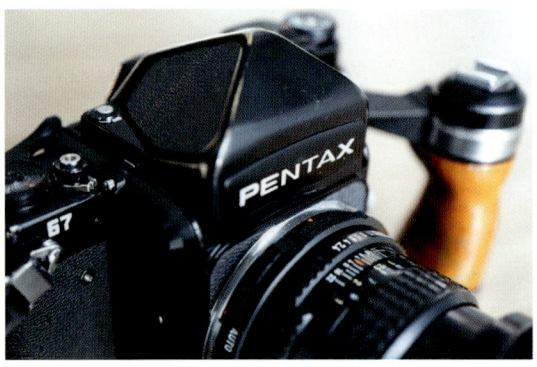

You'll need to spend some time in the gym if you're going make a beast like this your everyday carry. For some, however, it's worth the effort and the results speak for themselves—just don't expect to be a fast operator.

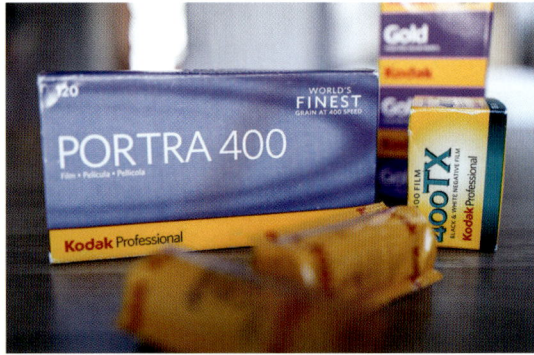

Film is back with a bang and is more popular than it has been for years.

SMARTPHONES

There is some excellent work being produced by smartphone shooters, and this approach to street photography shouldn't be dismissed. A smartphone is always with you and the latest models offer RAW shooting capability and levels of image quality which are previously unheard of. Phones are small, light, discreet, and they're always with you.

But they're not for me. Sure, it's good to be able to take a quick phone snap in an emergency—and it's better than taking no photo at all—but I never feel I'm a *serious* photographer when I'm shooting with my phone. The user experience gives me little joy, and even if I do manage to get a great shot, I never feel like I've actually *crafted* something special.

WHICH LENS?

As with most considerations about gear, lens choice is a very personal thing and you have to do what works for you.

My advice is don't faff around with lots of different lenses. Get to know one lens really, really well—well enough that your eyes start to see like that lens and your brain starts to think like it. Once you do, everything will feel so natural, so fluid, so instinctive, that by the time you bring the camera up to your eye, you'll already know exactly what your frame will look like. You'll know how that lens describes the world without even thinking about it. And that's when the magic starts to happen. It's liberating!

PRIME OR ZOOM?

I've been doing this for a long time and what works for me without any doubt is a wide-angle prime lens. By prime lens I mean a lens with a fixed focal length. But why a prime lens and not a more versatile zoom? Well, there are a number of reasons:

- Firstly, zooming inevitably takes longer. Those vital milliseconds could make the difference between getting your shot and missing it, and you really don't want to lose the spontaneity of the moment.

- Secondly, the image quality you'll get from a prime lens is nearly always superior to what you'll get from a zoom.

- Thirdly, as primes have far less glass than zooms, and often have less electronic circuitry, they tend to be smaller, lighter, and quieter. Consequently, they're usually more durable and reliable.

So, you're probably getting the message that I recommend using prime lenses. But what about focal length? Usually in street photography, we give some importance to context, and the background in our scene more often than not contributes something useful to the frame. Remember, you have a full frame to fill, not just that bit in the middle. A wide-angle lens will allow you to take in the wider picture and, more importantly, it forces you to get closer to the subject. By getting in close, your images will have much more sense of emotion, drama, or intimacy than they would have if you were shooting from across the road with a longer lens.

The whole shooting experience when shooting with a prime lens is more fulfilling than zoom photography. You need to get used to zooming with your feet!

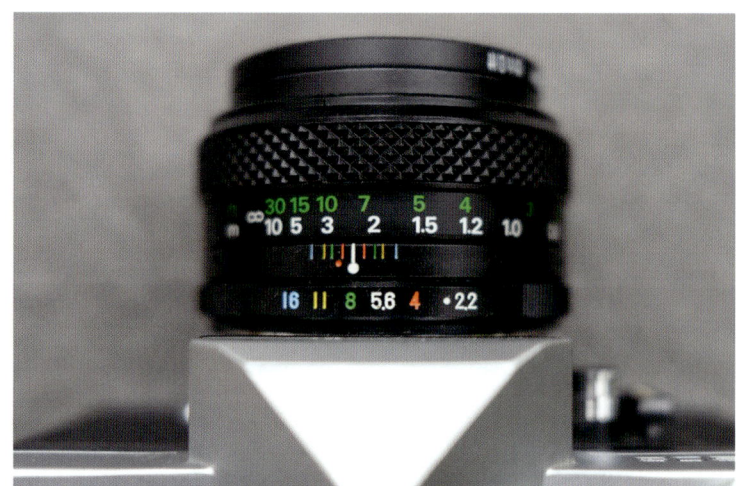

35MM

The sweet spot focal length for street photography is 35mm. This focal length offers you a perspective that isn't too far from what the human eye sees, so it's a *realistic* perspective. Try looking at a scene without a camera; now lift your camera (with a 35mm lens) to your eye and you'll be looking at a very similar view. This feeling of realism is a pretty good starting point to authentically document street scenes.

35mm lenses are extremely versatile and often relatively fast, typically f/1.8 and sometimes f/1.4, making them ideal for shooting street portraits. This is the one lens that will do most jobs well: street scenes, documentary projects, portraits, urban landscapes, and travel photography. If you have only one desert-island lens, it should be this.

THE NIFTY FIFTY

Some will say that if it worked for Henri Cartier-Bresson, then we should be able to make it work for us. The 50mm lens used to be called the standard lens and by default was often included in the purchase of an SLR camera. For many years this was seen as the obvious choice if you were to use only one lens.

We should remember, however, that Cartier-Bresson lived in a very different era, when the streets were less cluttered and crowded and he had much more space in which to operate. He could more easily step back to get more into his frame; today we don't always have that luxury.

For those in an early stage of their street photography journey, the 50mm isn't a bad starting point. You'll probably feel more comfortable shooting slightly farther away from your subjects. But as your confidence grows, you'll probably start to feel that this focal length is too tight and that you're not able to pack enough content into your frame. Many photographers use the 50mm as the gateway drug to something wider.

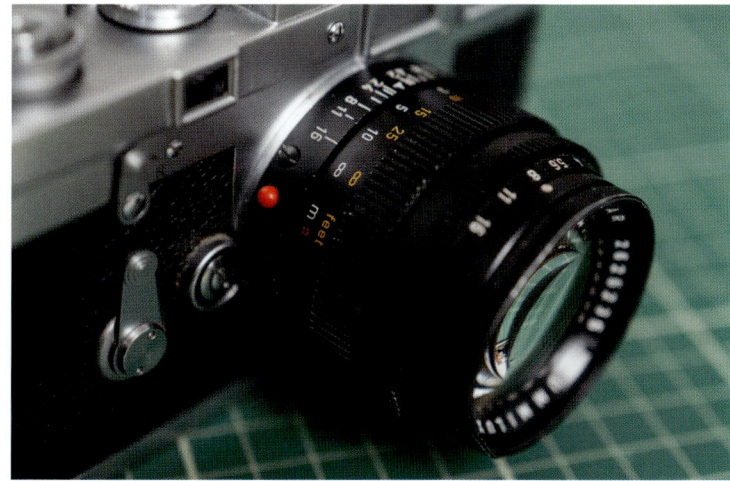

There's not much you can't do with a 50mm lens. It's a great all-arounder.

What to look for when choosing a camera

Here are some factors to consider when choosing a camera for street photography, in approximate order of relevance/importance:

1. **Portability and weight**
   Size does matter! You need a camera that fits comfortably in your hand, is easy to handle, and you'll be comfortable using for long stretches on the street.

2. **Lens options**
   The camera must be able to accommodate your choice of lens, whether that's a fixed or interchangeable lens. If you go for a fixed lens, bear in mind the type of street photography that interests you. There's no point in buying a fashionable street camera with a fixed 28mm lens if most of your preferred shooting is done at 35 or 50mm. If you go for a fixed lens, consider whether you need a fast lens (such as f/1.4) or a less expensive, slower lens (such as f/2).

3. **Ergonomics and feel**
   If a camera feels right, it will perform better for you. It should be a joy to hold, and you must want to pick it up off the shelf. Does the camera sit right in your hand? Will you truly enjoy using it? You're about to spend a long time with your choice in your hand, so both ergonomics and emotional connection are important factors to bear in mind. Ideally, you'll be able to operate the camera with one hand.

4. **Fast operation**
   The controls should be intuitive. Physical dials, buttons, and rings to control exposure are much faster to use than scrolling through menus. You'll sometimes need to make very quick adjustments in order to get the shot. The camera should be ready to use as soon as it's switched on, with little or no lag.

5. **Focusing options**
   If your camera only has manual focusing, that's no bad thing and you'll be able to practice zone focusing. If it has autofocus, the AF should be fast and quiet.

6. Stealth

Your camera should be as small and discreet as possible so as not to draw attention to yourself. Black models stand out less than silver ones. Also consider the need to work quietly; a loud shutter sound could draw unwanted attention. Aim for a camera with an electronic shutter, a leaf shutter, or both.

7. Weather resistance

Street photography is an all-weather pursuit, so it's good not to have to worry about your camera getting wet. Look for the IP52 rating, which means that the kit is well protected from water and dust ingress.

8. Battery life

You don't really want to be carrying lots of batteries around all day. Some cameras have better power management and battery life than others, so do your homework before you commit to buying.

9. Build quality and durability

Some cameras are built like tanks, whilst others can feel plasticky and flimsy. Street cameras can take quite a pounding!

10. Image quality

Are you surprised this is so low on the list? It's perhaps not as important as you think: Most modern cameras can take pictures that are more than good enough, and it's easy to get carried away with megapixels. For most purposes, 20mp will be perfectly adequate.

11. Low-light performance

If you intend to shoot after dark, this is a key factor, and it isn't always a function of the megapixel count. However, generally speaking, the bigger the sensor, the more likely it is to offer greater dynamic range and deliver acceptable image quality at high ISO settings.

12. Articulating screen

Whilst we should be careful not to overdo shooting from the hip (waist level), it's useful to have the option of using a flip screen for covert shooting.

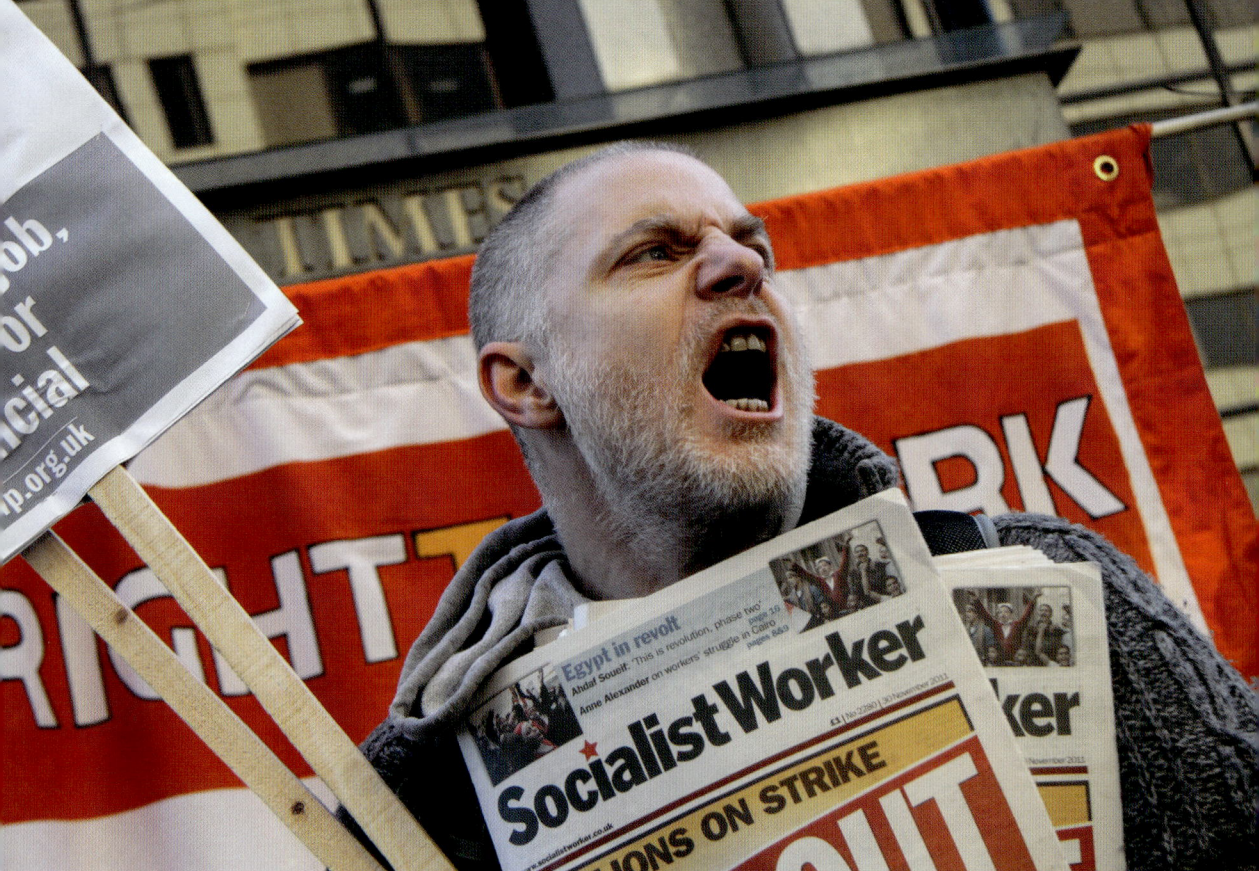

The 28mm is ideal for shooting in busy places where space is tight and you may not have room to step back.

28MM AND WIDER

You're probably familiar with the famous Robert Capa quote: *"If your pictures aren't good enough, you aren't close enough."* And there's something in that, particularly if storytelling is what you're all about. However, the wider your lens, the closer you need to get to your subject, which of course isn't for everybody.

For many, the 28mm is the perfect focal length, allowing them to build more complex, layered images with lots of information in the frame. Conversely, for those with a more minimalist style (Saul Leiter, for example), a much longer focal length will reduce that information to the point where the image relies much more on form and simple shapes than on complexity.

Another great benefit of shooting at 28mm is that you'll always get more depth of field, allowing for more context in the background (or foreground), which is often important in street photography. Then there's the matter of zone (or range) focusing: If you switch off the autofocus and set the distance to around three metres, shooting at f/8 will result in almost everything being in focus.

Should you go wider than 28mm? It's certainly not for the fainthearted. The wider you go, the more reality will be distorted—but it's certainly worth spending some time experimenting as you may uncover a distinctive perspective that becomes an important part of your personal style.

OTHER GEAR

One of the great things about street photography is that you don't need to carry loads of bulky or heavy gear around with you. Most of the time one camera, one lens, a spare battery, and memory cards is enough.

BAGS

Choosing the right bag is a big deal, and if you're anything like me, you'll spend a lifetime trying every bag on the market in search of the perfect solution. The ideal camera bag will be small, light, weather resistant, and comfortable to carry around the streets for extended periods. Avoid bags that look as though they may contain expensive gear, especially those with the name of a major camera manufacturer on the front.

Personally, I prefer a shoulder bag to a backpack, because I can access gear as quickly and stealthily as possible.

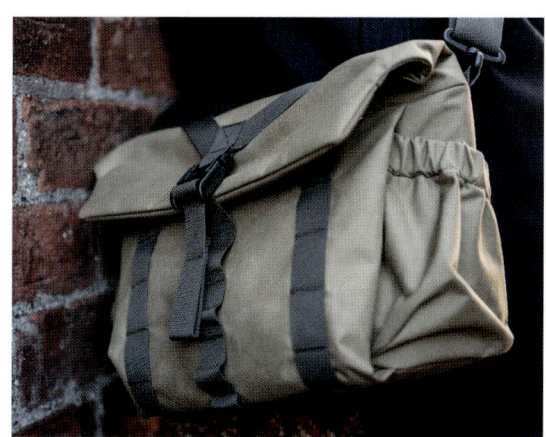

Shoulder bags, such as this Wotancraft Pilot, are discreet, comfortable, and weather resistant—all of which should be on your checklist when choosing a bag.

TO FLASH OR NOT TO FLASH?

Although relatively few street photographers use flash, it still has its place and can be used when the situation demands it. For photographers such as Martin Parr, Bruce Gilden, and Dougie Wallace, flash is an important factor in creating distinctive images, even in harsh sunlight, creating a very crisp, contrasty, and vibrant look.

But it's not for the fainthearted. When the flash fires, everyone around you will know that you have just taken a picture, not least the subject. Shooting this way requires a certain level of confidence and bravado.

When shooting the streets at night, I rarely use flash, preferring the natural look of the ambient lighting and making a feature out of available light sources. I sometimes carry a small flash in my bag, but only use it for the occasional street portrait.

STRAPS

Your camera strap should be secure, comfortable, and discreet (again, avoid those that brazenly advertise a camera brand). I advocate using a wrist strap rather than a neck strap, as the camera will always be in your hand and, therefore, more ready and prepared to take a shot. Also, wrist straps are more discreet because the camera won't be as clearly on display. There are lots of options available—I prefer those made from flexible climbing rope or soft leather.

FILTERS

Generally speaking, there's not much of a role for filters in street photography because they can easily destroy the authenticity of a scene. However, I usually protect the front elements of my lenses with a UV filter and, if shooting in monochrome, will almost always use an orange filter to increase contrast.

If you're shooting at night, then a diffusion filter can produce a pleasing atmospheric effect, creating a hazy glow around highlights such as street lamps.

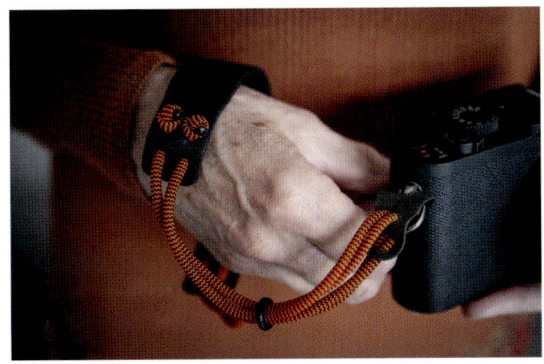

Wrist straps are generally more convenient than neck straps because they offer increased mobility and good security.

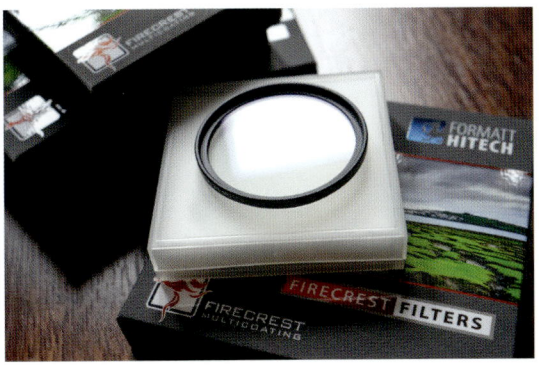

You definitely won't need a bagful of filters for street photography. Most street shooters use just a UV filter to protect their lens.

GETTING TO KNOW YOUR GEAR

It's essential that we have a good working relationship with our gear. In fact, we need to know it intimately and be able to operate it without thinking or looking at it. You should really be able to operate your camera with your eyes closed.

This is particularly relevant when you're shooting spontaneously and without the luxury of time to think about what you're actually doing. Your fingers should be able to make adjustments by feel alone, using muscle memory to control the camera's key functions. Being able to work quickly in this way means that you are less likely to miss shots.

There's no magic formula to achieving this, but you'll find that patience and practice will be time well spent.

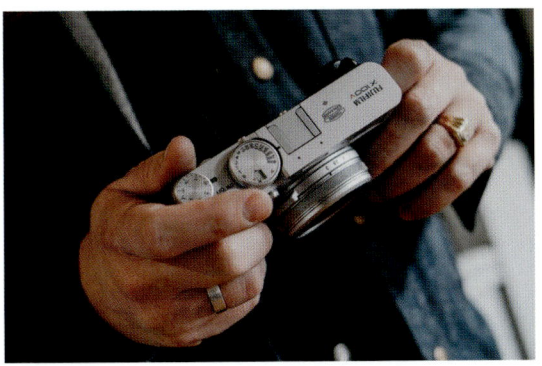

There's a lot to be said for consistently using the same camera and lens for street photography. Practice it until you can operate it with your eyes closed.

CAMERA SETTINGS

There's no right or wrong approach to how you set up your camera for street photography, and you must always do what works for you. However, I've found that a keep-it-simple mentality has always allowed me to operate quickly and instinctively, reacting instantly to anything that is happening around me.

It's nearly always best to set your camera up once at the beginning of the day, after which, with one or two exceptions, you should leave it alone. Don't get distracted by menu settings or by constantly making changes: Your mantra should be "set it and forget it." All your concentration needs to be focused on what's going on around you, not what's happening inside the camera. Get to the stage where it feels like you have a disposable camera in your hand and all you need to do is press the shutter button to be confident of getting a decent shot.

A good starting point is to prepare a default walkaround setting that will capture the shot you need in the majority of street shooting situations. You may not always get the perfect result, but it should be good enough. Of course, you can tweak those settings when the situation requires it, for example to deal with changing light situations or perhaps to achieve a shallow depth of field for a street portrait.

YOUR DEFAULT SETTINGS FOR EXPOSURE

These default (or failsafe or walkaround) settings amount to a combination of ISO, aperture, and shutter speed, which will almost guarantee you get the shot you need 95 percent of the time. You're now free to direct all your attention to the activity around you without having to think about what is happening in-camera. This way of working is designed to make your life easy and to shoot quickly and spontaneously. Here's what to do:

1. Set the exposure mode to **Aperture Priority**.

2. Set your aperture to **f/8 (average day)** or **f/11 (bright day)**.

3. Select **Auto ISO**.

4. In your auto ISO menu, **set the range from 200 to 6,400** and the **minimum shutter speed to 1/250th or faster**.

Let's look at the rationale behind this (bearing in mind the aim is simplicity and speed). We select a small aperture because context is often important in street photography and content in the background often contributes to the frame. Whilst you could take a lovely portrait of someone with an extremely shallow depth of field, it wouldn't tell you much about what that person is doing, where they are, or who they are with—all the context that adds depth and meaning to an image. An aperture of f/8 or f/11 (or even f/16 in really strong light) will give you sufficient depth of field to retain key information in the background while still letting a reasonable amount of light into the lens. Using f/8 is a good compromise aperture: It's an aperture for all seasons.

Let's now look at shutter speed. In street photography, a fast shutter speed is usually necessary. We live in a dynamic world where things are moving (perhaps we're moving ourselves), and we can't afford to risk losing a shot because of subject blur or camera shake. We therefore want a shutter speed of 1/250th second or faster to minimize the possibility of the image being ruined because it's not sharp.

Then we have ISO, which can be dealt with in one of two ways: You can set an auto-ISO range, allowing the camera to choose a high value if it needs to do so; or, alternatively, you can set a relatively high static value such as 800 or 1,200. We allow the ISO to run up to a high value so that we can maintain a fast shutter speed. Sure, this may result in a little extra noise, but it's a price worth paying if the alternative is a wasted shot because of subject blur or camera shake. Most modern cameras handle high ISO extremely well, and if you want consistently sharp street images, you will need to embrace this feature.

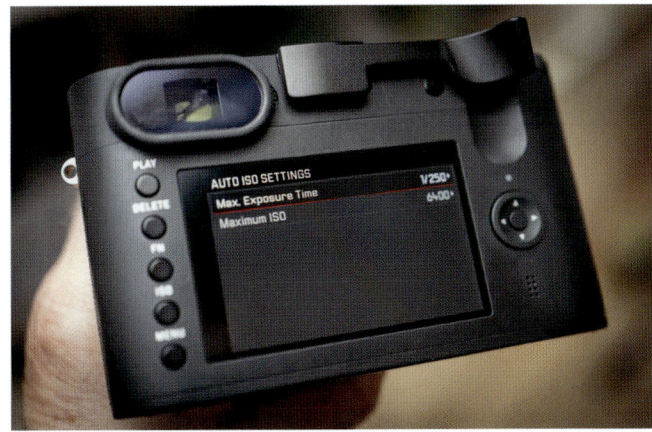

Most modern cameras allow you to set the parameters for auto ISO in the menu.

With these settings, you can forget about what's going on in the camera and direct all your attention to observing what's happening around you, searching for subjects, and ensuring you get the best possible composition. There will be times, of course, when these settings simply won't work for you and you may change them completely to suit the situation (shooting a street portrait, for example, may require a shallow depth of field). This method is a guide, not something set in stone.

Fine-tuning the exposure

Whilst these settings will work well most of the time, you will almost certainly need to make tweaks to the exposure. The quickest and most efficient way is to use your exposure compensation control, whether that is a dial, a thumbwheel, or a button.

For example, if you needed to darken your image, you would dial in a minus value in exposure compensation, say –1EV or –2EV. You will typically want to do this to protect the highlights, to intensify the shadows, or to saturate the colours. Conversely, if you were shooting toward the light, you could apply a positive (+) value to the exposure compensation to bring some detail back into shadowy areas.

The exposure compensation facility will allow you to fine-tune the exposure whilst letting you see the effect of these tweaks in real time (with a mirrorless camera).

Make friends with your exposure compensation dial; you should be constantly making tweaks.

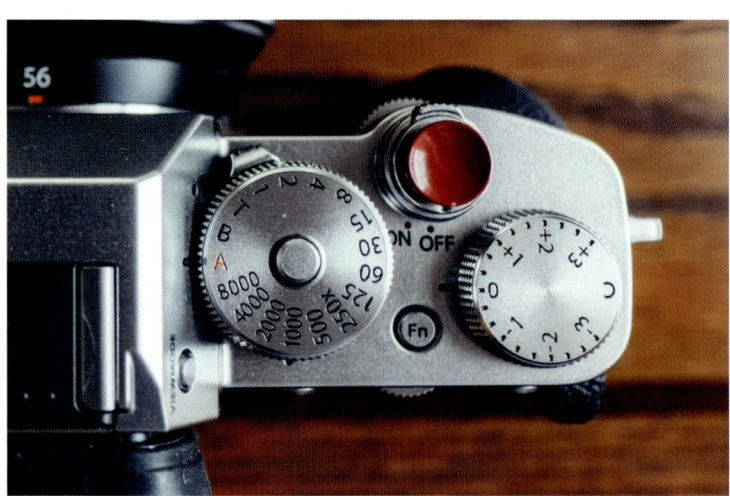

Metering

Don't overthink this! When metering, the multi-zone, matrix, or evaluative pattern (each brand gives it their own name) will give you a sufficiently accurate reading. This analyzes composition, colour, and brightness distribution to determine exposure, and it gets it right most of the time.

Some street photographers prefer to use spot metering, but I find this cumbersome and slow. The time spent obsessing about where to position the spot could mean missing that critical moment.

It's also worth mentioning light meters. An increasing trend for street photographers is to use older analogue cameras, many of which don't have a built-in exposure meter. There's something quite *wholesome* about measuring the light with a handheld meter before taking a shot, and many of us see it as an important part of the street photography process.

Decent light meters are fairly inexpensive and can be analogue or digital; there are also a number of smartphones apps, some of them free, that do the same job.

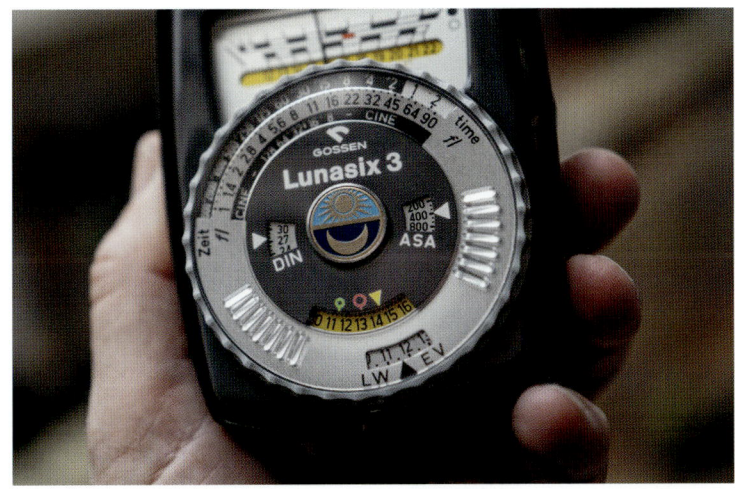

Exposure meters are either analogue or digital; each does the same job but one presents readings with a needles on a dial, like this one, whist others give you a digital readout of the exposure value.

RAW or JPEG?

Should you shoot in RAW or JPEG, or both? Personally, I usually shoot just in RAW, if only to keep all options open farther down the line, for example when it comes to making adjustments to white balance or when converting an image to black and white.

If your camera has dual memory card slots, it's probably worth shooting a RAW file to one card and JPEG to the other. This could give you the opportunity to use the camera's built-in presets or film simulations. Sometimes, particularly when working on projects, I'm looking for a consistent aesthetic and the film simulation can give me that aesthetic straight out of the camera. The other advantage of recording to two card slots is security: Memory cards can become corrupted without warning, and it is good practice to have a secure backup.

However, I wouldn't criticize anyone for shooting JPEG only; JPEGs take up less memory space, are easier to edit, and their read/write speeds are faster.

FOCUSING

The big question is manual or autofocus? The answer is it doesn't really matter, and you should do what works best for you. Focusing is a personal thing and there's no right or wrong approach. Some street photographers find it easier to use autofocus and others prefer focusing manually. Traditionally, street photography has always been associated with manual focusing, probably because of the genre's long association with rangefinder cameras (Leicas, in particular, which have never had an autofocus capability).

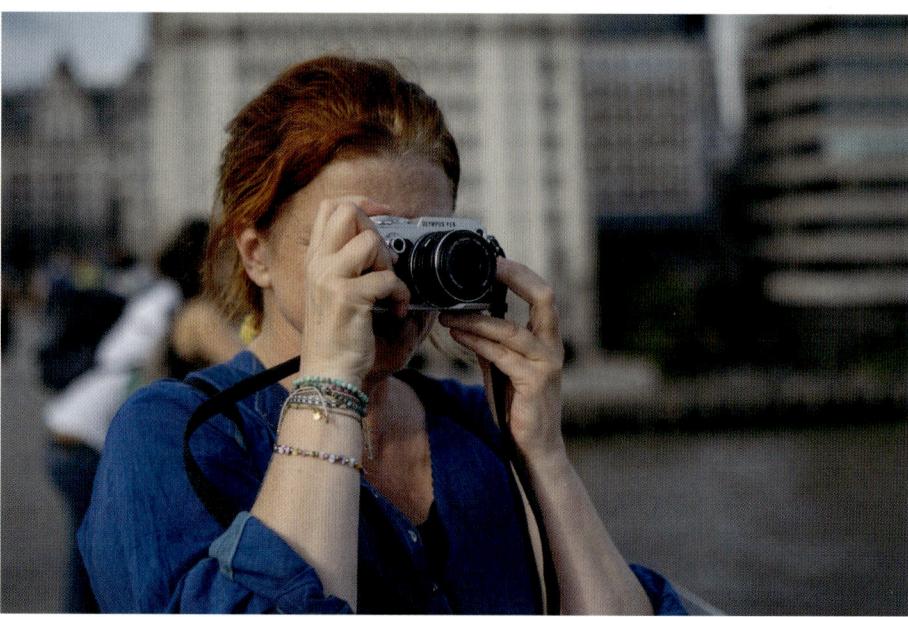

Purists still prefer to focus manually, but it doesn't matter whether you use MF or AF—do whatever's the fastest and most accurate method for you.

The autofocusing ability of most modern cameras is fast, accurate, and reliable, and you would be right to question why manual focus is even an option. However, street photography is often about speed and reaction times, and quite often autofocus simply isn't quick enough. That might sound counter-intuitive, but please bear with me.

The problem with autofocus is that the process of positioning the focus point on the appropriate part of the subject, then acquiring focus (locking on) with a half-press of the shutter button, and then taking the picture can take too long, and a decisive moment can easily be missed. This is why many street photographers prefer to focus manually, using the zone focusing technique, to ensure a sharp picture is taken in the shortest possible time.

Zone focusing

Zone focusing has been used by street photographers forever and a day. This is a technique whereby you manually pre-focus your lens at a specific distance (say, 8 feet) and use a small aperture to ensure good depth of field. This will give you an operating range or a zone of sharpness—say from 4 feet to 25 feet—and everything within this zone will be acceptably sharp. I use the term "acceptably sharp" rather than "pin sharp" to mean that sharp enough is good enough.

Once you've set up your focus distance and aperture, all you need to do is to make sure your subject falls within the zone. If you've never tried zone focusing you may feel that it requires a leap of faith, but if you can get over any initial reservations, you should find the process straightforward and most effective—if not liberating.

The key to making zone focusing work is to have deep depth of field. This is best achieved with the combination of a wide-angle lens and a small aperture. Zone focusing only really works well with a lens of 35mm or wider. The wider the lens, the more effective zone focusing will be; you'll probably find that the zone will be too small with a lens that is longer than 35mm.

Follow these three steps for zone focusing:

1. **Turn off the AF** and set your camera/lens to MF.

2. **Set a small aperture:** f/8 or f/11 is ideal.

3. **Set a focus distance.** Pre-focus your lens to a specific distance and leave it there (usually around 7 to 10 feet).

If you're using an older manual lens, it will probably have a depth-of-field scale on the barrel from which you can clearly see what's in the zone. Many modern cameras also have a digital scale in the viewfinder that does the same job. Either way, you'll be able to see how far your zone extends.

The barrel markings on traditional lenses make zone focusing a breeze (some digital cameras replicate this with a scale in the EVF or on the LCD screen). In this example you'll see that I have set the distance to 8 feet; then, reading from the white aperture markings, you can see that at f/11, everything between around 6 feet and 12.5 feet will be in focus. This is our zone.

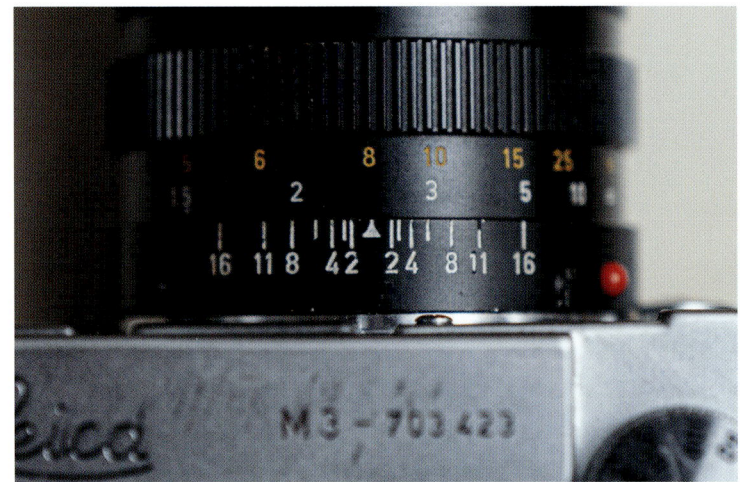

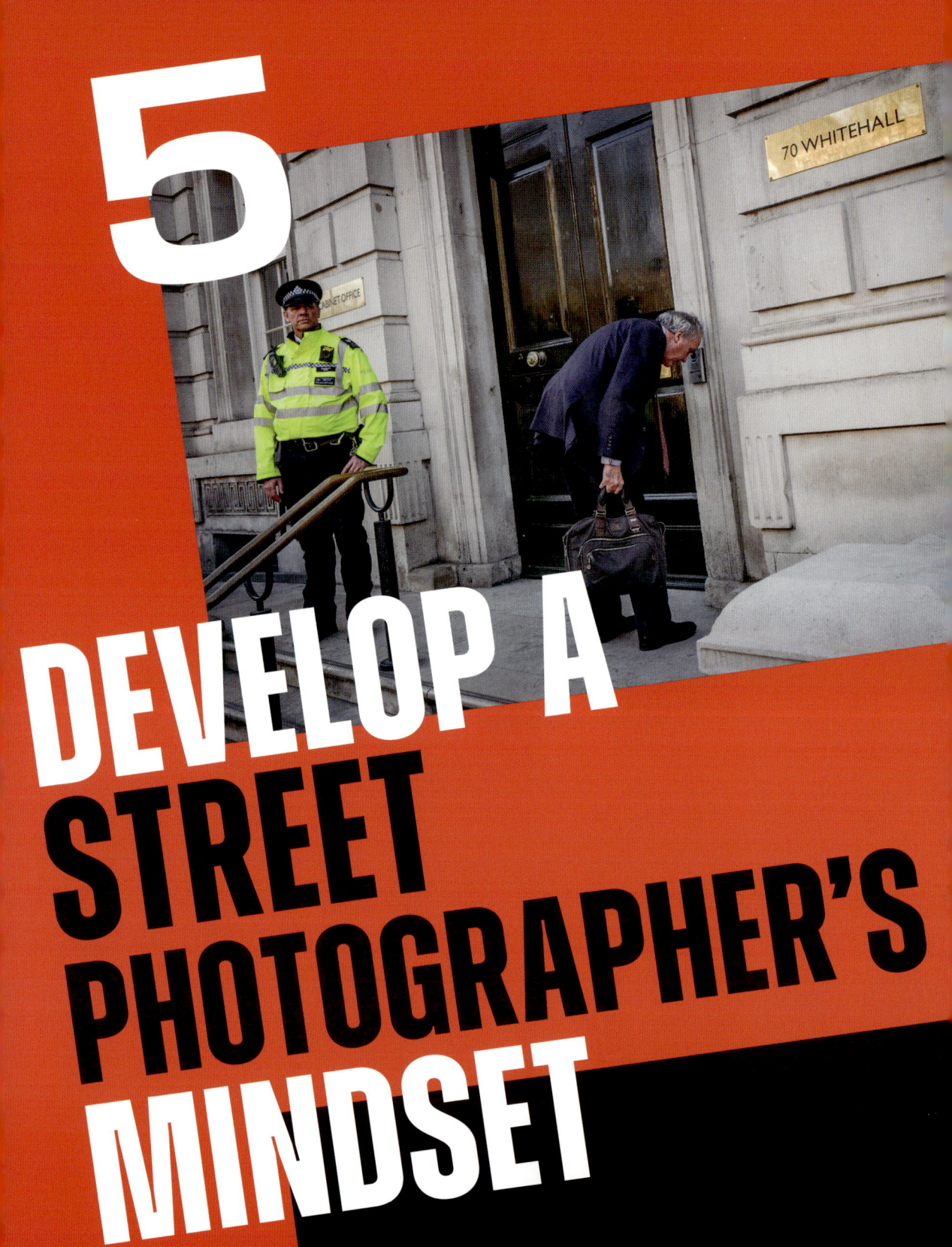

5

DEVELOP A STREET PHOTOGRAPHER'S MINDSET

What, exactly, is a street photographer's mindset?

Do landscape photographers have a mindset? Wildlife photographers? Portrait specialists? Perhaps they do, but not in the way that we do. Earlier we discussed personality types, and the question of mindsets flows naturally from that conversation. For most of us, street photography is more than taking pictures. It's a way of life, a subculture—perhaps almost a cult.

In this chapter, we'll dig deep into the soft skills you need to develop to become accomplished street photographers. I have identified the 15 skills we should all possess. The good news is that they are all easily acquirable. You could call this being streetwise.

Always be on the lookout for the unusual in the usual (like the politician apparently hitting his head against a brick wall). Once you start to think and behave like a street photographer, there's no going back. You'll develop a mindset that will stay with you.

RELAX!

I mention elsewhere in this book the importance of being warm, friendly, open, and relaxed when you're shooting on the streets. In encounters with others, your own demeanour is often reflected back to you, and people will respond to you in a like-minded way.

Be proud of what you're doing, and don't try to hide behind your camera. If someone does catch your eye and smiles at you, smile back—don't turn away and pretend you didn't notice. Whilst I generally prefer to work unseen, I inevitably have interactions with members of the public. If people want to stop and chat, then I'm happy to chat. You'll find that, with practice, you'll be making quick judgement calls about whether or not to engage with your subject. All this, of course, needs to be tempered with being invisible and discreet, but I think there is a happy medium. Occasionally, following a pleasant interaction, I'll offer to send the subject a copy of the photo. It's a nice *quid pro quo*.

I find that my mood often reflects the type of pictures I take. If I feel positive and upbeat (usually when the weather is sunny!), then I tend to come across happy, positive, and upbeat scenes. If I'm not feeling great, I'm grumpy, or it's raining, I'll probably take conceptually darker images; it's human nature, I guess.

DEVELOP YOUR OBSERVATION SKILLS

Do you think they're already good? Then make them better! There's a great little video on YouTube called *Basketball Awareness Test* (you should find it easily using that search phrase). In this test of observational skills, a team dressed in white and a team in black are playing basketball, and you are asked how many passes the white team makes. It's not difficult, and most people give the correct count—but how well did they observe? I won't give you the punchline! The video was produced by Transport for London to highlight the issue with drivers being unaware of cyclists.

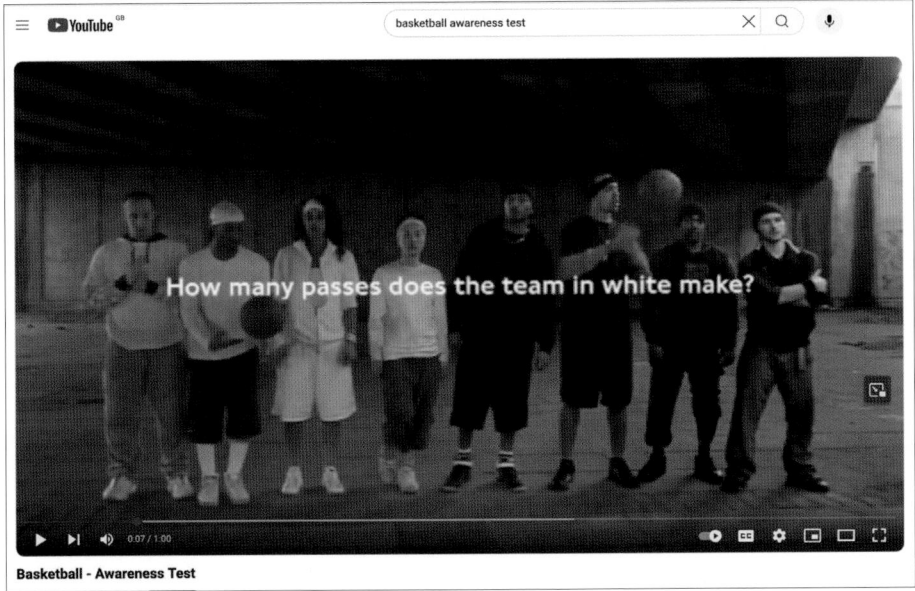

Basketball - Awareness Test

Check out this YouTube video to test your own observation skills.

The video also highlights an issue for us as street photographers. If there's one must-have personal quality we all need, it's exceptional observation skills.

When we talk about observation skills, we are simply referring to the act of paying attention, which most of us are capable of doing. It requires being present in the moment and fully engaged with your surroundings. It's not only about what is directly in front of you, it's about the bigger picture.

Observation is at the very core of street photography. It goes beyond just seeing; it involves truly *looking* and actively seeking out the details that make a scene into something special. As a street photographer, you need to be fully present in the moment, zoned into the sights, sounds, and events that unfold on the streets. This usually requires practice: Train your eye to notice the subtle gestures, the interplay of light and shadow, the juxtaposition of elements, and the nuances of human behaviour.

> *"I believe in the humanist spirit of photography, that the camera gives us a kind of passport to explore the world, and to really look at people and places with compassion and empathy." —Joel Meyerowitz*

TEN STEPS TO DEVELOPING YOUR POWERS OF OBSERVATION

Below are some tips to help you develop your observation skills:

1. **Be present and mindful.**

    - Avoid distractions like looking at your phone, listening to music, engaging in conversation, or dashing through the streets.

    - Engage your senses: Notice the light, sounds, movement, and even the smells around you.

    - Practice mindfulness techniques to train yourself to stay focused.

2. **Study human behavior.**

    - Observe patterns, commonalities, quirks, nuances, gestures, and emotions in people's behavior.

    - Study routines such how people interact in cafes, cross streets, or stand on train platforms.

    - Look for contrasts, such as someone calm amidst chaos.

3. **Notice light and shadows.**

    - Study how the light changes throughout the day and how it interacts with structures, objects, and people.

    - Observe reflections, silhouettes, and shadows.

4. **Focus on the detail.**

    - Look for textures, patterns, or unique objects in your surroundings, especially things in unexpected places or situations.

    - Train yourself to spot small, often-overlooked moments, such as a dropped item or an awkward gesture or glance.

5. **Work on your peripheral vision.**

    - When focusing on a subject, engage your peripheral vision to scan for complementary or contrasting elements.

    - Practice by observing a scene and note what's happening in the corners of your view.

6. Practice visualization.

- Imagine potential photographs as you walk the streets, even when you don't have a camera with you.

- Anticipate where people or objects might align to create compelling compositions.

7. Keep a journal.

- Noting down what you see can help you process and remember details better.

- Write down descriptions of scenes or moments that connect with you.

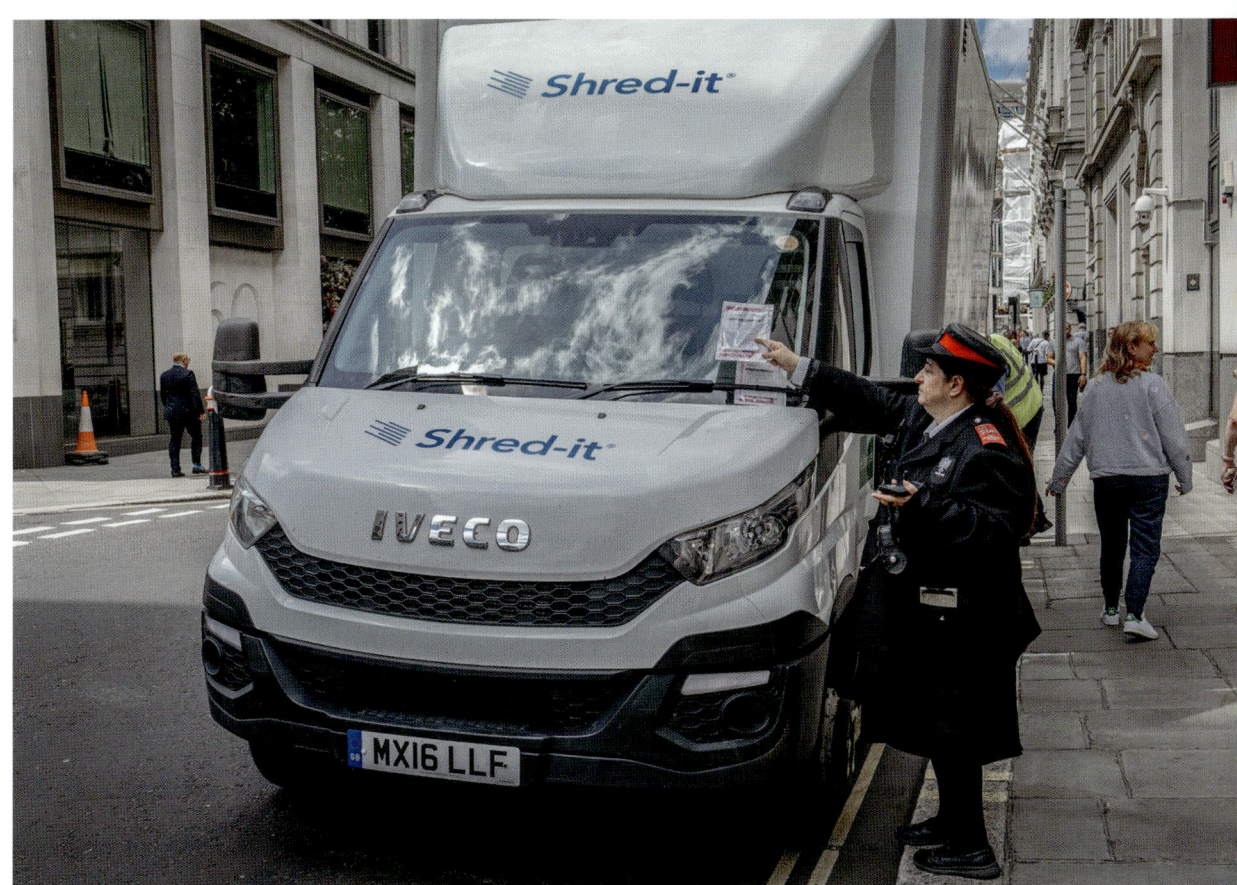

Using words is an easy way to make connections—you just need to have your wits about you and think quickly. Here I saw the words "Shred It" on the van and I noticed that it was being issued with a parking fine. Bingo!

8. **Study the masters.**

- Analyze work by the great street photographers such as Henri Cartier-Bresson, Helen Levitt, or Elliot Erwitt. Try to understand what they observed in an image.

- Notice how they record decisive moments and understand their motivations for composition and storytelling.

9. **Walk without a camera.**

- Train yourself to notice compelling scenes without the pressure of taking a photo. You will almost certainly see plenty!

- Mentally compose shots and identify what caught your eye.

10. **Practice patience.**

- Stay in one location for longer than you would normally linger and observe how the scene evolves or develops over time. This can help you notice opportunities others might overlook.

ALWAYS BE "ON"

There's a saying amongst financial traders: *"Snoozing is losing."* It's exactly the same for street photographers: We can guarantee that the second we let our guard down and lose concentration, the perfect picture passes us by.

Being always "on" works in two ways. Firstly, your camera needs to be switched on, set up, and ready to go. Use a wrist strap rather than a neck strap for fast access, disable your camera's sleep function, and have the camera preset with your preferred setting so that you don't need to think before pressing the shutter (refer back to Chapter 4 for the "set it and forget it" approach).

Secondly, you need to be always "on" and tuned in mentally, always thinking, observing, calculating, and considering the possibilities. Some street photographers like to shoot with a buddy or in larger groups, whereas I prefer to shoot alone because I can be much more in the zone without the distractions of conversation.

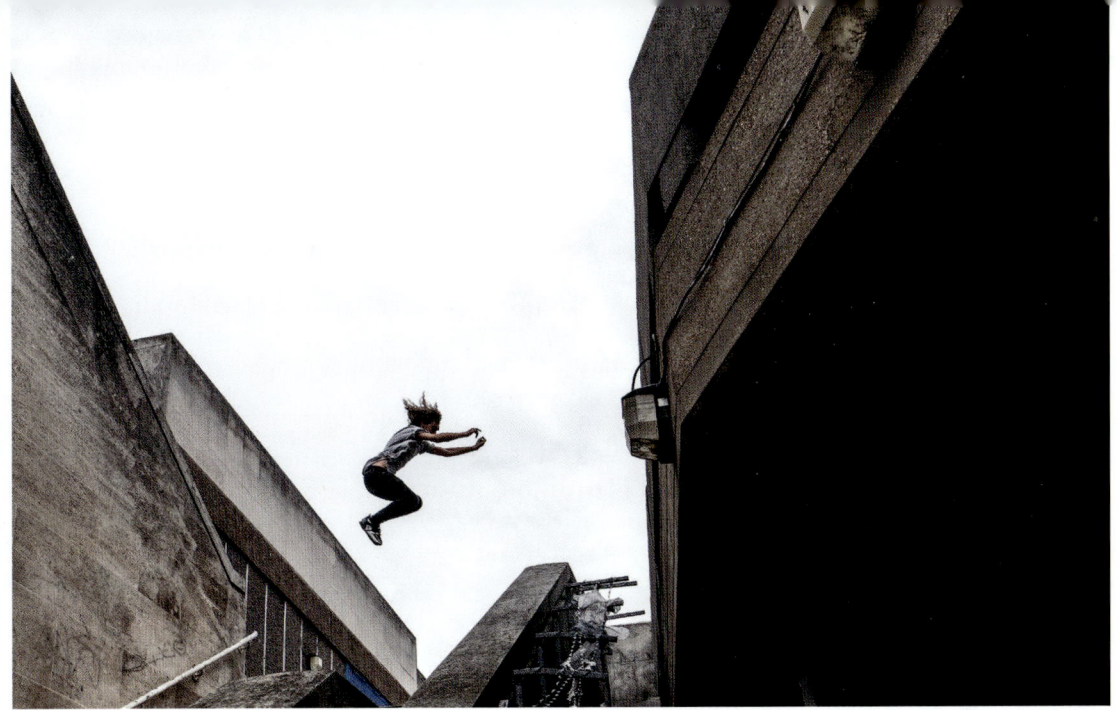

Had I not been in the zone and totally tuned in to my surroundings, I might have missed this guy in mid-air.

HUNT AND FISH

Street photographers are hunters or fishers, sometimes a bit of both. Whichever you are will be determined in part by your personality and in part by your preferred style of imagery.

I would advocate both hunting and fishing. Whatever your natural inclinations, the versatility of both approaches will stand you in good stead. Although I see myself as being much more of a hunter than a fisherman, I would probably do both in an average day's shooting.

HUNTING

The hunter is permanently on maneouvres, patrolling the streets in a state of high alert, looking for those elusive moments. The hunter is constantly on the move and won't be still for long, enjoying the unpredictability of what might appear around the next corner. They shoot a lot and often shoot while they are walking, without stopping, taking lots of pictures but getting proportionally few keepers.

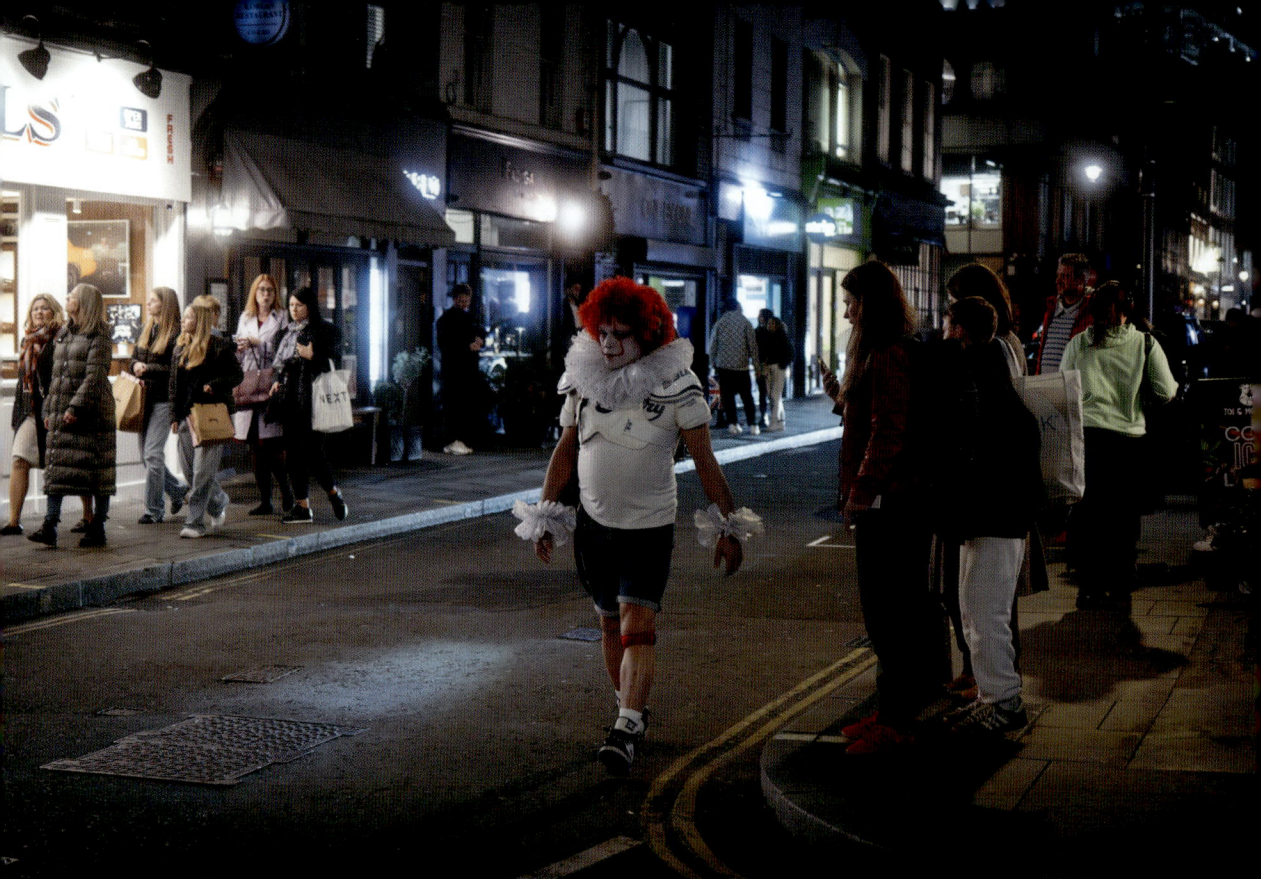

The hunter never knows what's around the next corner; they are always ready and they never hesitate.

Garry Winogrand was a great example of a hunter; he was once said to "sting" his subjects. He skillfully dodged and weaved amongst the crowds of people in the streets of New York with his Leica and 28mm, not merely observing, but actually being a part of street life. He composed impulsively and often improvised, in a way that was described by Jean-Luc Godard as "the definitive by chance."

Hunting doesn't work for everyone. Whilst it's more dynamic and exciting, it's more likely to lead to confrontation and is probably not best suited to the more cautious or introverted street photographer.

FISHING

As the name implies, fishing is an exercise in a much slower, laid back, and more patient style of street shooting. It's just like real fishing: You find a good place in the stream where you know there will be fish, you cast your line, and then wait for the fish to come. You know the fish are there, and you know they will eventually come; it's just a matter of time. This works just the same way in street photography.

The fisher will choose their spot and wait for the subjects to come into the frame. Location is critical here. The right location can mean a well-chosen background, some great light, or another factor that makes the image work.

Henri Cartier-Bresson was a good example of a fisherman, as was Fan Ho. Both knew how to find the perfect location and had the patience to wait until all the elements came together to make the perfect frame.

"Street photography is like fishing. Catching the fish is more exciting than eating it." —*Joel Meyerowitz*

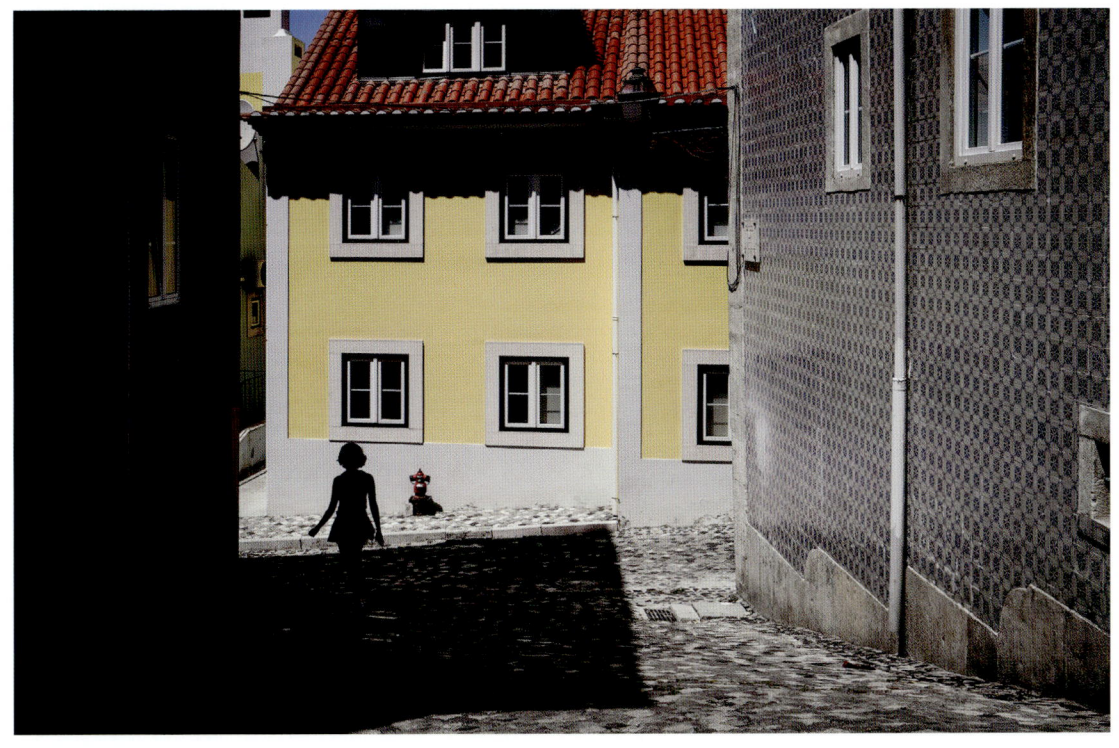

I immediately saw the potential in this background and I designed the space for a person to occupy. I waited for 5–10 minutes, and this girl walked into that space.

ANTICIPATE

"To me, photography is an art of observation. It's about finding something interesting in an ordinary place. I've found it has little to do with the things you see and everything to do with the way you see them." —Elliott Erwitt

Why is that guy going there? What's she about to do with that stick? Why is he walking backward? Strange things happen on our streets, and predicting what comes next is a kind of sixth sense that street photographers need to develop. We need to pick up on the tiniest of movements, the quietest of sounds, out-of-the-ordinary body language—anything that could influence either events or people's behaviour.

Anticipation does not mean waiting passively; it is an active and conscious engagement with what's happening around you.

We need to be students of body language. We watch, we listen, and we wait, second-guessing what might happen next: the peculiar gesture, the thrown punch, or the (slightly clichéd) jump over the puddle. Pay attention to the rhythm of the street, the movement of crowds, and the interplay between people. As you become more tuned in to these subtle cues, you'll start to anticipate interesting moments before they occur.

CHECK YOUR 5S AND 20S

To anticipate what's about to happen you need good situational awareness. There's a protocol in the British Army called "check your 5s and 20s." This refers to soldiers checking their 5-metre radius, then their 20-metre radius so they have a complete picture of their immediate surroundings to quickly assess any dangers. (This protocol later became known as the "0s, 5s, and 20s" rule during the Afghanistan War, when soldiers needed to check below the feet for IEDs when they stepped out of their vehicle.)

You can use this same principle in street photography, transposing "danger zone" for "photo-potential zone," to have a good basis for anticipating what's happening in your immediate vicinity.

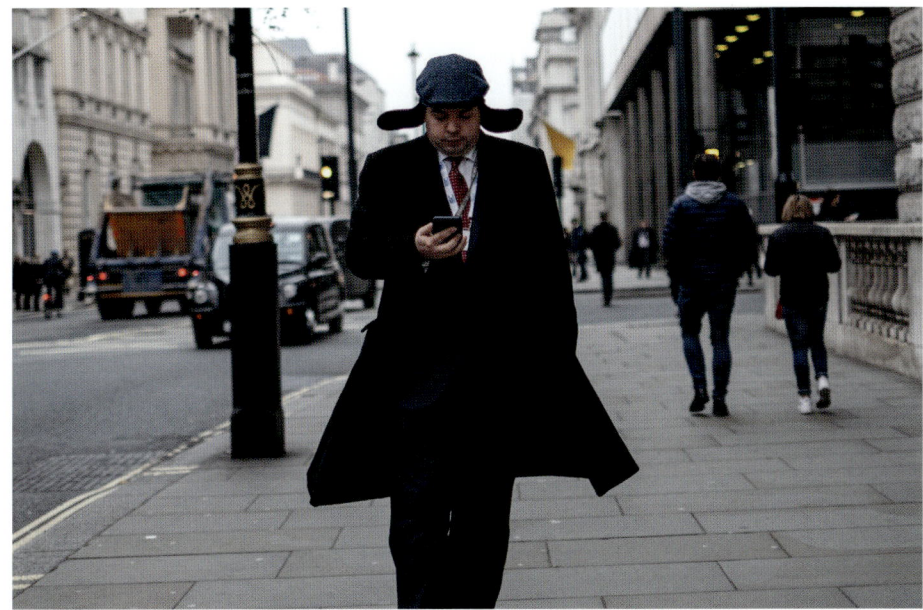

It was a windy day when this chap was walking toward me. A few moments before I took this picture, I saw one of the flaps on his hat blow up in the wind. I was then on high alert, anticipating (and hoping) the wind would catch the other flap—and it did!

FIND DETAIL

The ability to see potential in otherwise irrelevant detail is priceless, and it is the cornerstone of compelling street photography. It's often the subtle, barely noticeable, elements in a scene that can transform an ordinary image into one that resonates emotionally and visually.

Many of the great street images over the past 50 years came into being because of the photographer's ability to tune in to the minutest detail and then use it to their advantage. We need an acute sense of curiosity to see beauty in the mundane or unusual in the usual.

Actually seeking out detail needs to become a habit. Be nosy. *Think* about everything you see, look beyond the obvious, and question everything. The more you do this, the more it becomes an intrinsic part of your walking the streets.

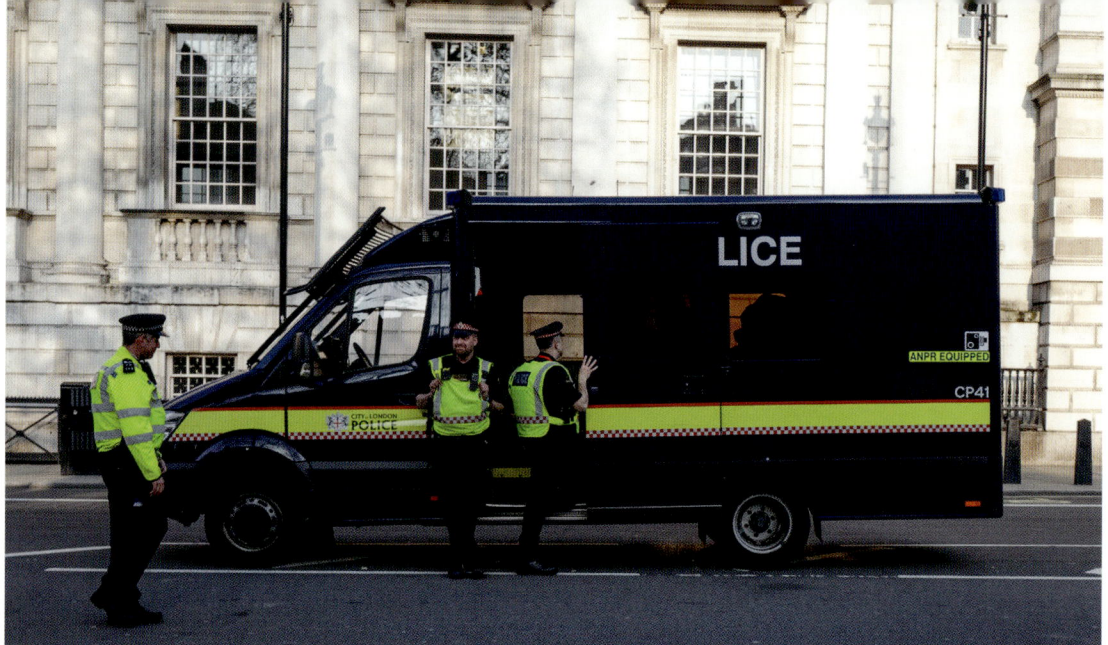

The detail here is all about the word "lice." This is, of course, not a dig at the police, but I couldn't resist making a connection!

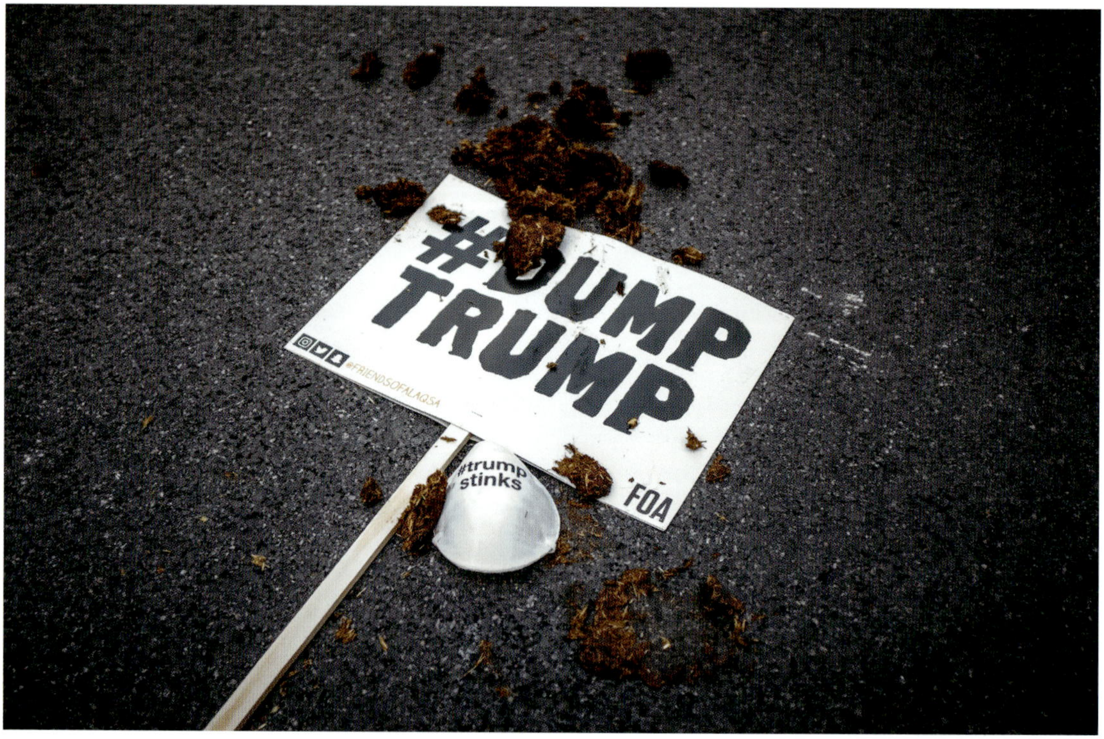

The sign on its own has little value—but when you connect the word "dump" with the horse manure, the wit is apparent.

MAKE CONNECTIONS

Connecting two or more elements in a frame has long been one of the pillars of street photography. A connection could be, for example, a simple juxtaposition or a visual pun (as in the Dump Trump image). Connections work best when the elements would not otherwise be related to each other, and bringing them together completes the circle.

We can consider three types of useful connections:

- Connections between people
- Connections between people and objects
- Connections between objects

Any of these can work, though the person-to-person connection is perhaps the most interesting. As human beings, we tune in to human interactions more readily than we do the non-human interactions. These connections could take the form of human contact, gestures, contrasting postures, body language, or eye contact.

Connections can be used to help tell a story, introduce humour, evoke an emotion, or provoke a reaction. Bear in mind that it is easy to stray into street photography cliché territory here (such as the trope of the homeless person sitting next to a swanky car).

BE PATIENT

I see so many street photographers give up on a scene before it has had time to develop into something more interesting. This is something that doesn't usually affect the natural fishers as, for them, patience comes as standard.

If you are not naturally patient, work on developing a more relaxed approach; hang around and wait for scenes to evolve, and don't move on until you've exhausted every option. Don't put pressure on yourself to shoot lots of great images every time you hit the streets; it will almost certainly never happen.

Linger more on street corners, walk more slowly, and spend more time waiting for the subjects to come to you, which they often do. I accept that this does not come easy to many of us, as we're so keen to get that next great shot. But some investment in time spent "hanging around" will pay dividends.

EXHAUST EVERY SCENE

Let's say you see an interesting scene evolving ahead of you. You get closer, take the picture, and then off you go. But don't do that—the job's not finished yet! Well done for reacting quickly and getting the shot, but there's still work to be done. We call this working the scene.

Assuming that your scene is still visually viable (nothing has much changed and there is still some shooting potential), you should now consider some alternatives: Try a higher viewpoint, take a few steps to the right, get a little closer, experiment with different settings. Whilst doing all this, maintain your flow of shooting. Take as many pictures as you can and try to resist "chimping," which will interrupt your train of thought. When you review the images later, there's a fair chance that at least one of them will be better than your first shot.

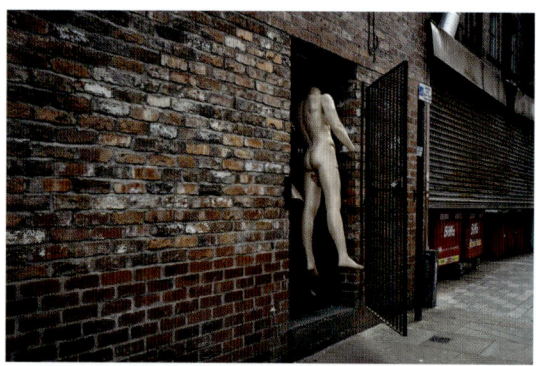
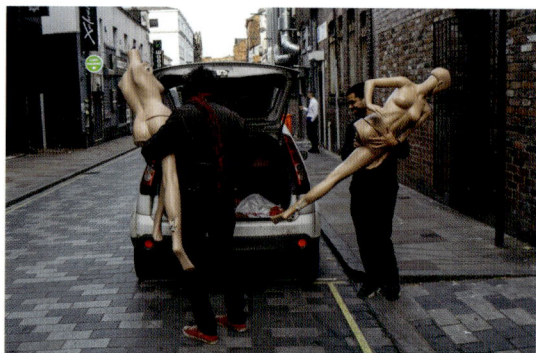
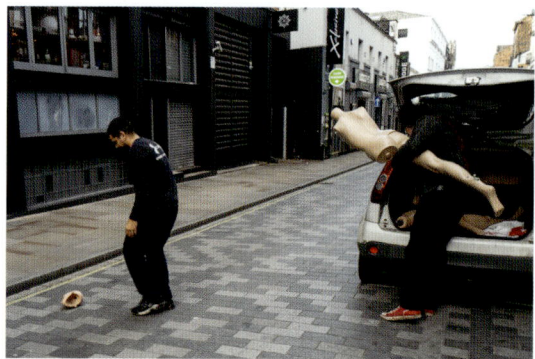
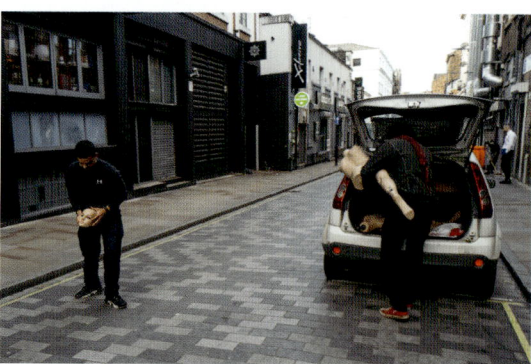

I saw these guys struggling to keep control of the mannequins as they tried to load them into the small car. Having taken one quick shot, I knew there would still be more photo opportunities to come, and I would end up with a good selection of keepers.

EMPATHIZE

"Photography is an empathy toward the world." **—Don McCullin**

Empathy helps give us a sense of perspective and allows us to establish a connection with our subjects. It involves seeing the world through the eyes of others and relating to their experiences. When you approach your street shooting with empathy, you go beyond capturing images; you tell stories that resonate with viewers and that evoke emotions.

Empathy also allows us to break down barriers and build trust with the people around us. It's about being respectful and considerate of their privacy and their personal space. Through empathy, we can capture candid moments without intruding upon people's lives and allow viewers to connect with our subjects more intensely.

Street photographers can be perceived to be uncaring and lacking in empathy. Don't let this be you. When the circumstances are right (when you won't forgo a candid moment), engage with your subjects on a human level. Take the time to interact with them, listen to their stories, and learn about their lives. Soak up all this wonderful human information. Through building empathy, you can not only enhance the quality of your images but also contribute to fostering understanding and empathy in the wider society.

FORGET PERFECTION

One thing that can hold street photographers back is a quest for perfection: the perfect composition, perfect light, perfect sharpness, perfect timing. Such obsessions invariably lead to missing the shot. An attitude of "close enough is good enough" should serve you well. It's better to have an otherwise strong image with slightly questionable sharpness than to have missed the moment because you were taking too long chasing perfection.

Study the work of Daido Moriyama or William Klein, two of the world's greatest street photographers. Many of their compositions were chaotic, unsharp, and compositionally wrong, but the spontaneity and the energy

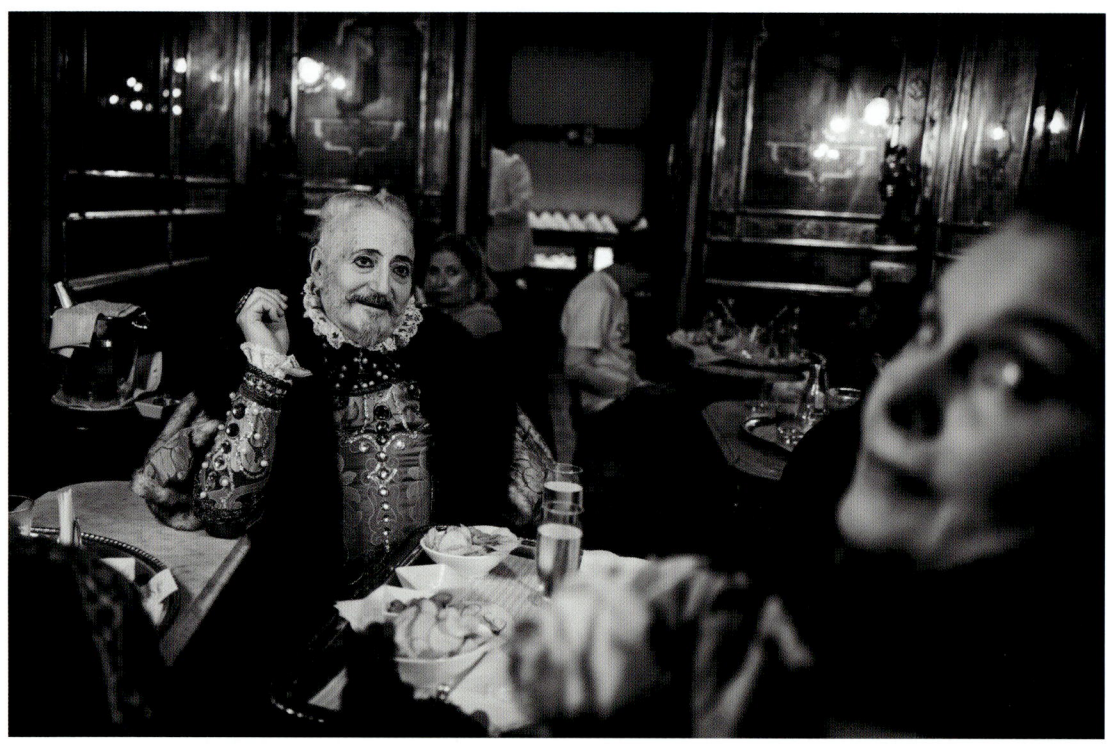

Take this image, for example: the horizon is wonky and one of the main subjects is out of focus. But I think it still works. The imperfection adds to the reality of the naturalness of the scene.

within the frame would overpower any misgivings about perfection. In fact, the opposite could easily be the case: An image with impeccable angles, perfect balance, and beautifully observed compositional rules could be so sterile and sanitized that it has little impact.

FIND YOUR HOTSPOTS

Discovering productive shooting areas is key to successful street photography. There's little value in spending time in locations that don't offer any opportunities. Skilled fishermen head to spots where they know the fish are likely to bite.

Every town and city have their share of more and less productive spots for street photography. A location might stand out because of exceptional lighting, an intriguing background, distinctive characters, or a unique atmosphere. Street corners, for instance, often provide fertile ground because they're vibrant intersections where lives overlap and the unexpected unfolds. The same applies to crossroad junctions.

Take the time to familiarize yourself with the areas where you plan to shoot. Identify the hotspots, high-energy zones, bustling corners, and places to avoid. Observe how people move through these spaces and note the times of day when activity peaks. Pay attention to the quality of light and learn the rhythm and flow of the location.

Lastly, don't overanalyze your choice of location. Many street photographers gravitate toward what they consider the best or must-visit spots (which tend to be where all the other street photographers are), but these areas are often over-photographed and may not yield unique results. Keep in mind that the most memorable moments often occur in the least expected places!

EXIT YOUR COMFORT ZONE

It's easy to fall into the habit of capturing the same familiar scenes, avoiding the challenge of venturing into more complex or unconventional territory, but stepping beyond your usual boundaries can be incredibly inspiring, rewarding, and even exhilarating. It can foster growth and creativity in your work.

Someone once said: *"The magic happens when you step out of your comfort zone,"* and this sentiment rings especially true in street photography. This doesn't mean putting yourself in harm's way, but it might involve exploring subjects that feel more demanding or uncomfortable in some way. For instance, you could take on a project in an underprivileged area, work with individuals who may be difficult or unpredictable, or simply challenge yourself to get physically closer to your subjects.

Another approach to refining your photography is to adopt a subtractive mindset. As you revisit a scene, focus on simplifying your composition: eliminate distractions, find better light, and arrange the elements in your frame to emphasize what truly matters. This process can transform a good shot into something exceptional.

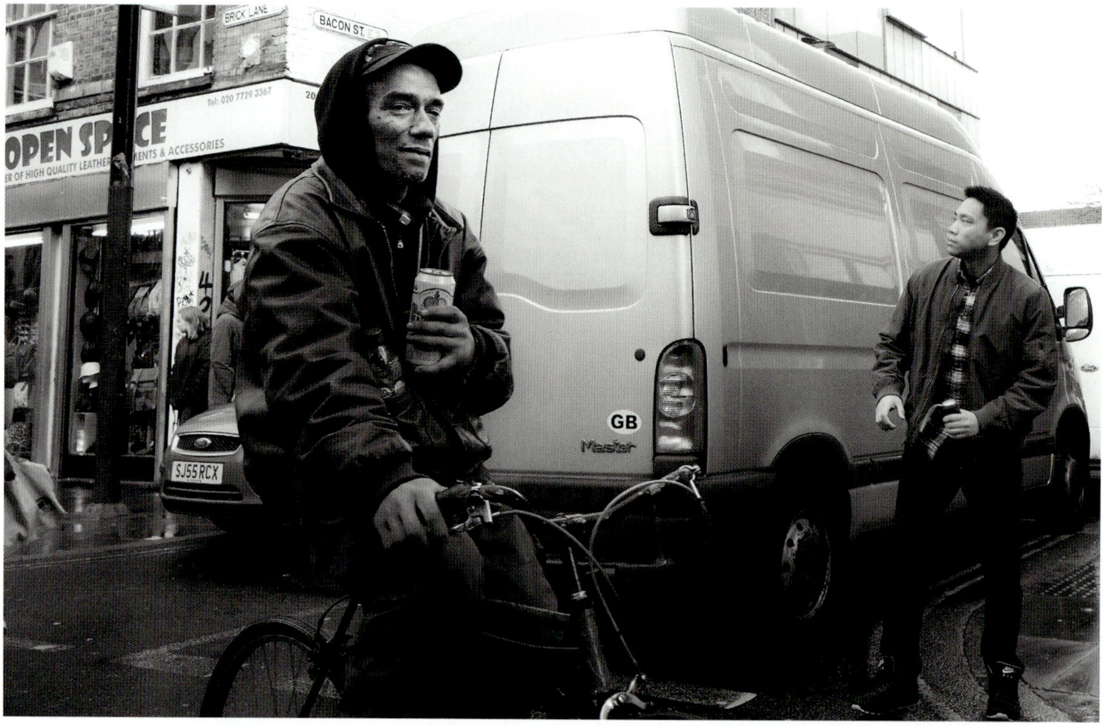
BRICK LANE
BACON ST.
OPEN SPACE
ACCESSORIES
GB
SJ55 RCX

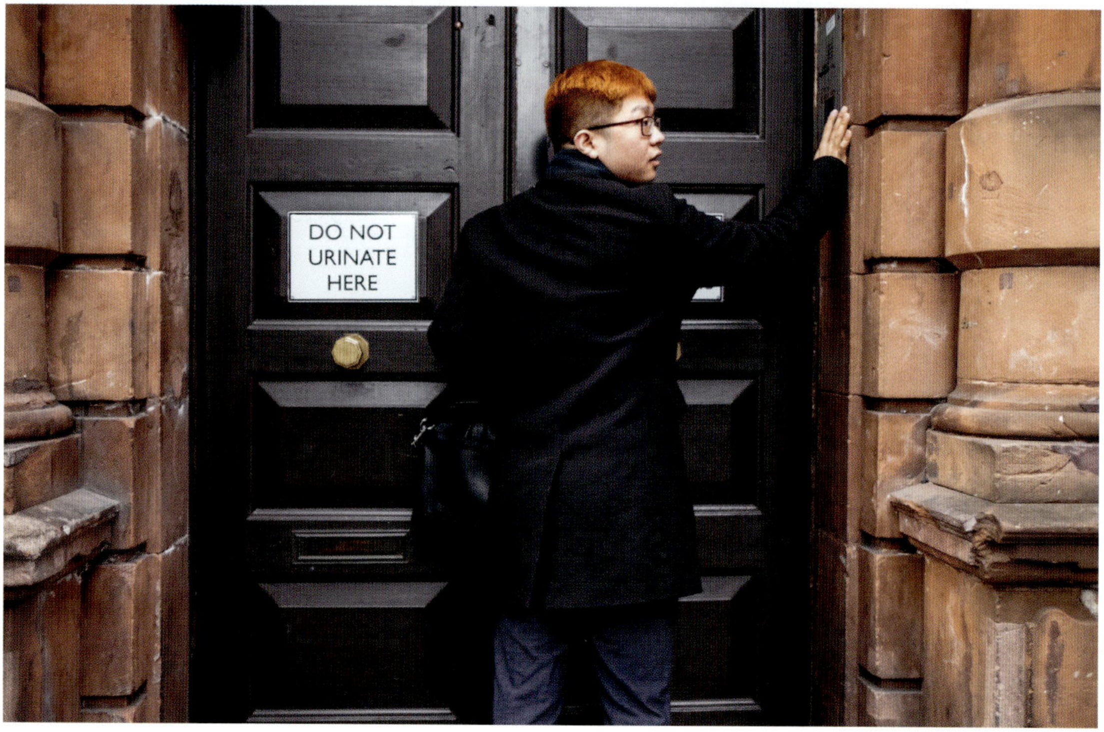
DO NOT
URINATE
HERE

BE COMFORTABLE WITH YOUR ETHICS

This principally refers to the ethics of street photography, which are generally concerned with balancing the creative freedom of the photographer with the rights, privacy, and dignity of your subjects.

Much has been written on this subject, and the question of ethics often prompts a strong response. There really is no right or wrong stance on this; we all have our own position on ethics, and it's not for me to tell you what yours should be. Personally, I wouldn't normally take pictures of homeless people or anyone who appears to be vulnerable in some way, and I wouldn't deliberately set out to ridicule someone (although I accept there is a fine between ridiculing someone and having a bit of fun).

Some key ethical considerations you should be aware of include:

- **Consent:** To preserve the authenticity of a scene, we usually work without asking for permission to take the picture. Whilst this is legal in many places, ethical dilemmas arise when subjects might feel exploited or uncomfortable (but they can only feel this way if they are aware you took their picture).

    A word about gaining consent: some photographers prefer to ask permission before or after taking a picture, especially if the image will be used for commercial purposes or widely shared. Whether this is required or not depends on the laws of the country or state in which the picture was taken (in most jurisdictions, consent is not required).

Opposite top: By putting yourself in situations you would normally avoid, your confidence will grow, and a sense of "I can do this!" will gradually take over.

Opposite bottom: Is he or isn't he? More importantly is it ethical? Is this chap portrayed in a bad light, or is it just a bit of harmless fun? Only the photography knows the real answer.

- **Context and intention:** Ask yourself why you are taking the picture. Does it tell a story, celebrate culture, or document history, or is it merely for personal amusement or shock value? There's not necessarily anything wrong with the latter, but do be aware of how your images could be perceived, especially in cross-cultural contexts.

- **Privacy and respect:** Generally speaking, if people are in a public place they have little or no expectation of privacy. However, we should consider whether an image may infringe on someone's personal dignity. For example, if they were having a private moment.

- **Exploitation:** It's best to avoid photographing people in vulnerable situations (such as people who are ill, homeless, or grieving) purely for artistic or dramatic effect. Also consider whether the image empowers or objectifies the subject.

- **Transparency:** If your work is part of a project or series, consider explaining the purpose behind it. This openness can help foster a sense of collaboration or understanding between you and the subjects.

- **Cultural issues:** Different cultures have varying norms around photography, and you may encounter cultural or religious sensitivities. People in certain cultures might associate being photographed with negative connotations or intrusion.

- **Damage limitation:** Avoid causing distress or putting subjects in uncomfortable situations. Be prepared to delete a photo if someone strongly objects to it, even if you took it legally.

- **Representation:** Consider how your images portray the subject and the wider community they represent. Are you reinforcing stereotypes or creating a biased narrative?

- **Honesty:** Avoid staging or altering photos in ways that misrepresent reality unless your intent is clear. Remember, street photography is all about authenticity.

- **Legal issues:** Whilst ethics and the law are distinct, you need to know the laws of the region in which you're shooting regarding photography in public spaces, especially around concerns with photographing children or private property.

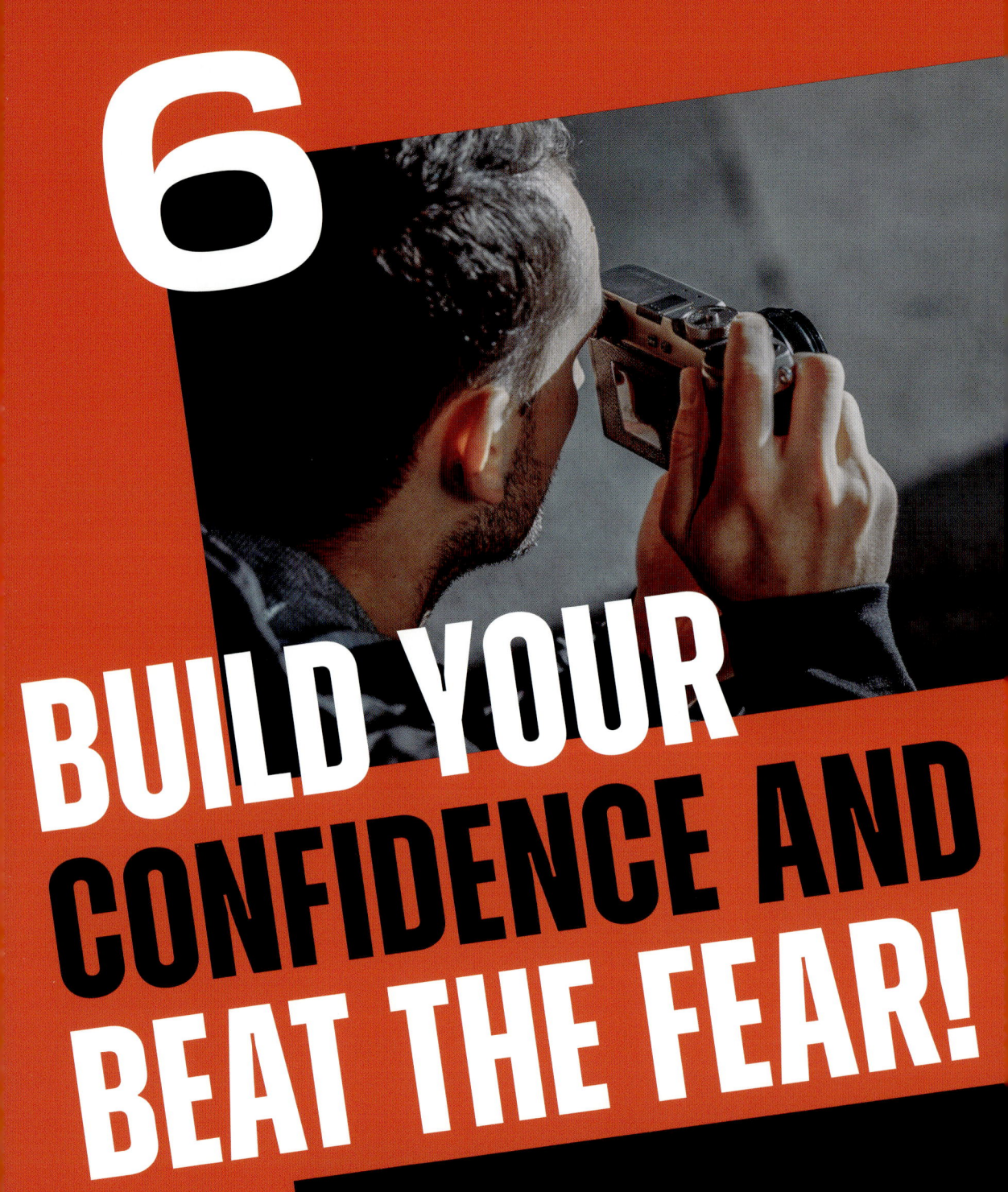

6

BUILD YOUR CONFIDENCE AND BEAT THE FEAR!

Many newcomers (and indeed experienced shooters) are fazed at the prospect of taking pictures of strangers out in public. What sort of reaction will we get? Will people be angry with us? Will they think we're weirdos? Will they hit us or grab our gear? Will they run and fetch the police? Sure, all of these things *do* happen, and they're reasonable concerns. However, most of them happen fairly rarely and some have never happened in my own experience.

However, some reservations such as these are, quite naturally, understandable, and we need to find a way to deal with them. It pains me to see how so many potentially good street photographers are put off or give up completely because of fears that are ill-founded or irrational. In this chapter, I will give you strategies to combat some of the common fears and reservations so you can hit the streets with confidence.

Most street photographers have suffered from a lack of confidence at some point. The good news is that with the right approach and lots of practice, we can all be fearless and confident shooters!

YOUR FEARS: A RATIONAL APPROACH

What are the common fears?

We all experience different fears and at different levels of intensity. Here are some of those most felt by street photographers:

- Fear of making people angry

- Fear of being challenged

- Fear that we're doing something illegal

- Fear that we're infringing someone's privacy or copyright

- Fear that what we're doing is ethically wrong

- Fear of rejection or criticism

- Fear of physical violence

- Fear of being robbed of your camera gear

- Fear of attention from the police or security guards

- Fear of being forced to delete images

- Fear of having your motives misunderstood

- Fear of people thinking you're weird or strange

Don't expect this sort of thing to happen when you're shooting on the streets! A fear of being subjected to physical violence when out taking pictures on the street is very much an irrational fear. If you're truly in fear, then you're probably shooting in the wrong areas!

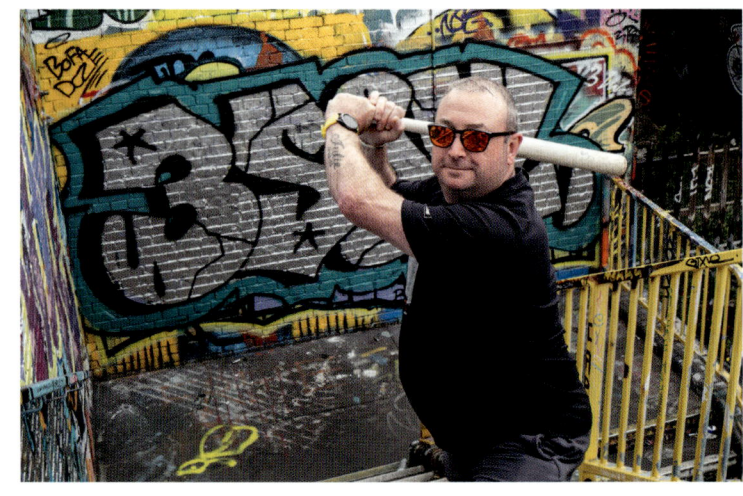

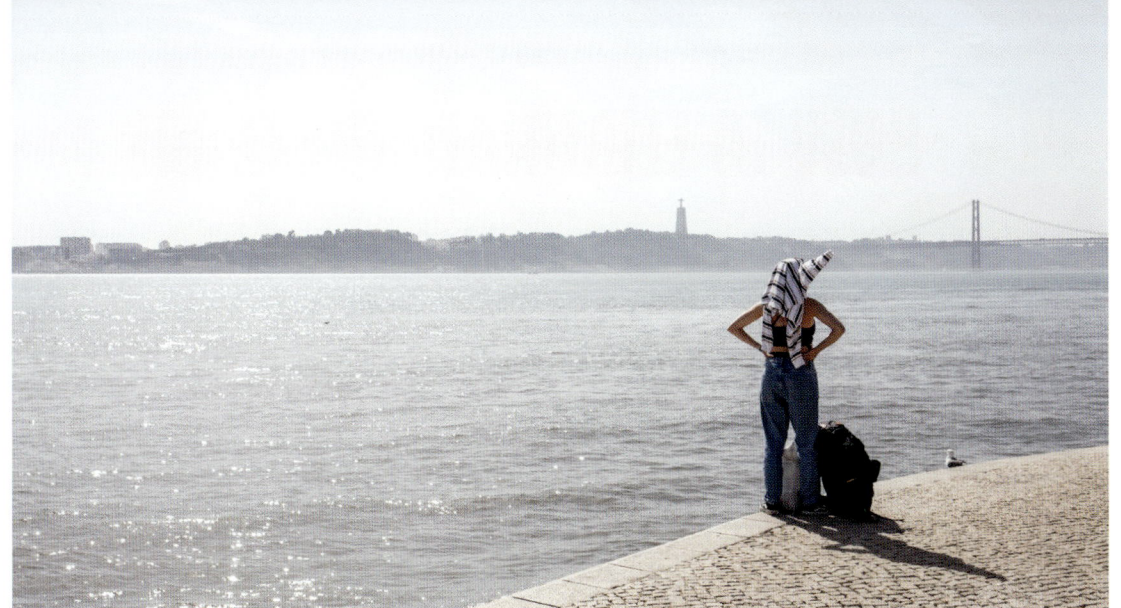

I'm generally not a big fan of shooting people's backs, but in this case the element of the unusual in the usual attracted me. And there's no way I'd have been called out for taking the picture.

CONFRONTING THE FEARS

Do you recognize some (or even all) of these common concerns? Don't worry, you're not alone; we all do from time to time. The good news is that there's plenty we can do about it.

You probably have already read, watched, or listened to plenty of material about conquering your fears, and there's no shortage of advice about how to best deal with the issue. Of course, for many people, conquering your fears is an exaggerated concept and we could easily replace it with the idea of building your confidence.

This fear/confidence issue affects most street photographers to some degree at some point on their journey. Some of us deal with it early on, some need to work hard at it, and for a minority of us, it will always be there.

A psychologist may suggest that fear is a warning system or a defence mechanism that aims to steer us away from danger. And it's not always a bad thing. Fear can keep us highly aware of surroundings and situations, and it can give us that quick dose of adrenaline that will spur us on to do the job. On the other hand, it can be debilitating and can hold us back in our quest to become competent street photographers.

HOW TO ELIMINATE THE FEARS

Recognizing the issue is a big step toward resolving the problem, and it's worth looking at the common fears list and working out exactly what's holding you back. Whilst all of these fears can be dealt with, it does take application, practice, and a determination to move forward.

Below are 12 steps that can help you reduce or eliminate the fear factor and build your street photography confidence.

1. FIND A SHOOTING STYLE TO SUIT YOUR PERSONALITY

There's no point in wanting to emulate Bruce Gilden if you're a shrinking violet and want to run a mile from any kind of confrontation. Our personality is deeply rooted in life experiences and psychological make-up and is difficult to change. So why fight it? Why not work with within your limitations and use them to your advantage?

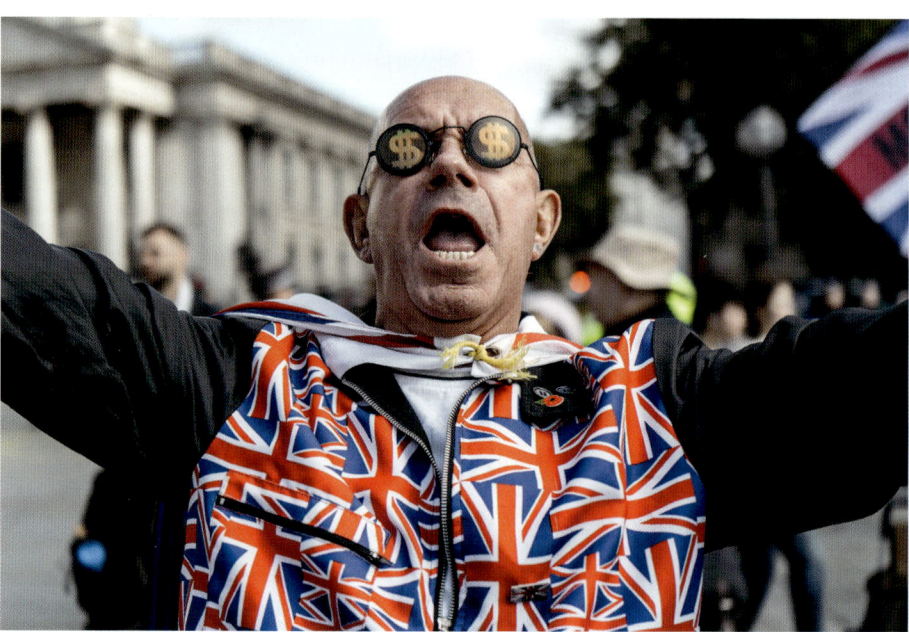

If shooting close-up is not your thing, why do it? Don't cause yourself unnecessary stress. Shoot subjects you feel more comfortable with.

Street photography doesn't have to be all about shooting challenging subjects, often at close range. For example, most of Saul Leiter's images were shot at a focal length of between 90mm and 150mm, and they very rarely included close-up shots of people's faces. In fact, he famously said: *"A window covered with raindrops interests me more than a photograph of a famous person."* Leiter would never have been truly comfortable shooting what we might consider to be traditional street photography, looking for random moments containing irony or wit; he was more concerned with making art, and this, in no small part, was driven by his personality.

One of the best street photographers I know *never* shoots people at close range. It's not in his personality and he would find it incredibly difficult, if not impossible. If he were to attempt to change his style to become more like that of, say, Bruce Gilden, it would cause him so much stress that he would probably give up street photography.

2. SHOOT EASY TARGETS

Taking the above concept a stage further, why stress yourself by shooting difficult subjects? It's easy to fall into the trap of assuming that if it's street photography, it needs to be raw, in your face, and up close and personal. But for many of us, it takes a long time to realize that street photography can be much more than that. You have probably seen Matt Stuart's iconic shot of the peacock and the rubbish skip, or his well-known picture of a leaf on the ground shaped like someone's lips. This is great observational street photography, and it's very comfortable to shoot because there are no people in the frame.

A good way to think of this this type of street photography is as "street still life." Going back to the previous point about shooting in a style which chimes with your personality, you'll probably warm to this approach if you have a playful or mischievous mind. Look for abandoned objects, signs, things that are not in their right place, coincidences, contrasts, irregularities—there is endless material out there, it just needs finding.

Another easy target is a protest or demonstration. Such events are (usually) heavily policed and provide a relatively safe shooting environment. Protesters generally want exposure for their cause and having their picture taken is all part of the game.

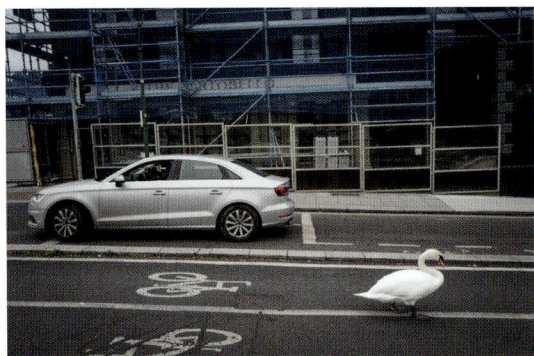 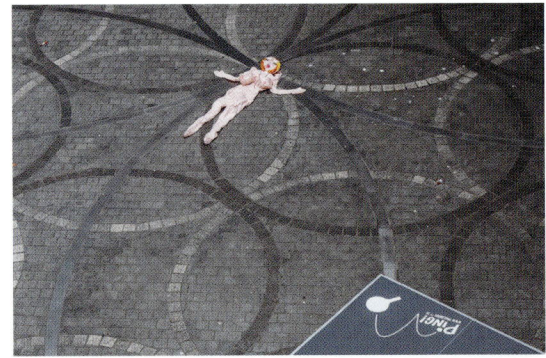

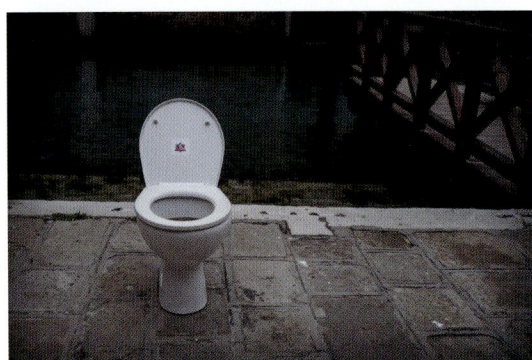 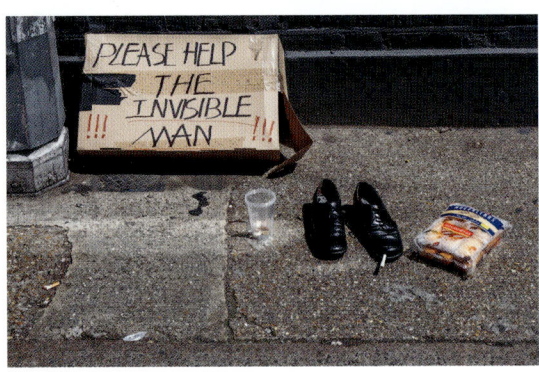

Try looking out for quirky, unusual, peculiar, or absurd things on the street. This observational style of street photography (I call it "street still life") is great fun to do and is never going to dent your confidence.

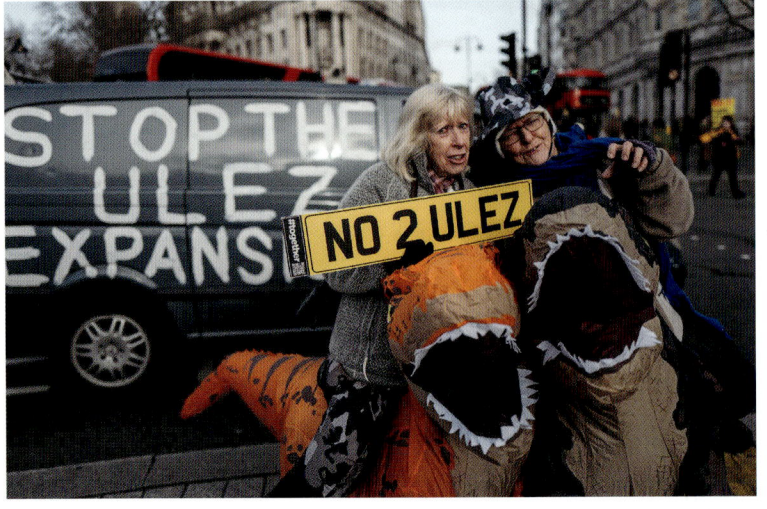

You'll see hundreds of photographers at many protests. Always be on the lookout for an offbeat or funny moment. It doesn't always need to be serious stuff.

Urban landscapes are also easy targets. These are all about the bigger picture, where buildings, structures, and the streets themselves take on more of prominent role in the image than do the people. For past masters such as Ernst Haas and Fan Ho, close-ups of people were rarely of interest. These photographers were more concerned with the fabric of the built environment around them.

Some purists may argue that urban landscape should not be classed as street photography as it doesn't usually feature a candid moment. However, as Nick Turpin, a well-known contemporary British street photographer who shoots a lot in this style explains: *"Architectural Street Photography is a newly coined phrase for Street Photography that gives equal weight to the built environment and to those that inhabit it. Architectural Street Photography combines the rigorous technical approach of the Architectural Photographer with the spontaneity and eye of the candid Street Photographer."*

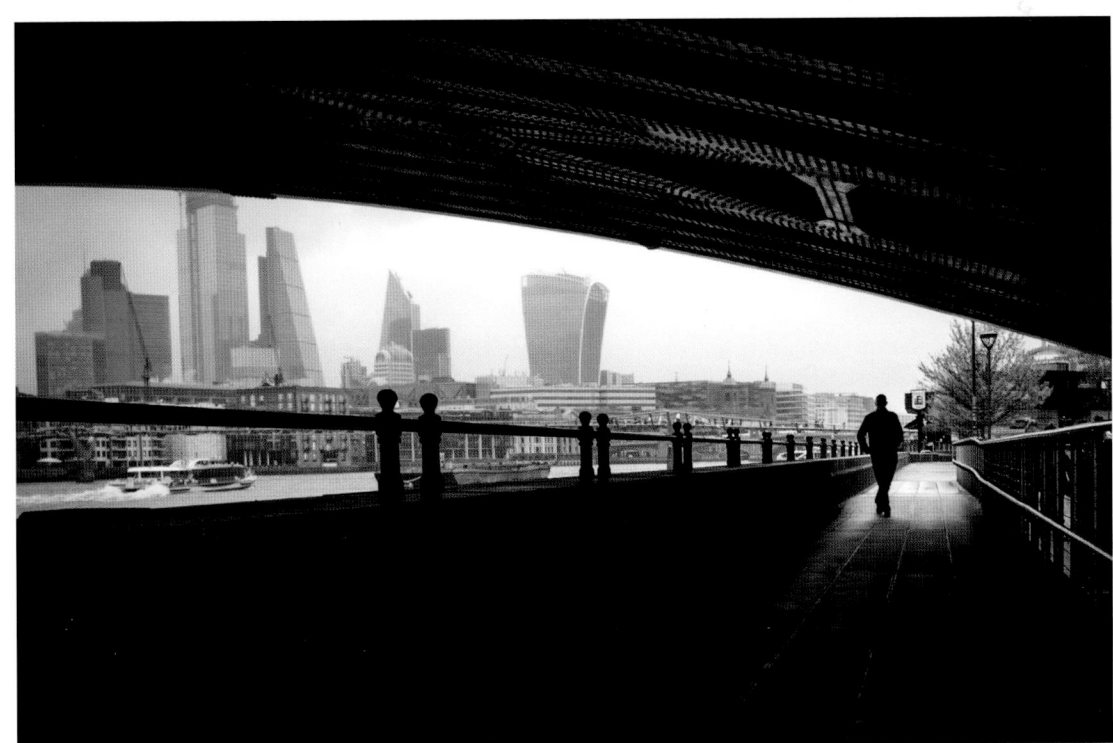

It's an urban landscape, in which the environmental content is perhaps more important than the human figure. Is it street photography? Does it matter?

3. JUST BE NICE

Next time you're out shooting on the streets, take a look around you and observe other street photographers. The chances are they won't be looking very happy, relaxed, or friendly; some of them may look tense, shifty, furtive, or even creepy. This is why street photographers sometimes get a bad name. But there is a better way.

It's a fact that those of us who appear to be the nice guy/girl generally have a far easier time on the streets. If we appear to be friendly, warm, open, relaxed, and "normal," people will behave in a similar way toward us. It's human nature. You will almost certainly find that a warm, friendly, and relaxed approach will make you feel more confident and in control—and you'll have a more enjoyable day. Furthermore, you'll be far more likely to avoid any kind of confrontation.

4. GO FISHING

We explored the concept of fishing in Chapter 2, and this calm, laid back approach can help reduce anxiety and build confidence.

Imagine the scene: You've found your spot and staked your claim to it. Your camera is set up and ready, and any people walking into your space are now incidental. The key phrase here is "your space." You couldn't possibly be accused of invading other people's space—they're coming into your territory. Furthermore, once you've anchored yourself to a spot, you'll become almost invisible and nobody will notice you.

5. BE A TOURIST, NOT A PHOTOGRAPHER

We generally aim to go unseen and not be busted as a photographer. We've all seen people shooting on the streets with several cameras, long lenses, and huge backpacks. It's enough to make your subjects run a mile! Use the smallest and most discreet camera you have. I'm a "one camera, one lens" kind of person, and everything fits either into my jacket pocket or into a small shoulder bag. My aim is to look more like a harmless tourist than a photographer.

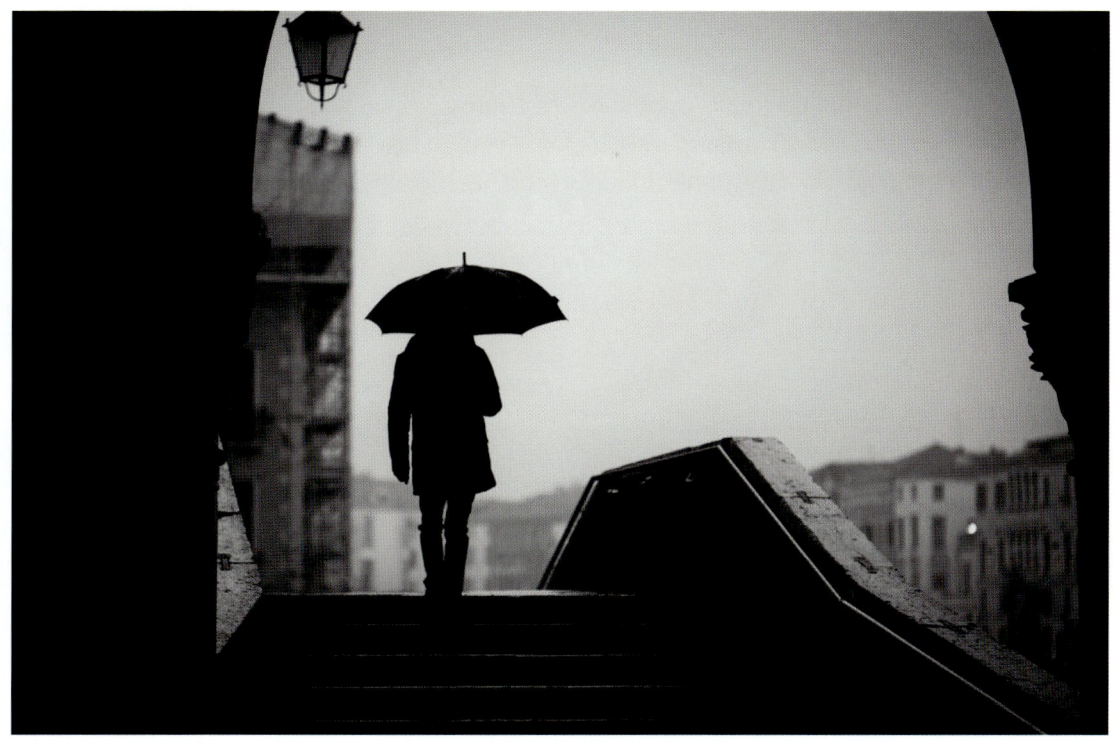

I knew exactly what I wanted here: a minimalist scene with one person holding an umbrella. It was quiet and raining, so it was only a question of time before someone came along. I leaned on a wall in the shadows, and I don't think a single person noticed me in all the time I was there.

Also, try to blend into your environment. People are less likely to notice you if you don't stand out in any way. You will blend in more easily if you wear dark clothing, carry minimal camera gear, and walk slowly, avoiding sudden, jerky movements.

6. DESENSITIZE YOURSELF

Psychologists define desensitization as the diminished emotional responsiveness to a negative, aversive, or positive stimulus after repeated exposure to it. In other words, the more you do something the more you become comfortable with it. Familiarity breeds acceptability and thus comfort.

So, if you were to start shooting from a distance and gradually, say over a period of weeks, move closer to your subjects, transitioning from using a longer

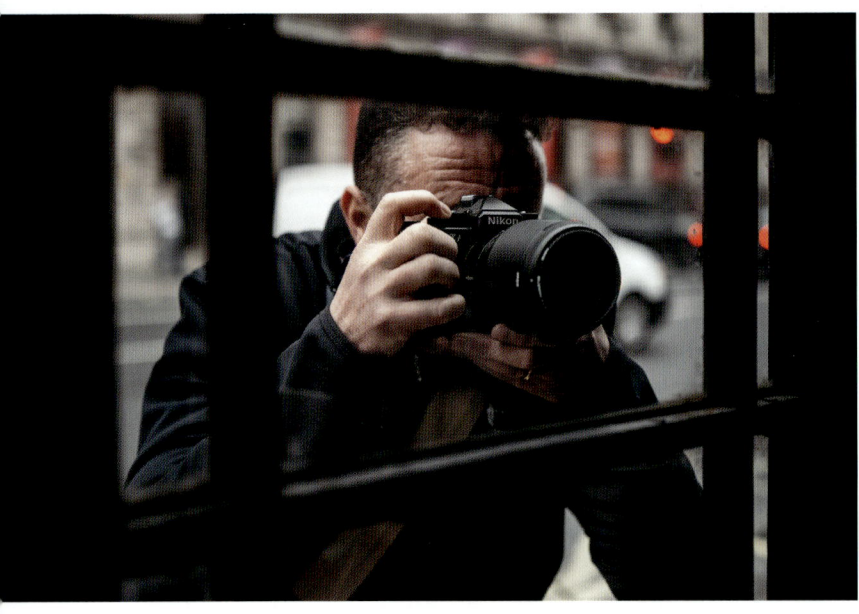

If you're feeling anxious, try shooting from further away with a longer lens, say 50mm or 85mm. Gradually get closer using increasingly wider lenses, eventually arriving at a sweet spot of around 35mm. This could take weeks or even months!

lens to a wider one, you would be desensitizing yourself to a point when, ideally, the fear of up-close shooting was either eliminated or unimportant. How long it takes depends on the level of fear and your own psychological make-up but do try it. It works!

7. HAVE A BACK STORY

Give yourself a reason to be there! This is another great by-product of shooting projects (see Chapter 9). You should find that projects give you a sense of purpose and the feeling of, *"I have a job to do here, and nobody can stop me."*

There will be occasions when we want to explain to people what we're doing, or when we *need* to explain ourselves (though in most situations, there is absolutely no need to justify taking pictures in a public place). But whether we explain ourselves or not is largely irrelevant here: The whole point is about being comfortable in the knowledge that we *can* explain ourselves if necessary.

When you're out shooting, you can expect people to ask you what you're doing (it doesn't happen often, but if does happen). A confident and purposeful reply will reassure people that you're not doing anything wrong and will help make you feel good about shooting. For example: *"I'm a photographer and I'm working on a project about street life in downtown Anytown. It's all about the buildings, the people, the lovely light—I'm hoping to turn it into a book."* Who could be offended by that kind of back story? And, of course, it's likely that you really are working on a project so your back story will come across with passion and authenticity.

8. SHOOT WITH A BUDDY

Street photography can be a lonely pursuit. Some photographers embrace the solitude whilst others can find it uncomfortably isolating. If the thought of shooting alone increases your anxiety, why not shoot with someone else?

Lots of street photographers struggle with the idea of solo shooting and there should be no shortage of street shooting buddies who feel the same and who would welcome the opportunity to meet up. Apart from the feeling of safety in numbers, shooting with others will usually give you a boost in self-confidence. Perhaps, most importantly, it can be great fun—and even competitive!

If you don't know any other street photographers, try asking around at your local camera club or join one of the many street photography groups on social media in your area.

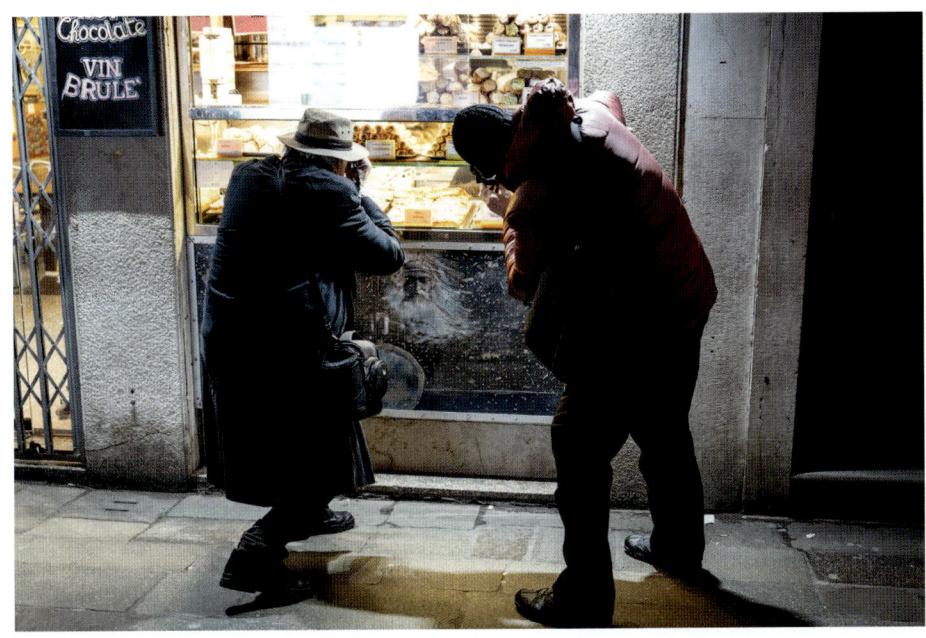

Street photography needn't be a lonely pursuit. Shooting with someone else is good fun, and you can share the learning experience. And of course have a drink afterward!

9. SHOOT QUICKLY AND COVERTLY

The less time you spend taking a photo, the less likely you are to be seen and, consequently, the less likely you are to feel uncomfortable. Here are some techniques you can use that will speed up your street photography and help you move around almost invisibly:

- **Have your camera pre-set and completely ready to go.** The longer you spend messing around with settings, the more likely you are to draw attention to yourself. A good rule of thumb is aperture priority, f/8, and auto ISO. These are my go-to settings that work for me 90% of the time (see Chapter 4 for a detailed explanation).

- **Make the composition in your head before bringing your camera up to eye level.** Frame the picture in your mind and only raise the camera when you are ready to press the button.

- **Use a prime lens rather than a zoom.** Time spent zooming may attract attention.

- **Use zone focusing.** Have your camera set on manual focus, and set to a pre-determined distance. Assuming you're working at a small aperture of at least f/8 and your lens is focused on a spot around 10 feet away, most of the subject matter within your zone of operation (probably between about 5 and 20 feet) will be sharp. Using manual focus will enable you to react more quickly.

- **Make sure your camera is switched on and awake at all times** (I recommend disabling the sleep mode). The downside is a reduction in battery capacity, but what use is a full battery if you're going to miss shots because your camera is asleep?

- **Don't hesitate.** Once you see a picture, press the button.

- **Use a wrist strap rather than a neck strap.** This way your finger will always be on the button and the camera will be ready for action.

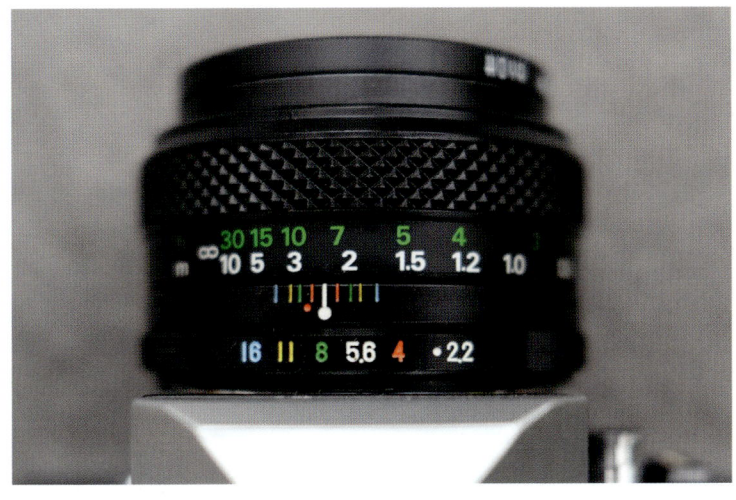

Zone focusing will allow you to shoot quickly, and therefore, unobtrusively. It may not be perfect every time, but in street photography, near enough is good enough!

It's good practice to shoot the streets with a cloak of invisibility, going largely unnoticed and without drawing attention to yourself. Whilst being busted as a photographer isn't necessarily a problem *per se*, your presence can change the dynamic of the scene: People may turn away, they may stop what they were doing, they may challenge you, or (even worse) they may pose for you. Joel Meyerowitz calls this "bruising the scene." Once you've been spotted, the spell is broken and you've probably missed that moment.

However, there's more to this than simply missing the moment. Being invisible or covert will almost certainly embolden you and will ultimately make you more confident on the streets.

Does shooting covertly make you feel awkward, like you're doing something wrong? It shouldn't. This is a perfectly normal and acceptable way to shoot. However, there's a fine line between shooting covertly and appearing to be weird or creepy. We've all seen the furtive street photographer, lurking in the shadows and taking sly shots of people; it's not a good look!

On the one hand, we should take pictures discreetly and without being noticed. On the other hand, we shouldn't hide or be ashamed of what we're doing. There's a balance to be achieved here, and that balance will usually swing toward being open and relaxed as your confidence grows with lots of practice.

Try some of the following techniques to help you go unnoticed:

- **Shoot "past" your subject.** This technique works particularly well when people are walking toward you and you are using a wide-angle lens (28mm to 35mm works well). Bring your camera up to eye level, ignoring the people in front of you, and let your body language suggest that you're about to shoot something in the distance. Don't make eye contact, focus your attention on the space behind them, and, when they walk into your frame, hit the button. Finally, stay in your pose: Keep the camera at eye level until they have passed. They will be none the wiser.

- **Shoot in "video mode."** This doesn't mean change your camera settings to shoot videos, it means panning your camera across a scene and pressing the button at the right moment as part of the sweep. People will think you're making a video about the wider scene rather than taking a specific interest in them.

- **Shoot from the hip with your camera at waist level.** With some practice you'll get to know exactly what shooting angle is required to compose the shot (or an articulating screen will do it for you). However, don't become overly reliant on this technique, and don't use it as a crutch. You should get into the habit of using the viewfinder in the normal way, only shooting from the hip when you really need to do so.

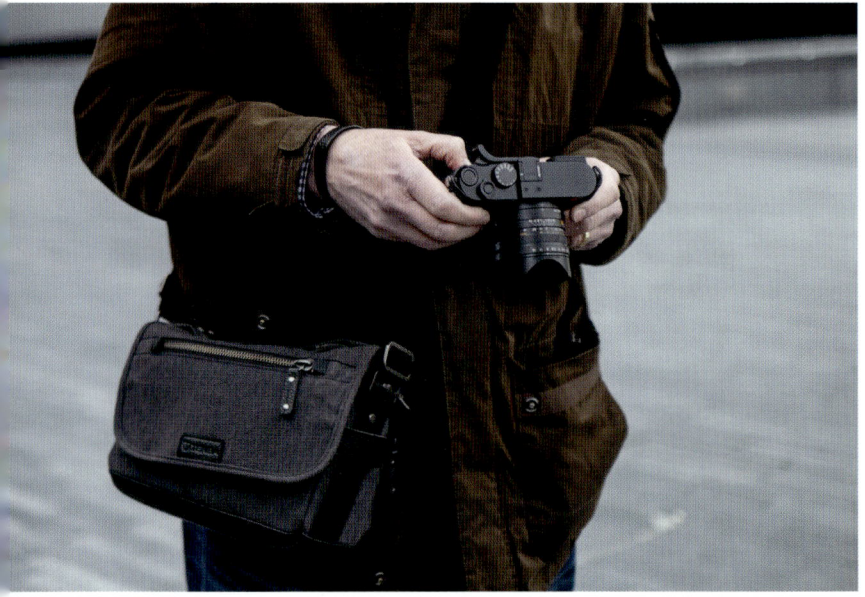

If you travel light and wear dark clothing, you'll blend into your surroundings and be less noticeable.

- **Go fishing.** If you stay in the same spot for any length of time, people will stop noticing you.

- **Travel light.**

- **Wear dark clothes, blend in, and walk slowly.**

10. AVOID EYE CONTACT

This is my killer tip and it can be a real game-changer. You'll probably be familiar with the situation: You see someone you want to photograph, you catch their eye, and. . . the moment has gone. That split second of hesitation resulting from the eye contact has killed the opportunity, and you move on, having missed the picture. The same goes for after the picture has been taken—eye contact could lead to a conversation you probably want to avoid, even a confrontation.

You need to get into the habit of avoiding eye contact before you take the shot, during the picture-taking, and afterward. You should immediately find that this makes the whole process so much easier and more comfortable.

Avoiding eye contact is difficult and takes some getting used to, but as a general rule, I *never* make eye contact with people on the streets. One of the few exceptions is when I need to engage with my subjects, such as when taking street portraits.

11. LEARN HOW TO HANDLE CONFRONTATION

Confrontation happens. Certainly, if you followed this chapter's steps, it's less likely to happen, and the more you engage in street photography, the more you will accept that being challenged really is no big deal. Hardly a week goes by without someone asking me, *"Why did you take my picture?"* or *"Did you just take my picture?"*

A key point here is that most people are asking out of simple human curiosity rather than out of displeasure or even anger; rarely are people offended. Of course, it's best to avoid being challenged in the first place, and it's less likely to happen if you work quickly and quietly, you don't get in people's faces, and you look more like a tourist than a photographer.

When people challenge you, you're under no obligation to explain yourself, and some street photographers refuse to engage in any way with their subjects (although this can seem a little rude). People's curiosity is often satisfied with a simple stock explanation, which you should have ready in anticipation of these situations. You might say you're working on a project, that you're doing a photography course, or simply that you are documenting urban life in that particular area. Just remember to smile, be nonconfrontational, and confident of your motives for taking that picture.

Should you ever delete an image if asked to do so? Much depends on the circumstances and how you feel about refusing. Did you photograph someone in a compromising or embarrassing situation? Were they doing something illegal? If you think a refusal may have unpleasant consequences, you should probably consider deleting the image and retreating from the situation, but you are under no legal obligation to do so.

Even if you do feel that you're under duress to delete an image, it can probably be retrieved later using card recovery software. If your camera is of the type that records to two memory cards, you could always have a back-up version on the spare card.

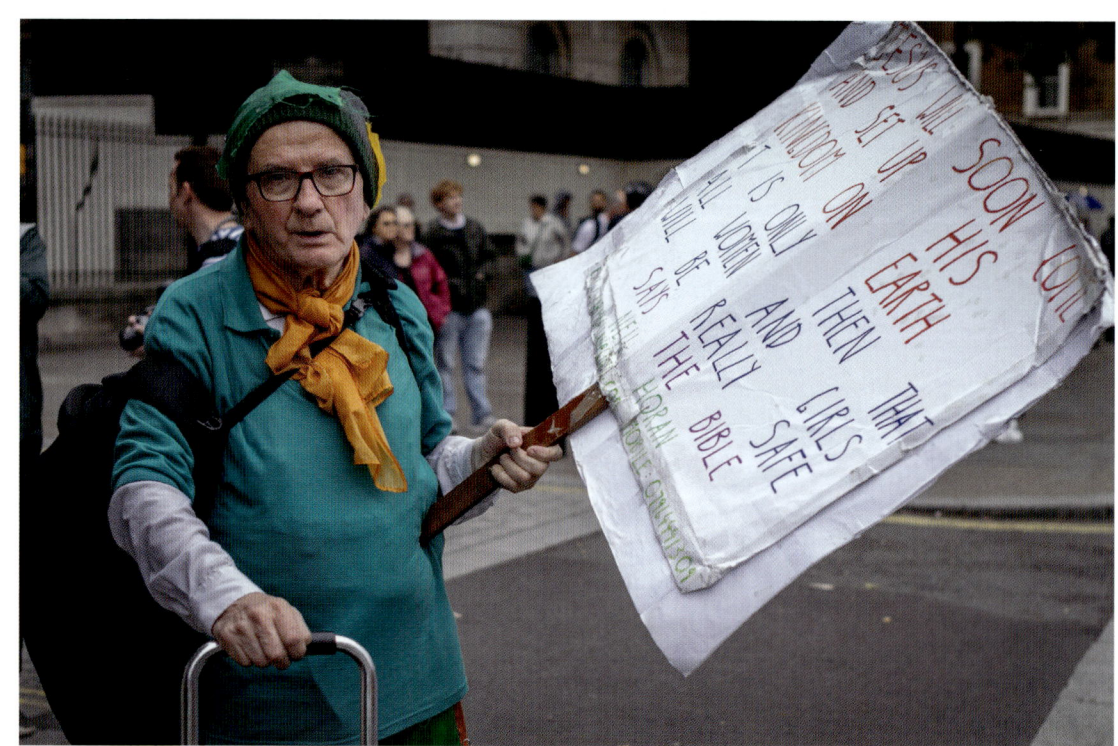

Despite any feelings of angst you may have, confrontations are actually quite rare and usually amount to nothing if you have a friendly, relaxed, and confident approach.

12. KNOW THE LAW

Knowledge is power! You will be a more confident street photographer if you know where you stand from a legal perspective. In the USA, UK, most of Europe, and, in fact, throughout much of the world, the basic legal premise is that if you are taking pictures in public, you do not need anyone's permission to do so.

Legally, if a person is in a public place, they have little or no expectation of privacy, which makes them fair game to be photographed.

USA and UK privacy laws are fairly relaxed, the key point being that everyone has the right to his/her private and family life. It really is a matter of common sense: If you think what you are doing may be infringing someone's privacy, then stop doing it. On the other hand, don't be bullied by someone on the streets who tells you not to take their picture. Unless they are doing something that compromises them, you can photograph them freely.

Always check out the local laws if you are visiting a different country. In France, for example, privacy is a completely different ball game and the creation and/or publication of images of a person without their consent could put you in a legally compromising position (perhaps this is why we see relatively little street photography in such a photogenic city as Paris). In Germany, there is a right to one's own image principle, which aims to strike a balance between personal privacy and freedom of speech. Whilst you can usually *take* the picture, you are more limited in what you can *do* with it.

Please be aware that some countries take a more harsh approach. In Hungary, for example, a new civil code outlaws taking pictures without the permission of every single person in the photograph. If you take a picture on the streets and someone randomly wanders into the shot, you are technically breaking the law.

But this section isn't really about the law itself—it's about your *knowledge* of the law. Once you accept that you are legally allowed to take pictures in a public place, taking them becomes easier. And this is the central point: You can shoot with confidence if you are sure of your ground.

PRACTICE

Practice is undoubtedly the key to becoming a more confident street photographer. The more you're out there with your camera, the easier it will all become.

When we start out on this journey, we see a wall to climb, and for many it can amount to an almost insurmountable problem. But familiarity brings contentment, and it really is worth putting in the hard miles, making street photography a normal part of your daily life.

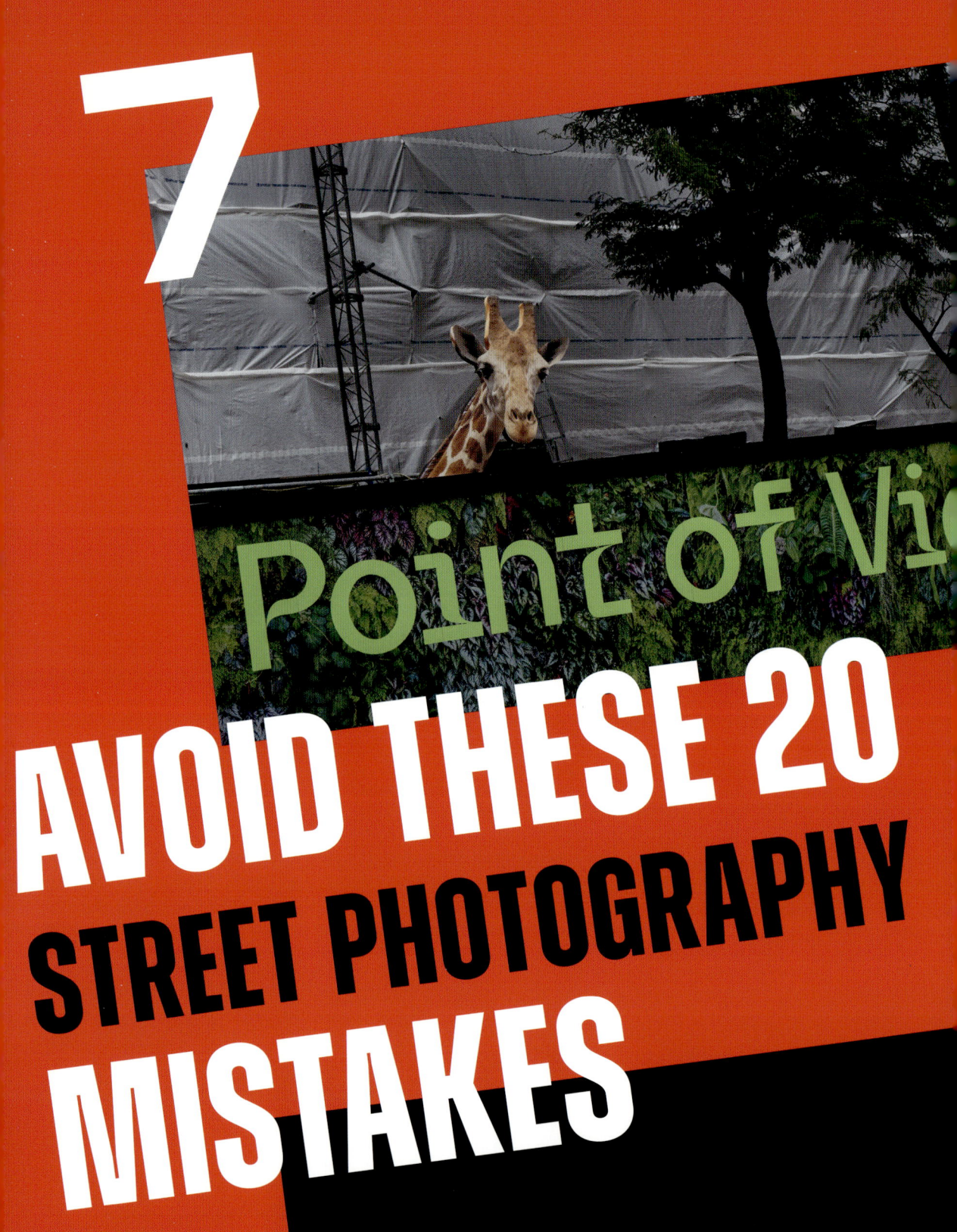

7

Point of Vie

AVOID THESE 20
STREET PHOTOGRAPHY
MISTAKES

We are only human, and we all make mistakes. One of the great (and not so great) things about street photography in the twenty-first century is that there is so much information available through books, forums, YouTube videos, and camera clubs. The problem is that disagreement is a common factor: disagreement about what gear to use, what to shoot, whether people are essential, whether it needs to be candid, and so on.

Inevitably, you will come across duff advice and you will make mistakes. It's normal; we all do. Having been teaching street photography workshops for the last 10 years, I have noticed patterns whereby people make common mistakes at an early stage of their street photography journey. The important thing is to recognize those mistakes so you can eliminate them from your shooting.

Here are some of the mistakes I regularly come across, and how you can avoid them.

A picture without people: Is it street photography? Or is it a mistake?

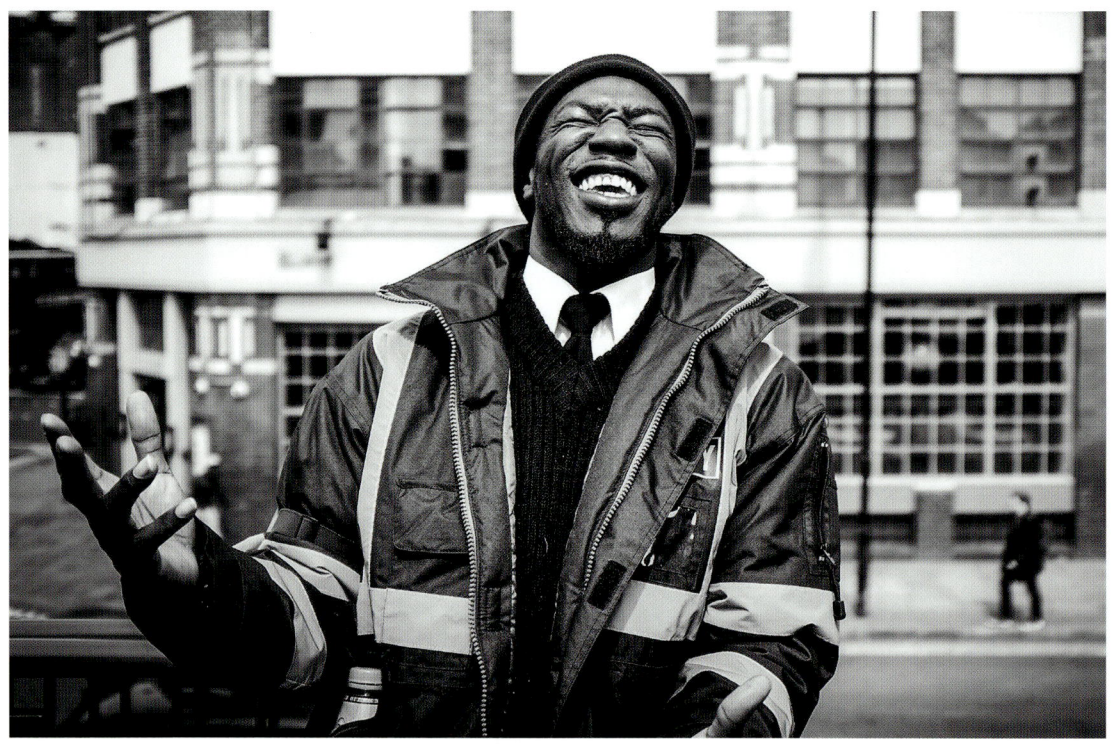

By getting as close as you possibly can, you'll be able to retain any intimacy or emotion in the image. I shot this using a 35mm lens.

1. NOT GETTING CLOSE ENOUGH

"Get in close" has long been one of the teaching mantras in street photography. Perhaps it's a little overplayed, and we certainly shouldn't treat it as an absolute, but I do see a lot of people (maybe they are new to street photography) who are just not getting close enough.

That's not to say you need to be in people's faces, but as Robert Capa famously said, *"If your pictures aren't good enough, you aren't close enough."* And that has some truth in it. This concept of close proximity in street photography often helps bring more drama, emotion, or intimacy to a frame. You wouldn't get this feeling or perspective from shooting from across the road with a long lens or, even worse, by shooting from across the road with a wide lens (which usually means there are lots of extraneous details in your frame, like expanses of pavement or sky).

If you're really concerned about getting too close to your subjects, maybe try shooting with a slightly longer lens, such as 50mm. With anything longer than 50mm, the perspective starts to become unrealistic and you lose any sense of intimacy.

So, when you're taking a shot, assuming you have the time, always think: Could I get any closer?

2. TECHNICAL ISSUES

Whilst street photography does not—and sometimes *should not*—need to be perfect, we should strive for a good level of technical competence. If an image is *designed* to be very underexposed, then fine, let it be underexposed. But it's not fine for the final image to be unintentionally dark due to technical errors. Let's face it: Street photography is hardly the most technically demanding genre, and getting most of the basics right is well within everyone's grasp. At the very least, make sure you handle the following elements to the best of your ability:

- **Focus:** The main subject of your image really needs to be sharp (unless a more abstract, blurry image is your intention, as in the case of the lovely work by Olga Karlovac).

- **Exposure:** It needs to be spot-on unless your intention is otherwise. Overexposed or underexposed images due to incorrect settings are unacceptable; try to get this right in-camera or, failing that, by making adjustments in post-production.

- **Slow shutter speed:** So many potentially good images are ruined by using a shutter speed that is too slow, often caused by setting the ISO too low (see Chapter 4 for more on this).

- **Composition:** Don't neglect it! Yes, street photography can be a bit cavalier when it comes to composition, but poor framing or cluttered backgrounds can distract from the subject and ruin an image. Remember, you have a big frame to fill, so use all the space wisely!

- **Shooting everything wide open:** Sure, there are times when we want an out-of-focus background, but this is rarely the norm. Overusing shallow depth of field can result in a loss of context in the scene.

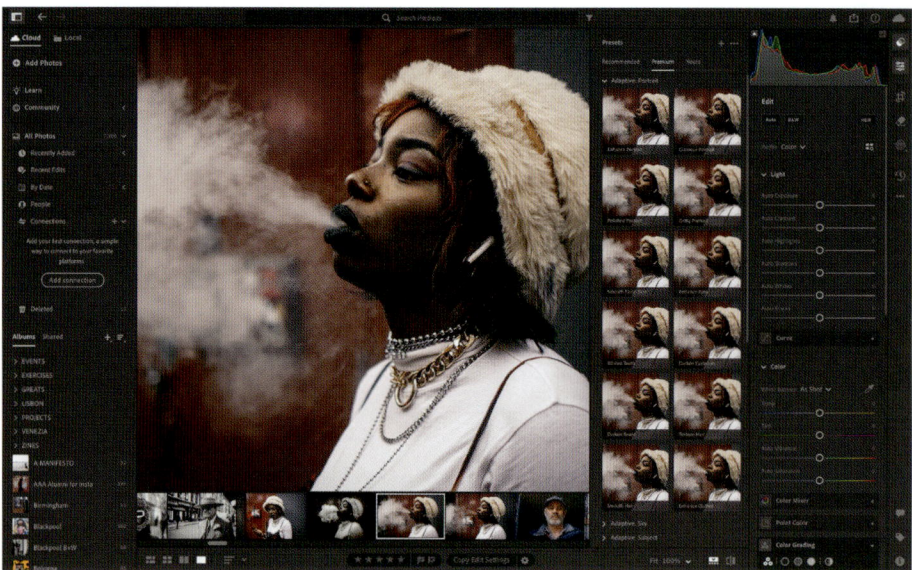

Get as much right as you possibly can, but don't compromise the "moment" by striving for technical perfection.

- **Shooting only JPEGs:** If your camera can shoot RAW files, why wouldn't you do so? Don't limit your post-processing potential by shooting only in JPEG.

- **Over-editing:** Street photography isn't really the place for creative filters or excessive effects in post-production. Try to avoid anything that could detract from the authenticity of the image. The same applies when it comes to buying presets to use in (for example) Photoshop or Lightroom; I wouldn't be totally averse to creating my own presets, but I would be less comfortable buying and applying someone else's creativity.

3. FOLLOWING THE HERD

We street photographers really do have tribal instincts and a herd mentality. We all like to buy the same gear, some like to wear similar clothes, we all read the same books, and so on. More problematically, many of us shoot exactly the same stuff.

You will see this happen all the time: A well-known Instagrammer or YouTuber discovers a new location or shoots in a particular style, and within days, the world if full of similar images. Where's the originality in that?

We saw a good example of this happening shortly after Nick Turpin published his *On the Night Bus* project (Hoxton Mini Press, 2017). This was an inspirational and original body of work, shot through London bus windows at night. It has since been widely copied (other photographers have even produced very similar books). There is nothing at all wrong with taking *inspiration* from others' work, but we should all try to find our way and create something original.

Try to block out what others are doing; shoot the world as *you* see it. Shoot what pleases *you*. Find your own way. You will only get so far if you adopt the herd mentality. And don't try to please or impress others—shoot for yourself!

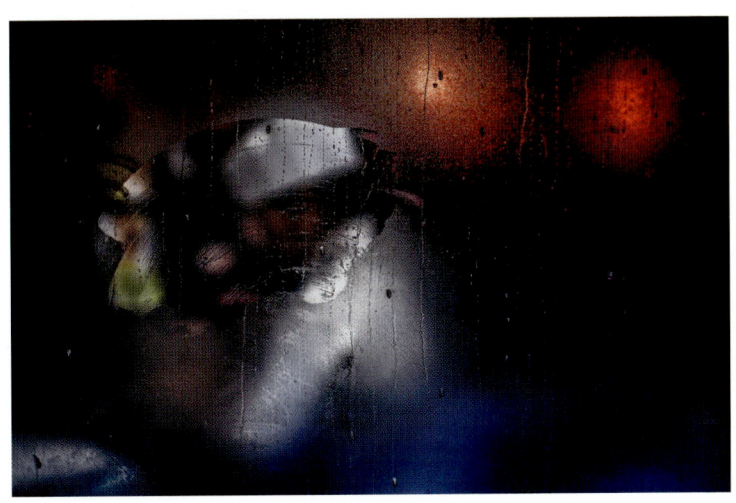

If you have ever shot in London's Chinatown, you'll probably have taken a picture of this scene, which is a sort of rite of passage for street photographers. But should you take the picture just because everyone else does?

4. LACK OF CONCENTRATION

Something I witness a lot is a real lack of concentration. If you want to be a good street photographer, you can't afford to let your concentration lapse. You really need to be in the zone—in the *moment*—and be totally focused on what you're doing. If you've ever watched really good street photographers at work, you'll notice that they are keenly focused on what's going on around them, anticipating, observing, and making connections. Here are some tips that may help you focus:

- **Don't listen to music or podcasts** whilst engaged in street photography; it takes edge of your concentration and you'll be focusing on the wrong things. Joel Meyerowitz once said that he often hears a picture before he sees it, and this can be so true.

- **Leave your phone in your pocket.** If you really need to check emails or make calls, get your phone out at, say, hourly intervals or (ideally) during your coffee or lunch break.

- **Shoot alone.** Even if you're out shooting with a buddy or in a group, give yourself plenty of space. Don't get distracted by chatting because you will inevitably miss shots.

- **Try to clear your mind** of things that could get in the way of being in the zone: Problems at work, picking the kids up from school, buying a new car, the divorce—whatever the distractions are in your life, now is the time to put them to one side and focus on what's going on here and now. Not only is it more productive, it's good for your mental health!

- **Stop chimping!** If you constantly look at the pictures you've just taken on your LCD screen, you're removing yourself from being in the moment and you'll inevitably miss shots.

- **Stay completely focused** on the job at hand. Try not to let your mind wander.

5. HESITATION

This is a big one and it's a common challenge. Even the most confident and experienced street photographers hesitate occasionally, and we have all lost potentially great shots as a result.

So why do we hesitate? It typically happens because of concerns about potential confrontation, invading someone's privacy, or self-doubt. Maybe we feel ethically compromised or we're unsure about the legalities of street photography. *"Will they see me taking a picture? What will they think? Will they think I'm a creep? Will they be angry?"* In reality, you're not going to be noticed, and these questions are most likely all in your head.

You need to get into the mindset of hitting the button as soon as you see the possibility for a shot, reacting instantly, and *then* thinking: *"How could I do it differently or better?"* So don't overthink it—just get your shot.

We all deal with hesitancy and worry. With a little practice, however, you can eliminate them from your street photography psyche. "Shoot first, think later" should always be your mantra.

Here are some tips for overcoming hesitation (also see Chapter 6 about building your confidence):

- **Have self-belief in your intent:** Reflect on why you're photographing strangers. Is it to capture a unique moment, tell a story, or express your artistic vision? It's unlikely that you're doing it to ridicule or harm them, and being comfortable and clear about your purpose can help justify your actions to yourself and others.

- **Start low-key:** Begin in places where photography is expected or accepted, like markets or public events.

- **Be warm and relaxed:** Smile and be friendly and approachable. If someone notices you taking a photo, a nod and a smile can help lower the temperature. If they ask what you're doing, explain it confidently and politely.

- **Practice stealth and discretion:** Shoot quickly and quietly, and shoot from the hip if you need to.

- **Analyze your hesitation:** Are you afraid of rejection or confrontation? Most of the time, people either don't mind being photographed or are flattered. Remind yourself of this to reduce fear.

6. MESSING WITH YOUR CAMERA

I often see street photographers messing around with their cameras while, in the meantime, things are happening around them that they should be paying attention to.

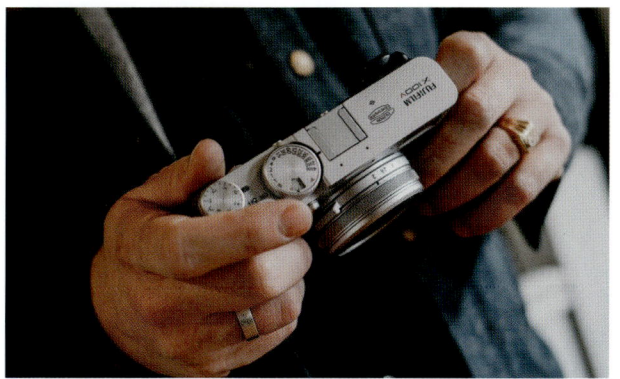

Don't take your eye off the ball by faffing around with camera settings. Your focus needs to be on what's around you, not camera knobs, dials, and menu settings.

You should be so familiar with your gear that you could operate it with your eyes closed. In Chapter 4, I suggested a "set it and forget it" approach whereby the only camera setting you are regularly adjusting is exposure compensation. Everything else is preset.

7. SHOOTING CLICHÉS AND TROPES

It's very tempting, sometimes, to fall into cliché territory with street photography. And yes, I accept that initially everyone goes through this phase. It's almost a rite of passage. But some of these tropes are very overused—at risk of causing upset, here are some of the common tropes and clichés you should try to avoid:

- **Street performers:** Someone simply playing a guitar is *not* interesting.

- **Umbrellas:** A solitary person with an umbrella in a wet cityscape—we've all seen it.

- **Funny signs:** Okay, this one could go either way. If there's a *really* witty connection to be made, then you could have a great image, but most of what we see barely raises a smile.

- **Silhouettes:** This is a controversial one. Although they are popular, unless there's another extra element, silhouettes *per se* can be repetitive and uninteresting.

Silhouettes are becoming quite controversial; are they another street photography trope? Alex Webb, Constantine Manos, and plenty of others would say not.

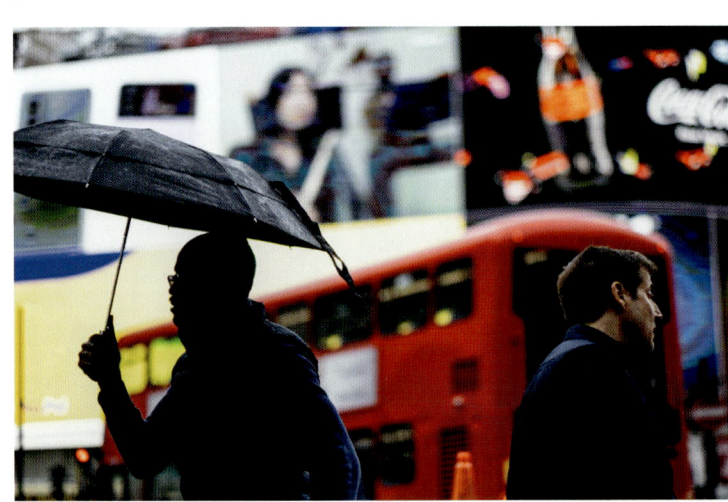

- **Colour matching:** A woman in a red hat who's also carrying a red bag. Why is that interesting?

- **The walker:** Do we really need to see any more pictures of people walking past a wall?

- **The phone call:** Someone standing on a street corner doing nothing except being on their phone is *not* worthy of our attention!

- **Homeless people:** Why? They're having a bad enough day without you poking your camera in their face.

Here's a good test you can apply to your pictures: Is there an interesting moment? Is there a very strong aesthetic? Or does the image convey a narrative? Tick any one of those boxes and you're on your way to a good picture. This is the quick litmus test I use if I'm unsure whether an image is going to have any real appeal.

8. NOT CONSIDERING THE BACKGROUND

I often hear photographers say: *"I quite like this picture but it's a pity about the background."* Of course, there are times when you have to react instantly to a scene and there's no time to consider the background. More often, however, we do have the time, we just don't pay the background enough attention.

Think about whether the background adds to or detracts from the image. Is it overly distracting? Does it dominate? Is it too fussy or busy? Is it completely irrelevant?

Getting this right is often a quick fix; maybe you need to wait a moment until the background changes, or maybe you need to move a few feet to your left or shoot from a higher viewpoint. This is one of the great things about the fishing approach: You are effectively designing the frame by choosing the background in advance so it's not left to chance.

9. MOVING TOO FAST

Most people walk too quickly, and they miss out on so much of what's going on around them. You really do need to be in the zone or in the moment, and that's much more likely to happen if you move slowly. You'll find that you see, hear, and even smell things you'd otherwise miss. Your senses will become more alert, and you'll really start to read the streets. This is when the magic starts to happen. So *slow down*!

10. CONVERTING EVERYTHING TO BLACK AND WHITE

Some people think that it is a street photography norm or a convention that images should be in black and white. It isn't.

Street photography began its life in black and white, naturally, because colour wasn't available in the early days. But today, we can capture that world in colour; black and white is an abstraction. That's not to say it's a bad thing—much of what I shoot is in black and white. But it's done that way for a specific reason and with a sense of purpose, not because of a belief that street photography *should* be in black and white.

Try to make the decision to shoot black and white before you press the shutter, so that you're shooting this way with intent: It's a creative choice rather than a desperate afterthought to try to make a boring picture look interesting. In my case, it tends to be dictated by projects. It's one of the decisions I make when I'm at the conceptual stage of putting a project together (see Chapter 9 for much more about this).

11. MISSING THE DETAILS

If you're going to be a good street photographer, then you must be 100% tuned into your surroundings and aware of everything that's going on around you. A big part of this is paying attention to life's small details, the things other people

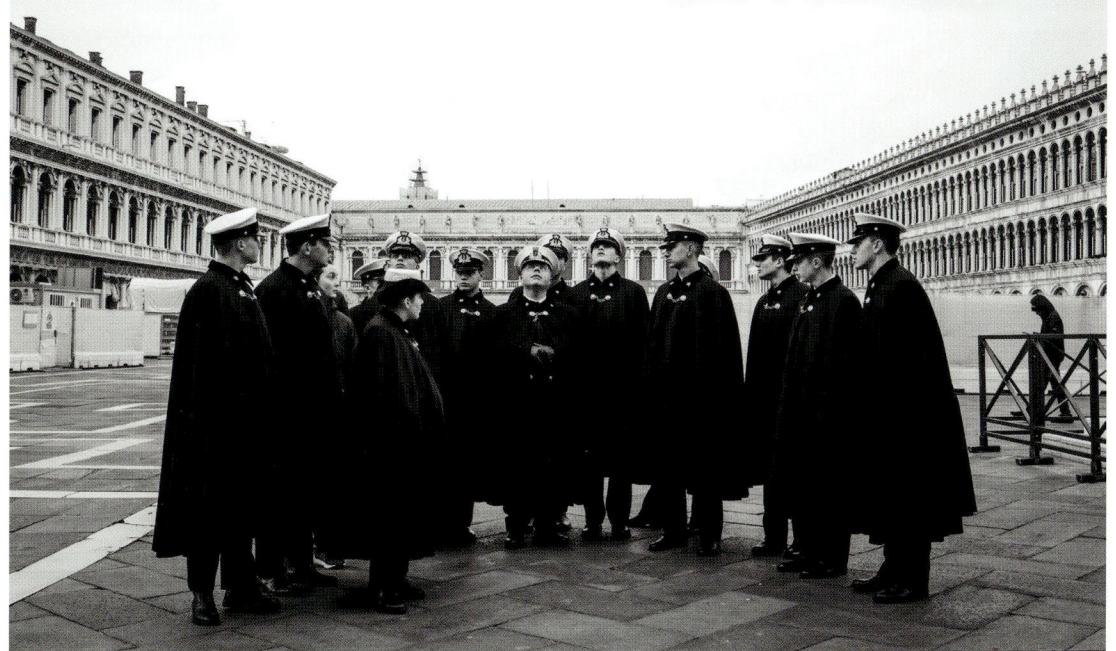

Sometimes an image just needs to be shot in black and white. This shot forms part of a series about the timelessness of Venice, and it simply would not have worked as well in colour.

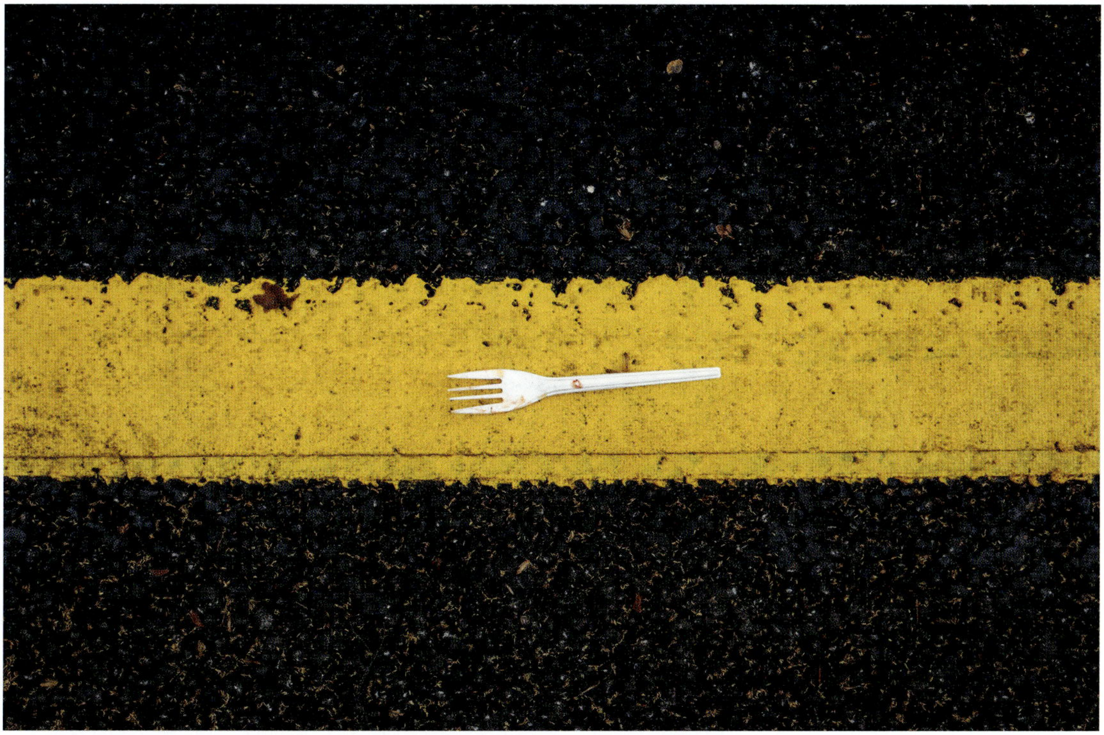

Who would give this a second glance? Maybe it's my strange sense of humour, but as soon as I saw it my first reaction was, "Oh look, there's a fork in the road."

would pass by and not even notice. Some of the world's greatest ever street images rely on one small detail to make them work. So, we need to be curious, inquisitive, and nosy, questioning everything and accepting nothing at face value.

12. BEING CREEPY OR FURTIVE

We've all seen the furtive street photographer, lurking in the shadows, hiding behind his camera, and always shooting from the hip. This person looks like they're up to no good. The way they move, the way they give you a sideways glance, their closed body language—it all tells you they're doing something they shouldn't be doing.

Don't get me wrong. Being stealthy is a good thing, as is a degree of invisibility. We all need to shoot quickly (and ideally not be noticed), but if you take this too far, it will have the opposite effect and you could end up looking like a weirdo. So just be proud of what you're doing and don't worry too much about being outed as a street photographer. Remember, the more normally you behave, the less you'll stand out.

13. BEING CONSPICUOUS

Photographers attract attention. The guy with the big DSLR around his neck with a 70–200mm lens on the front, pouches round his waist, and a huge rucksack on his back will look like a photographer. He's conspicuous. On the other hand,

Travel light, ideally with a small camera and one lens, so that you'll look more like a tourist than a photographer. Small mirrorless or rangefinder cameras are ideal for street photography.

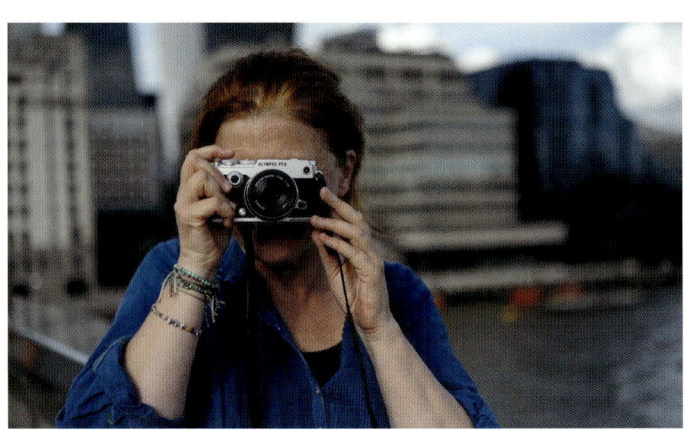

the woman carrying the small pocket camera will look like a tourist. People tend to notice photographers, whereas nobody pays much attention to tourists.

The problem is that when people spot you as a photographer, they are on alert. Once they're aware of your presence, there's a danger that you'll miss that interesting candid shot. So always be the tourist; carry minimal gear, and try not to look too much like a photographer.

14. RANDOM SHOOTING WITHOUT PURPOSE

Street photography can seem pretty hard, and many people make it even harder for themselves because they have no direction. If you head out onto the streets with no real idea of what you're looking for, you're more likely to go home empty-handed.

We've all been there: You walk around all day and you don't see much that's interesting. There's a lot of luck involved in street photography, and sometimes things just don't happen for us. But, if you use projects as a vehicle for organizing your work, you're much more likely to be productive and fulfilled. So hit the streets with a couple of projects in mind, but still focus on the activities going on around you. That's the bonus!

15. SHOOTING TOO MUCH OR TOO LITTLE

I had someone in a workshop recently who took over 2,000 pictures in one day; on that same day, another participant took fewer than 30. There is, of course, no right or wrong number of images to capture, but there should be a happy medium.

It's unlikely that the guy who took 2,000 shots was putting much thought into what he was shooting; he took an indiscriminate "spray and pray" approach, hoping to get lucky. Whilst you could argue that, statistically, the more you shoot the more success you'll have, I suggest that with this approach, your focus is too broad and you cannot possibly be *thinking* enough about what you're shooting.

Conversely, if you take too few pictures then you're probably being inhibited by *over-thinking*. You could say it's a case of "paralysis by analysis".

There's no right number of pictures to take as what works for me may not work for you. It's all about experimenting and finding the right balance.

16. UNREALISTIC EXPECTATIONS

I see a lot of street photographers putting pressure on themselves to come home at the end of the day with a card full of great images. Honestly, it's never going to happen, so don't cause yourself stress by putting pressure on yourself to shoot loads of great images every session. If I spend a day on the streets, I'm more than happy to get one or two keepers. Sometimes it's none, which is fine. And that's a good mindset. I'll walk 30,000 steps, drink lots of coffee, have a beer or two, have some interesting conversations, pop my head into a gallery, and whatever number of good pictures I take, I'll consider it a great day.

So don't let unrealistic expectations put you off or hold you back: A low hit rate is perfectly normal. Street photography is a long game where patience really pays off. Be patient and the results will come!

17. NOT CONSIDERING THE LIGHT

Don't take images that are in poor light! This sounds like such an obvious point that it's hardly worth mentioning. But I see a lot of images that were ruined because the photographer didn't think carefully enough about the light. For landscape, studio, or fashion photographers, light is seen to be critically important, but for some street photographers, it's a secondary consideration.

Whether you're using frontal lighting, side lighting, or backlighting, do it *by design*. Think about the effect the light is having on your frame and be in control of it. Decide what effect you want from the light and position yourself in such a way to achieve it.

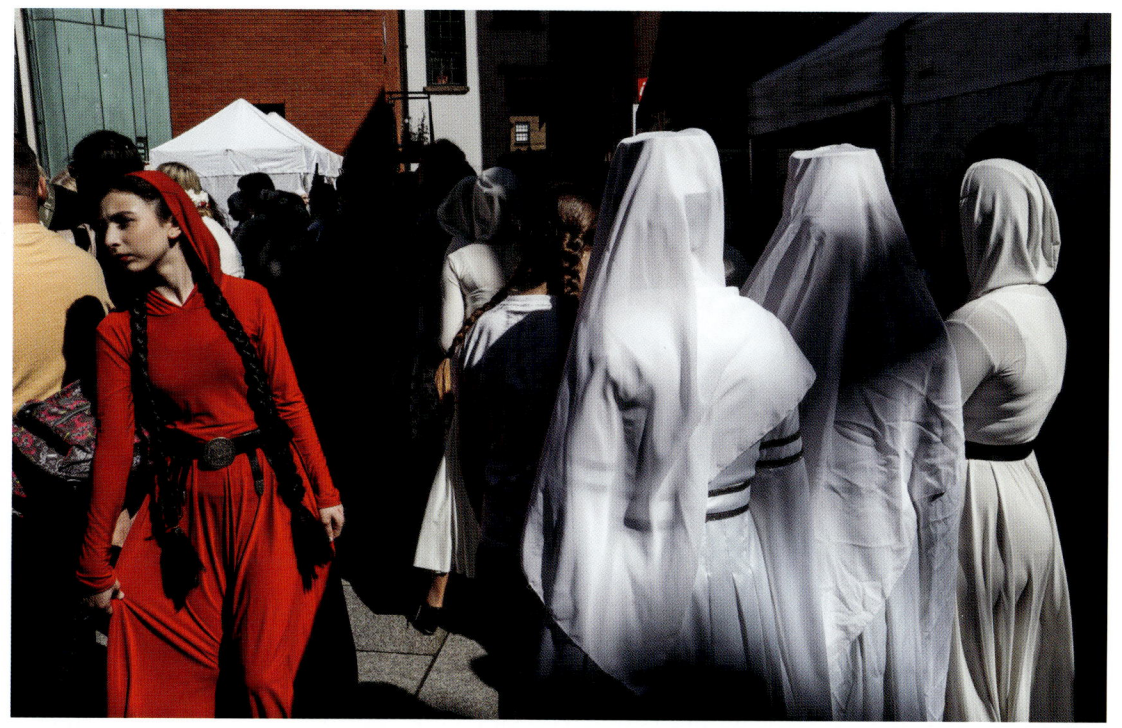

Sunny days are perfect for street photography. Strong frontal lighting can help enhance colours and boost contrast.

18. SHOOTING EVERYTHING FROM THE SAME PERSPECTIVE

It's too easy to put the camera to our eye every time and get all our shots with the same perspective. Some would say it's the easy option that doesn't really require any thinking. Street photography is very fluid and relaxed, and you'll find that by varying your perspective you can bring so much more energy and spark into your street photography. My advice is to mix things up a bit! Try something dramatic, unusual, maybe even uncomfortable, and just see what happens. Shoot from a high viewpoint, shoot from the hip, or get down low (the rat's eye perspective, like Elliott Erwitt with some of his pictures of dogs).

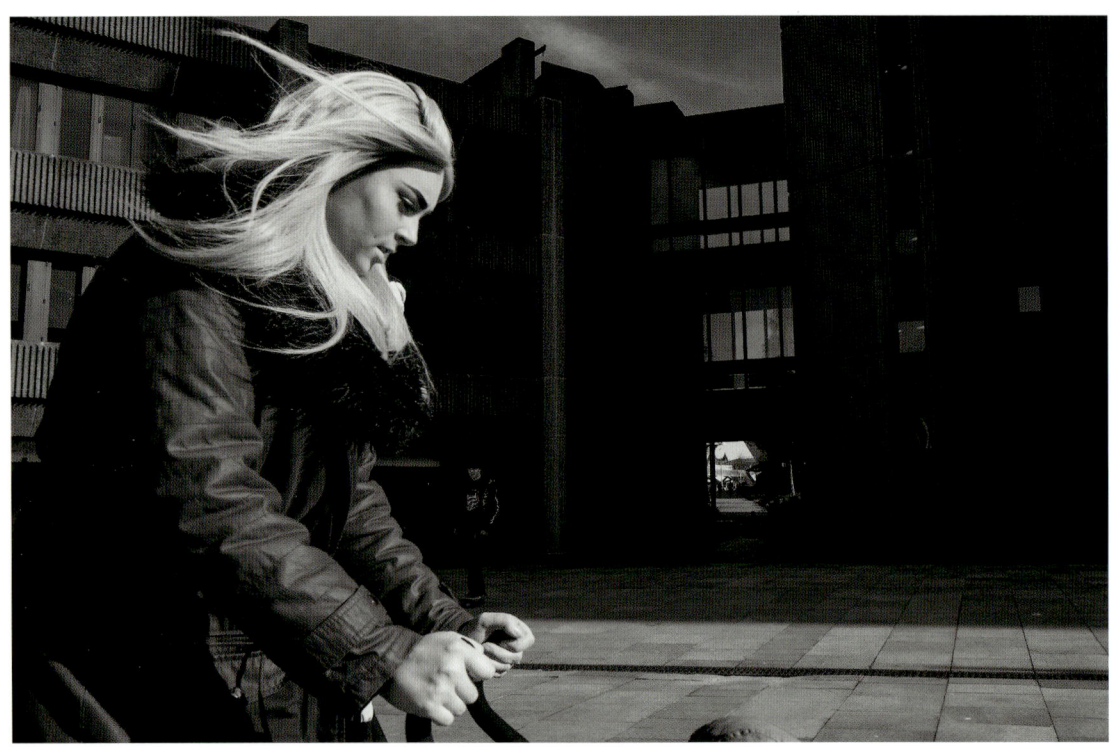

A different viewpoint, such as shooting from the hip, can give you a more dynamic and engaging perspective.

19. LETTING FAILURE HOLD YOU BACK

As I mentioned in point 14, street photography isn't easy (and if you think it *is* easy you're probably not trying hard enough). Many potentially good photographers fall by the wayside at an early stage, giving up because it all seems like an uphill struggle.

One of the problems is that it's so unpredictable. Will it rain? Who might walk through that door? Will that great juxtaposition happen before your eyes? Who knows! The chances are that none of these things (or other interesting things) will happen, and you end your day of street shooting thinking: *"Well that was boring, nothing happened,"* thus feeling that you failed as a street photographer.

Welcome to my world! This is all quite normal, and it's all part of the fun. Enjoy the serendipity of the occasional successes, and don't make failure an excuse or a reason to quit street photography. It's certainly not failure, and it happens to the best of us. Consider this great quote from playwright Samuel Beckett: *"Ever tried? Ever failed? No matter. Try again. Fail again. Fail better!"*

20. DON'T MAKE GEAR AN EXCUSE

Gear really doesn't matter. Pretty much any camera will do, and you really don't need expensive gear to be a good street photographer. I know a guy who shoots film on a little old Olympus Trip whose images are substantially better than another guy I know who shoots with an $8,000 Leica. So don't make the gear an excuse.

Sure, good gear can sometimes help you a little—shooting in low light, for example—but it's never going to make you a better street photographer. Use what you've got, get to know it inside out, and let it become part of you. This will always be a far richer experience than constantly buying new stuff and using gear you're not familiar with.

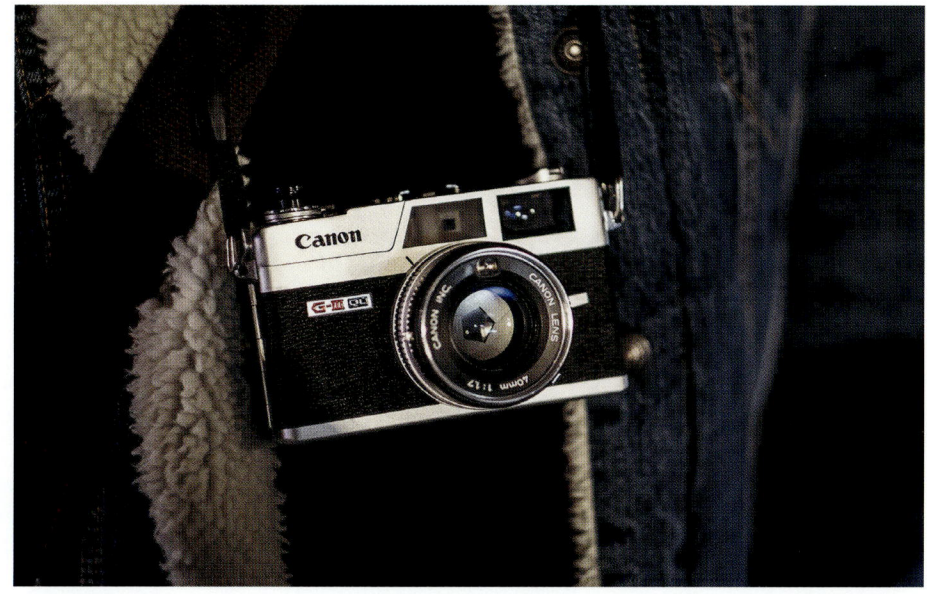

You don't need the latest, most expensive gear for street photography. In fact, I recommend going back to basics. Buy an old analogue camera and some film, and let the magic happen!

8

THE RECIPE FOR A STRONG IMAGE

Just like any other art form, street photography is, of course, subjective. The maxim, "One man's meat is another man's poison" is apt; a strong image for me may not be a strong image for you. Nothing causes more friction and angst on internet forums than the question of whether a particular street image is good or not.

However, to use a food analogy, there are some key ingredients which come together to create a satisfying result. You wouldn't want to put every single one of them into your recipe, so treat the following points as a list of options from which to choose.

Once you start to think and behave like a street photographer, there's no going back and you'll develop a mindset that will stay with you.

NORMAL ISN'T INTERESTING

You'll have gathered from the previous chapters that I'm no fan of the typical, one-dimensional shot of someone walking through a shaft of sunlight or past some street art. This is "normal." A picture of a street performer, a homeless person, someone on their phone—these capture what we *expect* to see in ordinary life. We, as street photographers, need to present our viewers with something unexpected, unusual, funny, beautiful, provocative, absurd, or in some way striking.

By any measure, this is not an interesting image! It's a woman standing next to a wall. How could that be considered interesting?

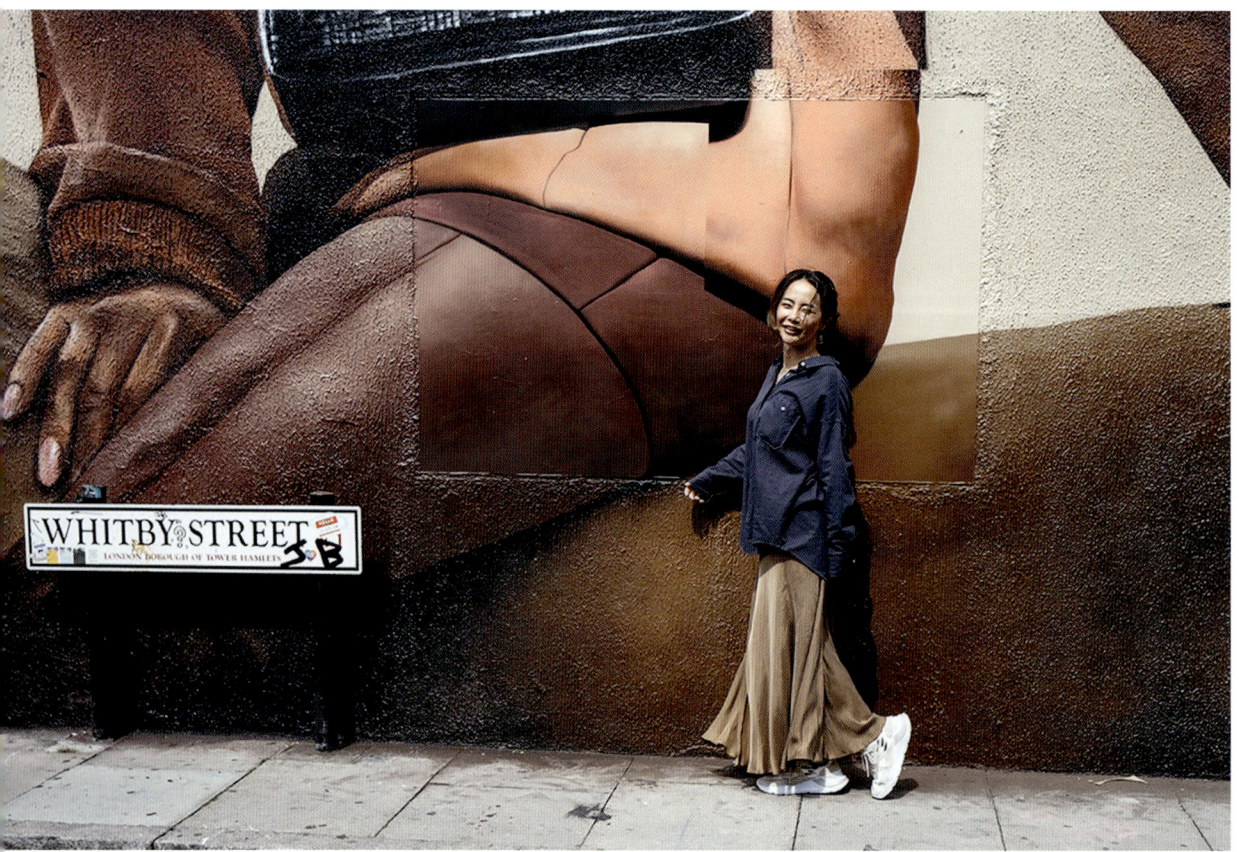

COMPELLING COMPOSITION

Striking compositions are all about capturing the raw energy and narrative of the streets while maintaining visual balance. We can use some of the conventional rules of composition, and we can also break them. Don't feel too hidebound by rules. Some of these rules are pretty essential, some are nice to have, and some are best ignored.

USE THE TRADITIONAL RULES OF COMPOSITION

- **Rule of thirds:** Divide your frame into a 3 x 3 grid and position your subject or key elements along the intersections. This creates a naturally balanced composition.

- **Leading lines:** Leading lines are one of the pillars of compositional theory, and they add depth to your image by giving the viewer directions as to where to look. Think of them as visual signposts. You don't (usually) want the eye constantly scanning the image and looking for a focal point, so you use the concept of leading lines to direct the viewer's attention to what is important. You can use the natural or man-made lines you'll come across on the streets, such as roads, fences, railway tracks, shadows, railings, or the edges of buildings, to lead the viewer's eye toward your subject. You can also find coincidental leading lines in hand gestures, arrows, street signs, a vanishing point, information on posters, or even the direction in which someone's eyes are looking. Lines can be straight or curved, and they can be pointing at any angle. The whole point of them is that they must direct the eye to something interesting.

- **Frames:** Find natural frames (doorways, windows, arches) within the scene to focus the viewer's attention and add depth. Take a look at Saul Leiter's work for inspiration—he used frames extensively and to great effect.

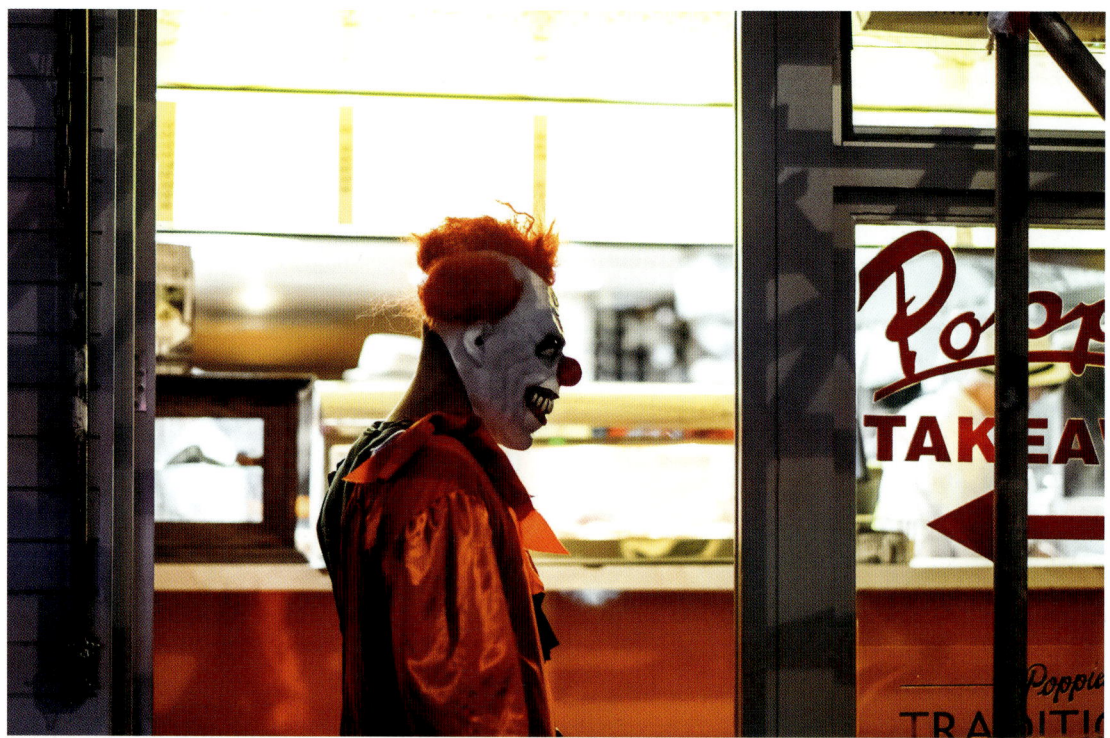

Make your subject important by putting it in a frame. In this case, the doorway makes the creepy clown stand out more.

. . . AND THEN BREAK SOME!

Who needs rules? As someone once said to me, *"Street photography is the jazz of photography,"* which I think is quite apposite. My own view is that the rules are there to be broken when the situation demands it. If you look at the work of William Klein or Daido Moriyama, you'll see that many of their compositions were chaotic and disruptive, but the spontaneity and the energy within them overpowered any misgivings about an imperfect composition. In fact, the opposite could easily be the case: An image with impeccable angles, perfect balance, and beautifully observed compositional rules could be so sterile and sanitized that it has little impact. We frequently see this with the ubiquitous shot of a small, silhouetted figure with some office buildings in the background.

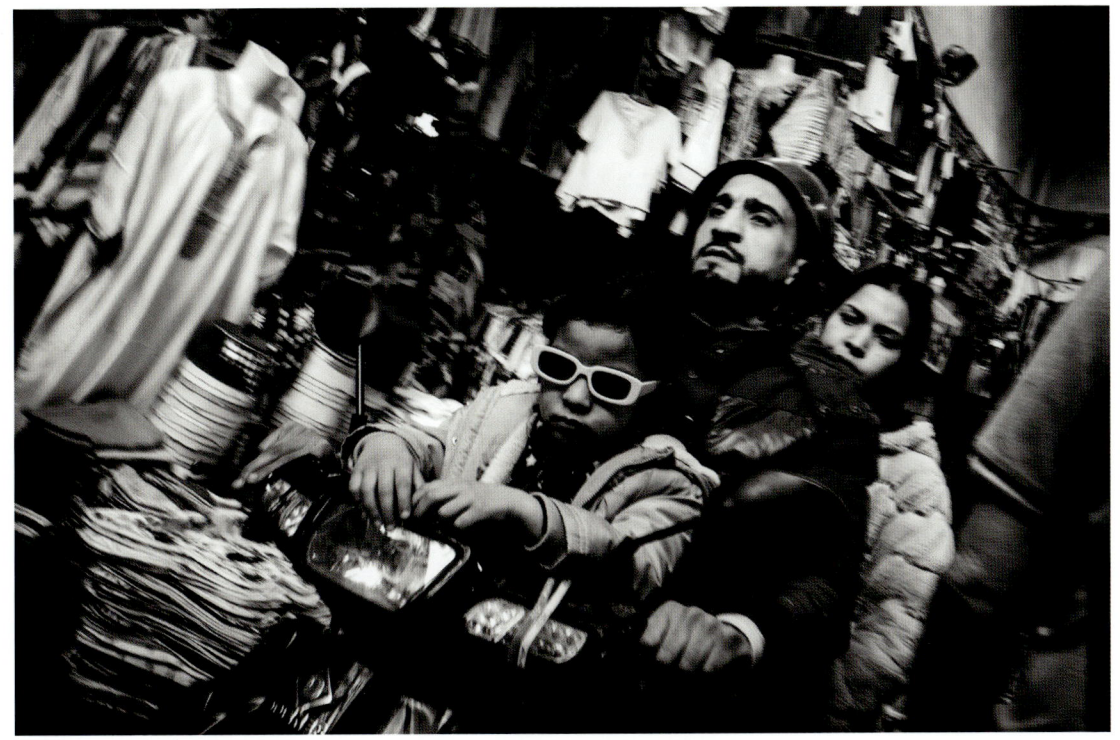

I like the imperfectness of this shot. The angle is wonky, it's grainy, and it's not sharp, but would it work as well if everything was perfect?

SHOOT LAYERS

For clarity, shooting layers is a compositional technique you deploy at the picture-taking stage, rather than a post-production editing technique. For example, photographs taken *through* something can provide a rich artistic interpretation of an everyday street scene. To see this technique in action, look no further than Saul Leiter, who would often shoot through misted-up windows, using the window itself as the primary, in-focus layer, with the main subject being almost incidental.

Using layers will add volume and depth to your images, and it simply means having a number of separate scenes located on different planes, usually from front to back (and sometimes from side to side), throughout the frame.

Aiming for three layers is a good starting point. Alex Webb uses this technique to great effect, with many of his iconic images being made up of a strong foreground, middle-ground, and background. Each layer in your image has an important part to play and should make a contribution to the overall effect.

When every layer contains some relevant information, they will come together to form the complete image, which has much more depth than an image with a single layer (such as the proverbial "person walking past a wall" shot).

Right: This is how Saul Leiter might have used layers: combining reflections with reality to create visual confusion and an element of abstraction.

Below: A different approach to layering. Taken in Marrakech, this shot and shows how we can use information in the foreground, the background, and also from the sides to add depth and context.

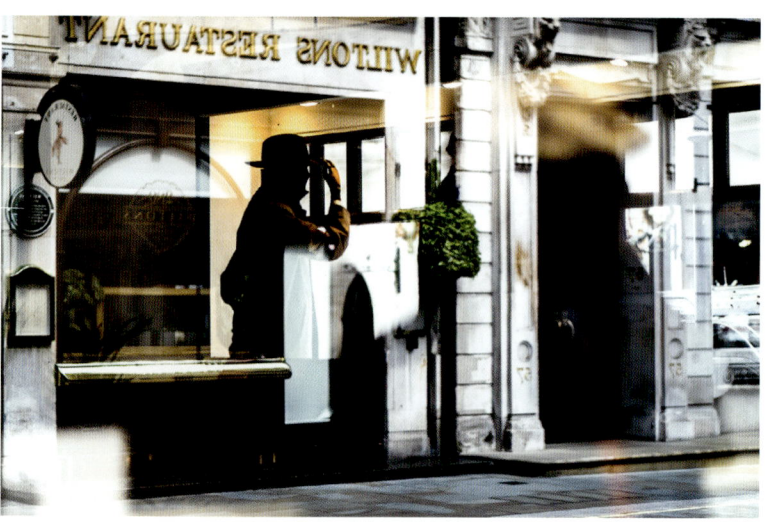

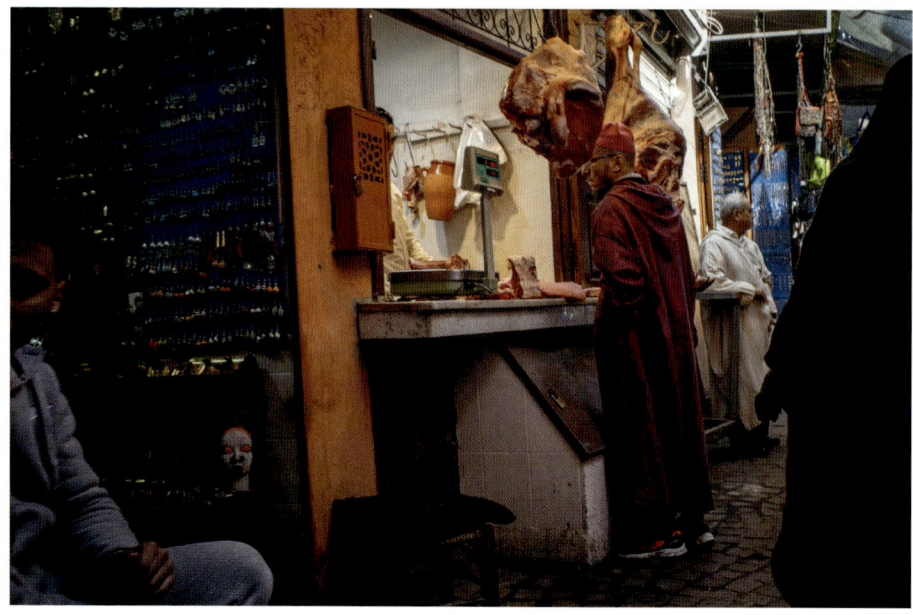

SIMPLICITY

Our brain will usually attempt to reduce an image to its simplest form. The Gestalt law of simplicity explains that it's important to simplify an image to help the eye and the brain feel comfortable in interpreting what we are trying to present, so your image should be as easy as possible to understand. For example, a cluttered background can detract from the subject, so finding clean or out-of-focus backgrounds can help the subject stand out.

When you're considering a scene, therefore, look for its simplest form to make it easy for the brain to interpret. Then, after a while, the viewer's mind will work harder and will comprehend the real meaning of the image.

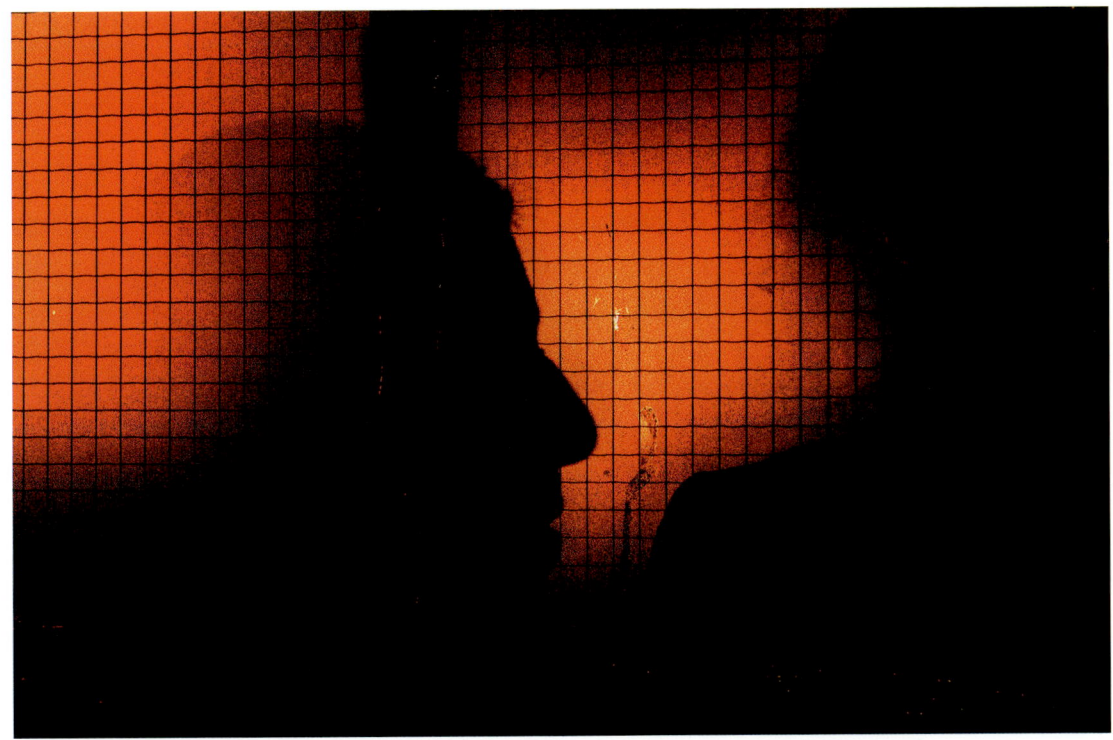

Minimal, simple, and clear shapes will always do well on Instagram and can help create striking images. I shot this image through the window of a bar at night, and then increased the contrast in post-production to emphasize the form of the two heads.

FIGURE-TO-GROUND RATIO

Another of the Gestalt laws, the figure-to-ground ratio refers to the relationship between the subject (figure) and the background (ground). An image with a strong figure-to-ground ratio will have good separation between the subject and the background.

It is sometimes difficult when we want to draw attention to our main subject, but the viewer can't see it clearly because the subject merges too easily into the background. The figure-to-ground principle helps us to explain which element will be perceived as the figure and which element will be the ground. Our mind will perceive the smallest or the most contrasty area as the figure and the larger area as the ground.

This principle is particularly effective when you are shooting in busy places like big cities, when it's difficult to isolate your subject from all the background noise. You can create a strong figure-to-ground ratio through the use of focus, contrast, or differences in colour.

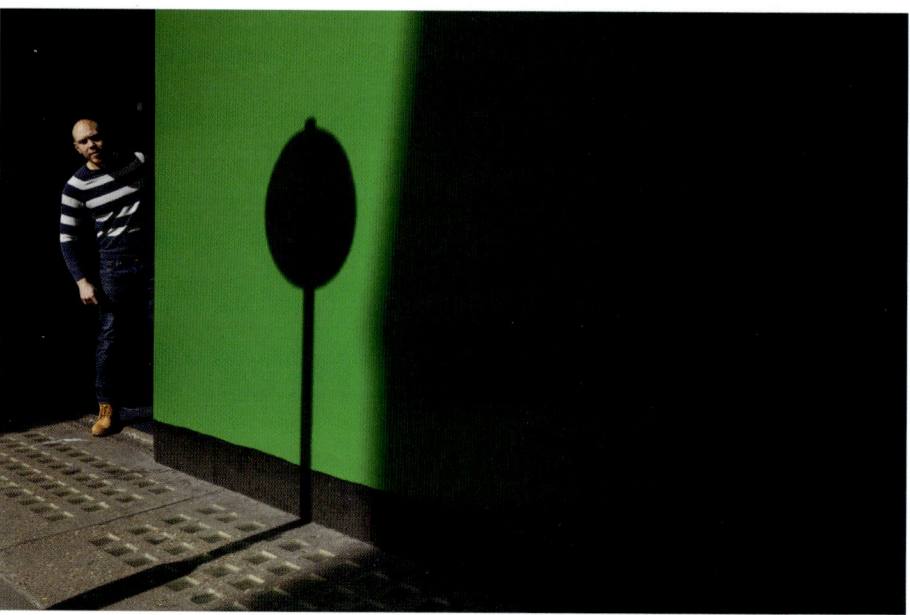

Although the figure is relatively small in the image and offset well to the left of the frame, there's a strong figure-to-ground ratio because his stripey top stands out against the dark strip of background.

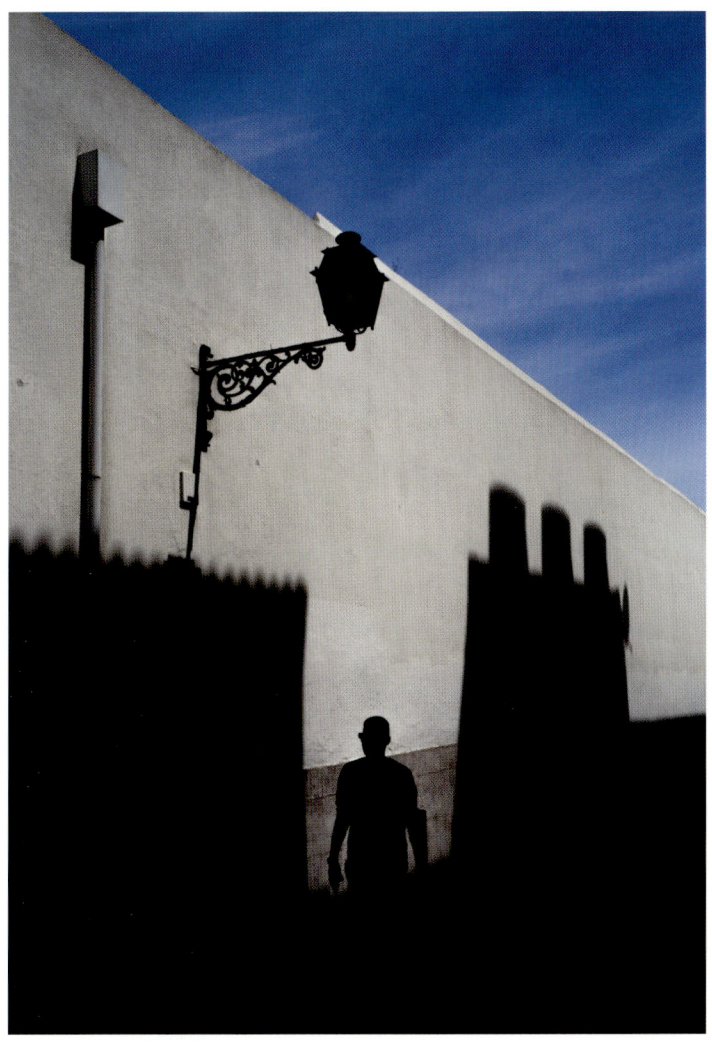

There's nothing wrong with using the qualities of light and shadow as the basis for constructing an image. This shot works particularly well because of the well-defined shapes of the shadows; in this case the shadows are a deliberate design feature of the image.

USE LIGHT AND SHADOW

Can a street image rely on light and shadow alone? Or is more needed, such as a story or a cute observation? There are plenty of examples from the masters of street photography that demonstrate how an image can pass muster just on these aesthetic qualities. Using light and shadow as the primary element in street photography images is a powerful way to create mood, drama, and visual interest. The sections that follow outline some of the factors I would look out for to make this kind of image work.

LOOK FOR HIGH CONTRAST SCENES

Find areas where light meets darkness. These areas create natural vignettes that can direct the viewer's attention to your subject whilst creating a good figure-to-ground ratio. This is particularly important if you're shooting in black and white because you need a much higher degree of tonal separation.

SHOOT SILHOUETTES

Images which rely solely on silhouettes seem to polarize opinion amongst street photographers. Some love them and rely heavily on them (often a little too much), whilst others deride them. I think silhouettes *do* have an important role to play in this genre, and it's worth analyzing the ingredients of a good silhouette shot:

- The starting point is to have a strong light source behind the silhouetted figure. This could be direct light (such as the sun) or indirect light (such as a bright wall).

- Next, your silhouette needs to make a strong and interesting shape, such as a person wearing a big hat, a flowing coat, or carrying something. Aim for a crisp, well-defined, elegant shape.

- If there is more than one figure in your shot, there must be good separation between them to avoid them looking like a big, dark blob.

- You may need to experiment with exposure (I do this using the exposure compensation dial). The crucial element to get right is the black point on the figure. It doesn't matter too much if, for example, the highlights are blown out.

THE SPOTLIGHT EFFECT

Observe how light filters through windows or through gaps between buildings to create focused beams of light that isolate your subject and create a cinematic feel. I would caution against over-using this technique, however, because it has become something of a cliché.

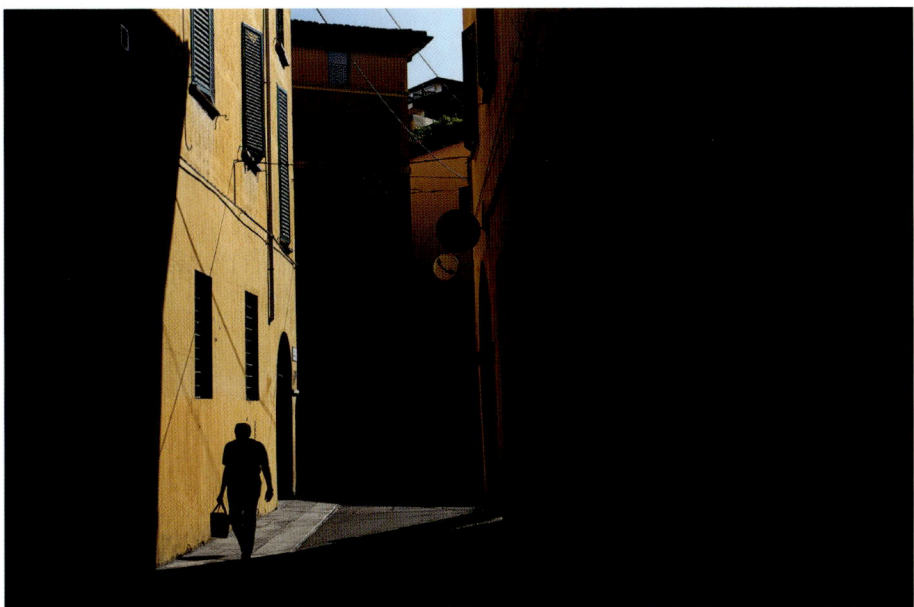

Always be on the lookout for strong, well-defined shapes for your silhouettes. Make sure there's good separation between them and the background.

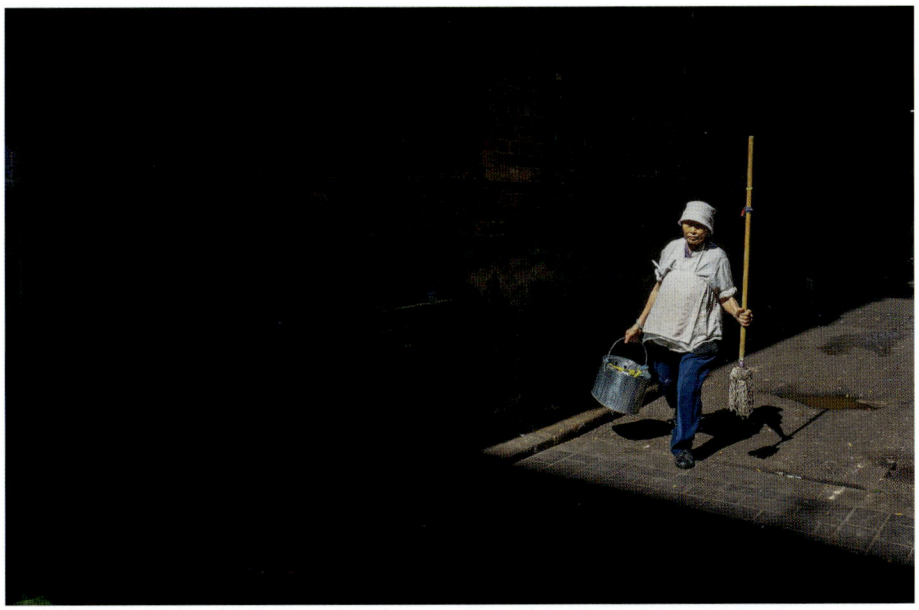

This is a popular, but perhaps over-used, technique that can highlight an interesting or visually appealing subject.

SHOOT DURING THE GOLDEN HOUR

Shooting during the golden hour can be magical. The soft, warm light at sunrise or sunset creates long, dramatic shadows and beautiful contrasts, making everyday scenes feel extraordinary.

OBSERVE PEOPLE INTERACTING WITH LIGHT

Watch people move through the light. See how they step into light or shadow patches to create dynamic compositions. Look for slivers of light falling across faces or mottled patches of light on their skin. This is a good opportunity for fishing (as described in Chapter 6), whereby you find some nice light and then watch and wait.

UNDEREXPOSE TO ADD DRAMA

This is a technique I use a lot, and I find that slightly underexposing an image can deepen shadows and enhance contrast (a nice byproduct is protecting the highlights); generally, the brighter the light, the more I'm likely to underexpose.

This effect is most easily achieved by shooting in aperture priority mode (or shutter speed priority, if you prefer), then making the adjustment on the exposure compensation dial. I do this much of the time and my thumb is never far away from that dial.

A DECISIVE MOMENT

Street photography is often all about the decisive moment, an early concept coined by the great grandfather of street photography, Henri Cartier-Bresson. He maintained that capturing the exact second when all the elements align is crucial. There is something quite electrifying in an image that has a strong decisive moment; that moment is there for a split second, then it's gone forever, never to be repeated.

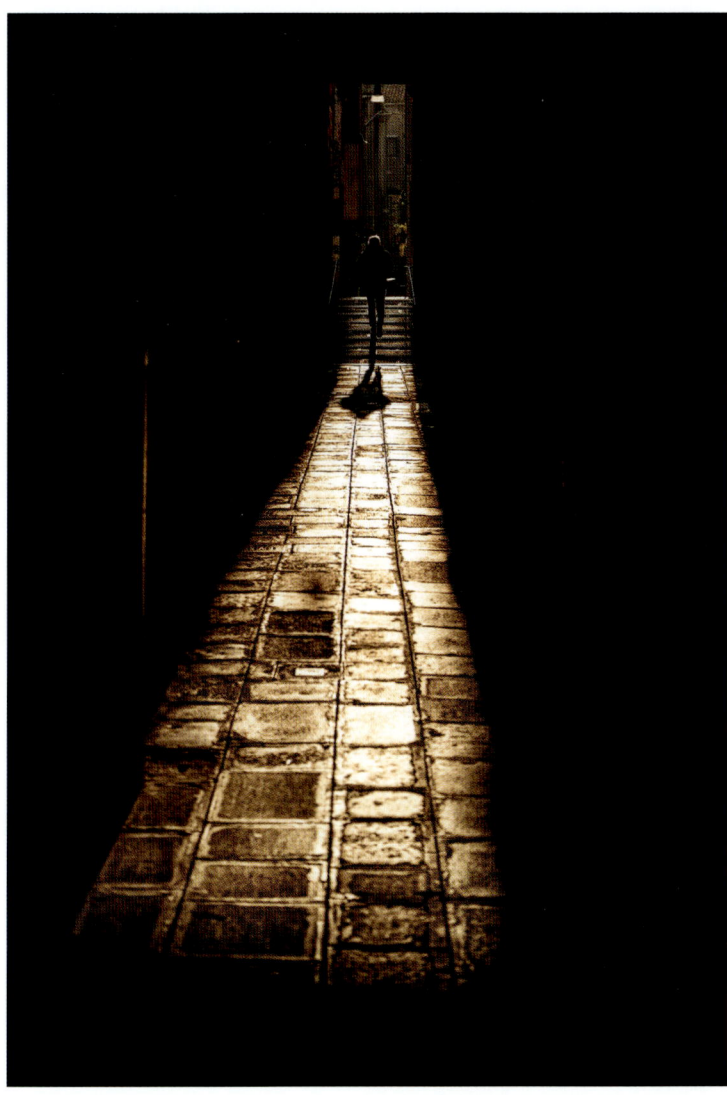

This shot was underexposed by 2 stops, which protected the intensely bright highlights and added to the overall drama of the scene.

Sometimes it's down to good planning or canny anticipation, and sometimes it's just a case of getting lucky. You must hit upon that split second when all the elements—light, composition, emotion, and movement—come together in perfect harmony to help tell a compelling story. To maximize your chances of capturing a decisive moment, you need good observation skills, a keen sense of anticipation, patience, and quick reflexes.

*"I am not interested in capturing the 'decisive moment.' I am interested in the accidental moment." —**Brassaï***

CONNECTIONS AND JUXTAPOSITIONS

The closely related concepts of connections and juxtapositions have always been a big deal in street photography. This is where we make a connection between two (or more) apparently unrelated elements in a frame. It's an essential skill for street photographers. It's a simple concept and one which has been superbly executed by contemporary practitioners such as Vineet Vohra, Pau Buscató, Nils Jorgensen, and Matt Stuart.

Connections (good connections, at least) can be few and far between. A good place to start is by studying the words you see on the streets. The written word is all around us: In shop windows, street signs, advertising posters—the possibilities are endless. Look for words that are strong in themselves, such as the word "absurd." If the graphical representation of the word is also strong, the effect is even more impactful.

Of course, there's more to it than simply using words. Words are a good starting point but can be a bit clichéd. Most street photographers move on to make more complex connections that may not be quite so obvious. (See Chapter 5 for more on connections.)

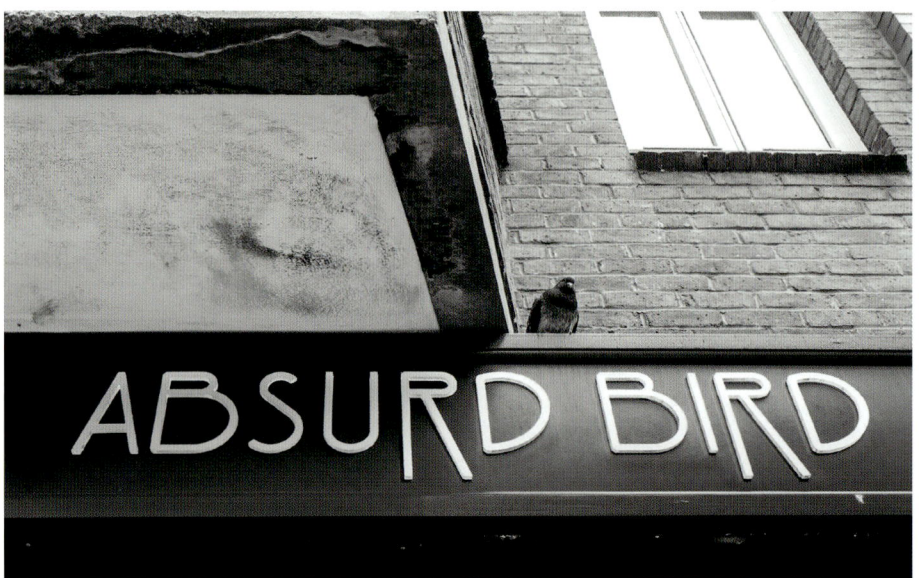

The pigeon made the perfect connection with the "Absurd Bird" sign!

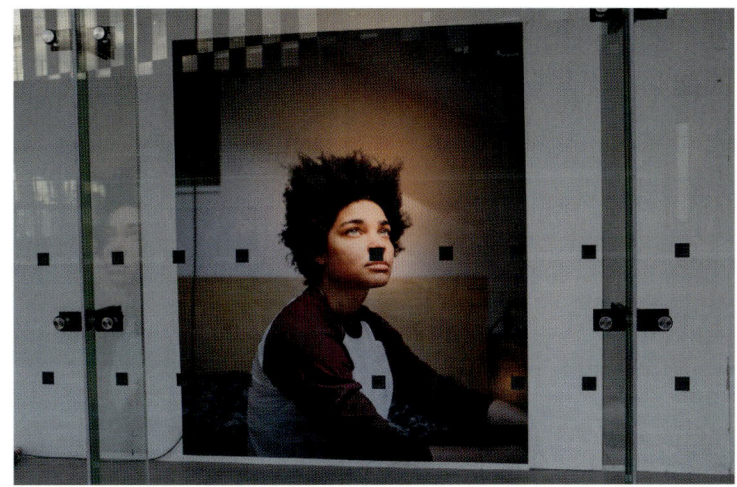

Juxtaposition has been a mainstay of street photography for many years. This involves placing two or more contrasting elements within a single frame to highlight differences, provoke emotions, or tell a story. The great Elliott Erwitt was very good at juxtaposition, and his images often promoted humor, irony, or unexpected meaning. He would often pair people with dogs in ways that made the animals seem to mirror human behavior or vice versa. His iconic knee-level photo of a woman's legs standing between a Chihuahua and a Great Dane's legs is a perfect example of how he uses scale and framing for comedic juxtaposition.

A good starting point is to look for contrasts: modern versus old, big versus small, colour versus monotone, moving versus still. Or, seek out generational or cultural clashes or ironies. These opposites can create striking visual interest.

SIMILARITY, COINCIDENCE, AND REPETITION

Other important ingredients are the notions of similarity, coincidence, and repetition. We tend to perceive elements as belonging to the same group if they look like each other. We can apply the principle of similarity using colour, size, texture, form, tone, or any other visual attribute. The important thing here is that unconnected elements that have similar attributes will be perceived as the same group. By using this law, we can more easily make correlations between unconnected elements.

We love the unexpected, and coincidence in street photography can result in some of the most captivating and surprising images. It often happens when unrelated elements within a scene align in unexpected ways, creating humour, intrigue, or a narrative.

For example, we could have the perfect alignment, when someone stands at the perfect angle with an advertising billboard, creating the illusion of interaction or a surreal juxtaposition.

Alternatively, we could use matching or repeating colours, like a person wearing a red coat that matches the colour of a bus in the background and also a telephone box in the foreground, all coming together with glorious serendipity.

Always watch people for how their behaviour mirrors that of others around them, such as three people all sneezing in unison.

The idea is that we make viewers do a double take: *"Can this be for real?"*

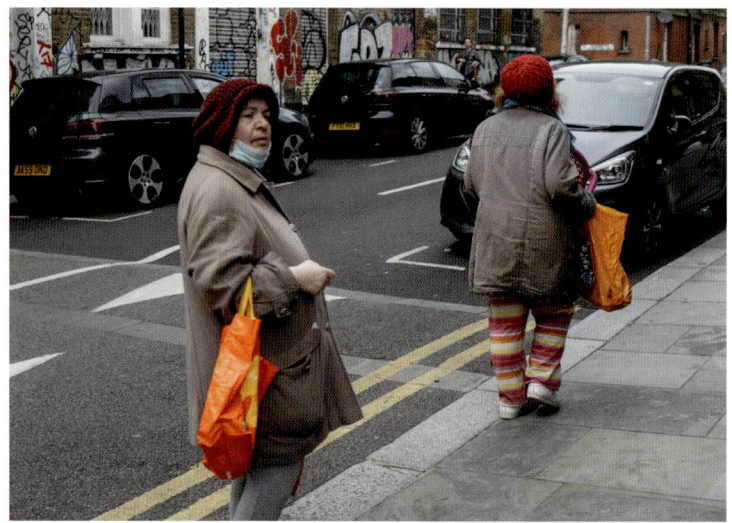

Keep your eyes open for simple visual similarities, such as these two women with similar coats, hats, and shopping bags.

STREET PORTRAITS?

The big question about street portraits is whether or not they are street photography. It's a matter for debate, and I would place them into the margins of what we think of as street photography, although they don't come close to any conventional definitions.

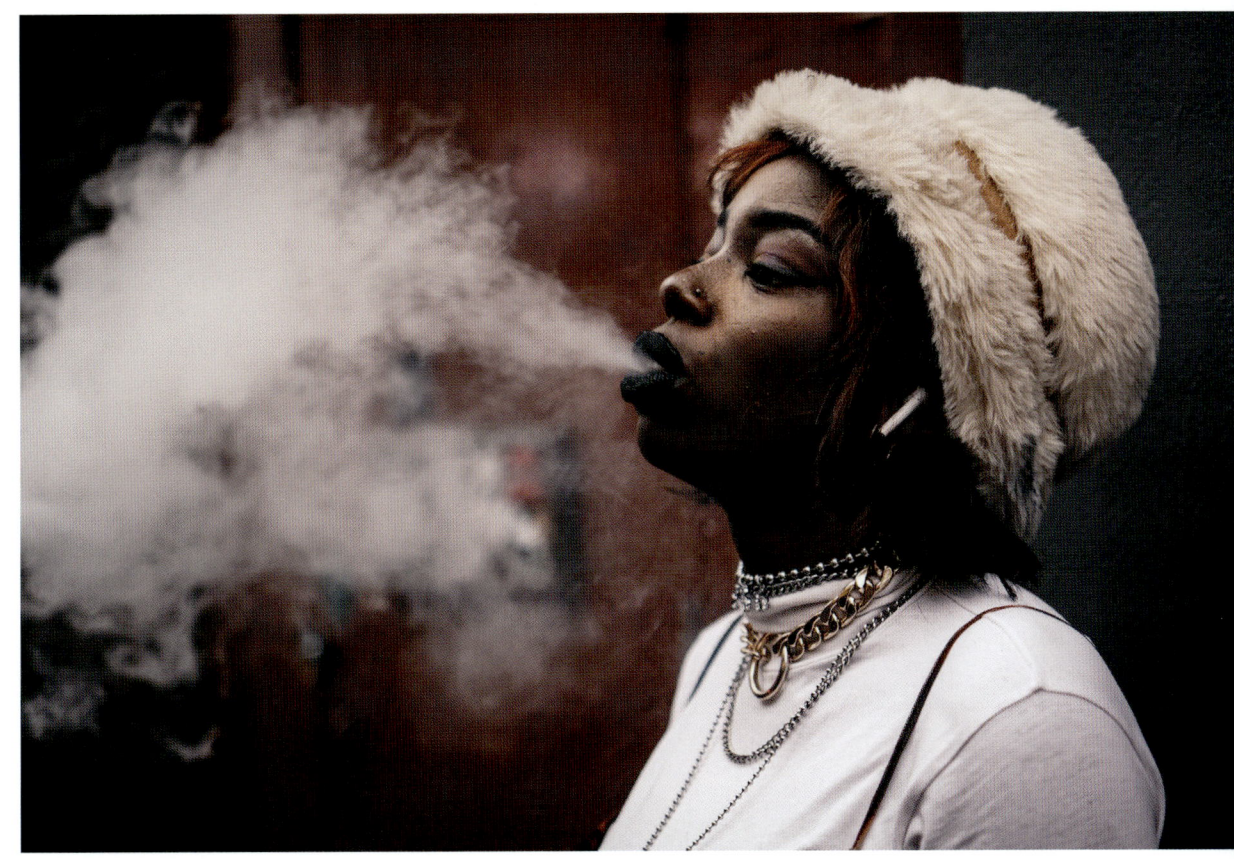

Street portraits are not for everyone, but the process of engaging with strangers—and the resulting images—can be highly rewarding.

So, should you ask strangers if you can take their picture? And, if so, is this really *authentic* street photography? Street portraits are extremely popular, and most of the street photographers I know shoot them to a greater or lesser extent.

A street portrait is a posed, rather than candid, portrait of a stranger on the street; typically, you'll see someone who looks interesting, and ask them if you can take their portrait. You may be surprised to know that most people say yes, and the whole process can be a rewarding experience for both parties.

We generally think of street photography as a candid pursuit, so engaging with a subject would appear to fly in the face of convention. But who cares? If you enjoy it, do it! It may not be conventional street photography, but shooting street portraits is great fun, and it's actually quite addictive.

AUTHENTICITY

Street photography really should be about authenticity, and this chapter wouldn't be complete without discussing it. This isn't a rule, but it's a widely accepted convention, and we should go to the greatest lengths to preserve the authenticity of a scene. Street photography shines when it captures real, serendipitous, unaltered life. Authentic street photography captures candid moments of everyday life in public spaces, emphasizing real, unposed interactions and the raw essence of humanity. It's about finding beauty in the mundane, the unusual in the usual, and the unexpected in the expected. We should be looking for honest, real moments that tell a story, evoke an emotion, or reveal something unique about the human condition.

This generally (but not exclusively) means that the following are off limits:

- Scenes that are staged or set up in any way (notwithstanding street portraits).

- Using post-production to substantially alter an image. This means no cloning to move elements around, no adding of things (such as a bat flying past a full moon), and no extensive colour grading. The biggest no-no is the colour pop, whereby an image has been reduced to black and white with the exception of one colour element, such as red umbrella. Leave that to the people who don't know what they're doing.

- Anything involving models.

- Interference in a scene; observe but don't get involved. It's our role to document, not to direct.

9

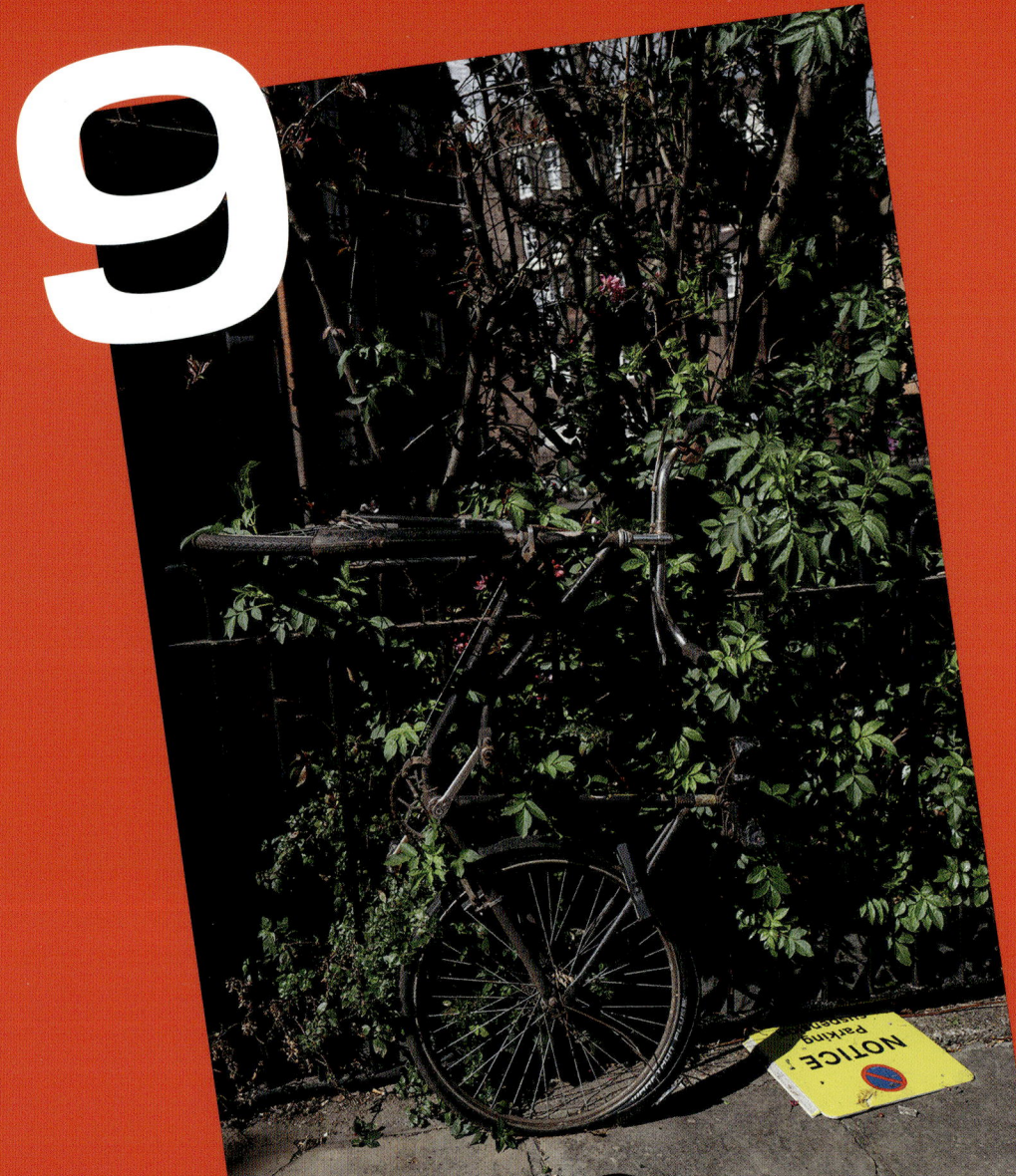

PROJECTS

If you study the work of the great street photographers (Winogrand, Meyerowitz, Gilden, Gruyaert, Maier, Erwitt), you will discover that they all shot projects. Like most of us, they also shot wonderful standalone images that didn't fit neatly into a project silo. You could say we all get lucky, and maybe they would have said the same. I guess some get luckier than others!

Of course, projects are not the only way to motivate your sessions in the field. Some people prefer to enjoy the unpredictability and serendipity of unplanned shooting. Plenty of excellent street photographers work like this, waiting for that one-off decisive moment that makes the whole day worthwhile.

One of my ongoing projects is about abandoned objects. This is more of a fun project than a serious one. Discarded items are so prevalent that wherever I am, there will potentially be material for this project.

However, great images don't come our way with any great frequency, and if we leave everything to chance and shoot randomly, we may go home disappointed. For some people, this can lead to feelings of frustration and despondency, and the lack of regular, consistent success may cause some people to give up street photography altogether.

It's common to meet rookie street photographers who are disillusioned with the results they are achieving; others struggle to find interesting material on the streets and don't feel they are being particularly productive. Or maybe they think their pictures look boring. Does this sound familiar to you? How often do you come back from a day's shooting with a card full of uninspiring images? Not enough keepers? Whilst it happens to us all at some point, these hurdles can be overcome by using projects. This is the preferred approach of most established street photographers.

One could say that this is the approach of the more serious street photographer, or at least the photographer who wants to be taken more seriously. (By serious, I don't necessarily mean good—it's all about intent, aspiration, and longer-term goals.) Let's call him or her the "project photographer."

The project photographer will use projects as a means to produce a consistent and connected body of work that has more depth and more compelling content.

I am a committed project photographer, and a major part of my street photography life involves shooting projects. I hope you'll be inspired to adopt a similar approach.

"Most of my projects seem to start as exploratory journeys with no visible end in sight" **—Alex Webb**

WHAT IS A PROJECT?

A project is a collection of images on a theme—a cohesive body of work based around a central idea or narrative within the genre of street photography. Unlike the random shooting approach, a project adds focus, direction, and intent to your work, helping to tell a story or to explore a concept in depth.

Your project could be comprised of six images or 600—the scale of the project doesn't matter so much. More importantly, there needs to be a common thread, a sort of visual glue or connective tissue that binds the images together as a body of work.

What does the end point look like? A project could manifest itself as, for example, a set of framed prints, a set of greetings cards, an exhibition, a zine, or a glossy coffee table book.

In terms of timespan, projects can take anything from a few days to several years; they can develop into long-term or even lifelong endeavours. Robert Frank's seminal book, *The Americans*, is a good example of a long-term project. This project, finally whittled down to 83 images, probed beneath the surface of mainstream American life to uncover some of the social issues and injustices of the mid-1950s and was as much an exercise in social documentary as it was street photography. This is the perfect illustration of how a project can shape up, with Frank taking around 27,000 images to arrive at the 83 in his book (first published by Grove Press in 1959).

A popular and cost-effective way of bringing your project to life is by producing a zine (more about this in Chapter 10). I frequently publish my own projects as zines, a low-cost and easy alternative to book publishing.

START WITH A CONCEPT

It all starts with a central idea or proposition, around which the project revolves. Your theme could be based on virtually anything: a specific location, a subculture, a cultural phenomenon, a social issue, a visual motif, or a particular aesthetic. For example, you could:

- Document street life in your own neighbourhood or on a particular street.

- Capture candid moments, such as focusing on how tourists behave.

- Capture human emotion or interaction through gestures.

- Explore juxtapositions, such as things covering people's facial features.

- Focus on a particular aesthetic, such as the effects of the light on street corners.

These are just a few random ideas, and you should now be thinking about developing your own concept(s).

A CONSISTENT APPROACH

Your project images should have a consistent aesthetic, visual or thematic style (such as similar subject matter), composition, or colour palette. Avoid, for example, mixing black and white with colour in the same project or having too many different aspect ratios. The images should all look connected and part of the same family.

STORYTELLING

Though not always the case, a street photography project may tell a story or present a perspective about life in the public realm, giving viewers insight into the photographer's vision.

TIMESCALE

Projects can be short term (anything from one day to a few weeks) or long term (spanning months or years), depending on their scope and complexity. I shot a project in Prague that I completed in 48 hours and had a zine produced within a week. At the other end of the spectrum, I have an ongoing project in its seventh year that is nowhere near completion. The important thing is not to rush projects and to let them develop and mature where necessary.

PHYSICAL OUTPUT

You will ideally have an idea of how your project will manifest itself even before you start shooting. Projects usually culminate in a tangible or shareable result, such as:

- A photo essay or zine
- An exhibition
- A photo book
- An online article, blog, or page on your website

WHERE TO FIND INSPIRATION FOR PROJECTS

If you struggle to find ideas and inspiration for your projects, you're not alone. Finding the right theme or concept is the first hurdle where projects often fall. It's best not to stress about this as your anxiety will probably inhibit your ability to generate fresh ideas. Don't force the ideas, but allow them to evolve naturally and in their own time.

The following are some examples of how I find inspiration for my own projects.

THE TYPOLOGY PROJECT

This is perhaps the most straightforward type of project to undertake. Typology projects are well defined, and you'll have a good idea of exactly what your subjects are and where to find them. You need to find a subject that interests you (for example, subway stations, street portraits, the beach, the colour yellow, reflections, and so on) and develop your project on that theme. I recommend to always be working on at least one typology project, because whilst you're tuned-in to possible material as you're walking the streets, you'll be open to all the other serendipitous opportunities that come your way. This style of shooting will also help refine your observation skills and your eye for detail.

LOCATION-BASED PROJECTS

My starting point for a project can simply be a location, which could be a street, a town, a district, a city, or a country. The location itself is the main subject ingredient and is the key part of the concept. You'll need to set out what it is about the location that interests you. Is it the people? The architecture? The vibe? As with typology projects, these are fairly easy to scope out, but you do need to have an interesting angle.

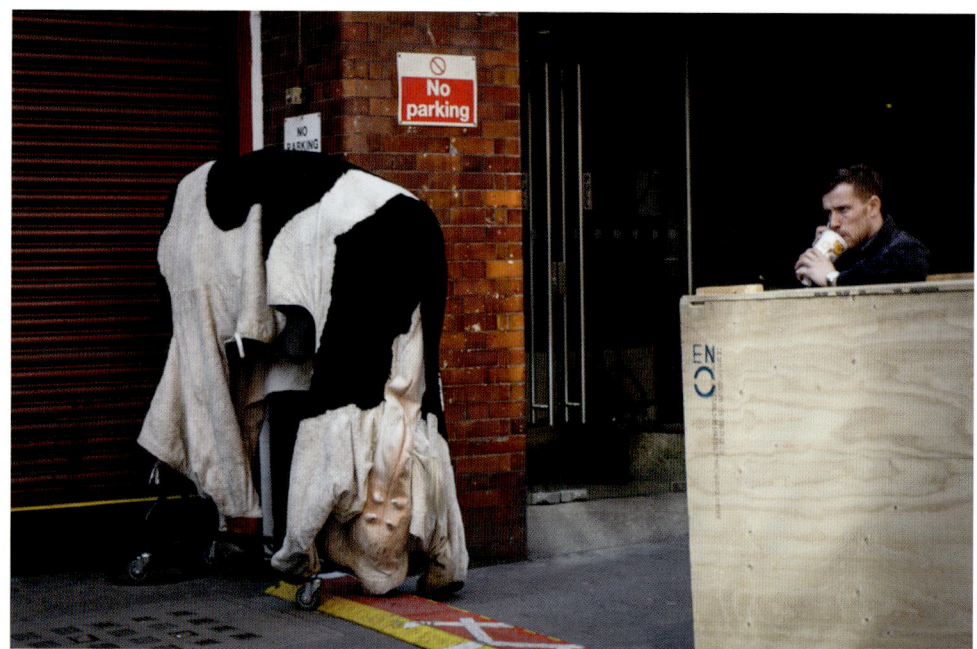

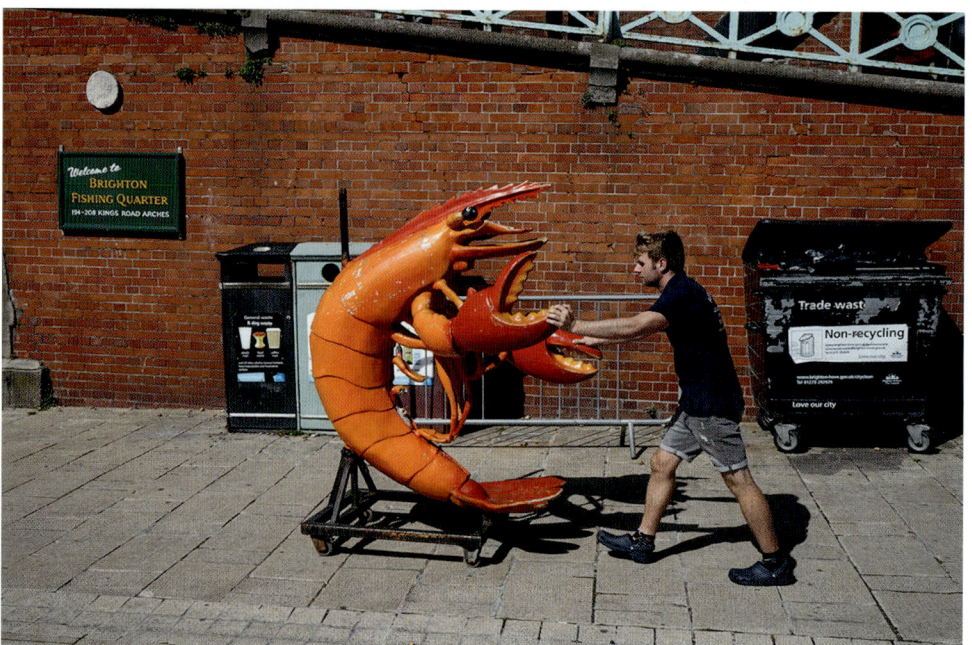

These two images are from an ongoing project called *Urban Jungle* that features animals we wouldn't normally expect to see on the street. The great thing about this type of project is that images can come from any location; wherever I am in the world, I'm on the hunt for animals.

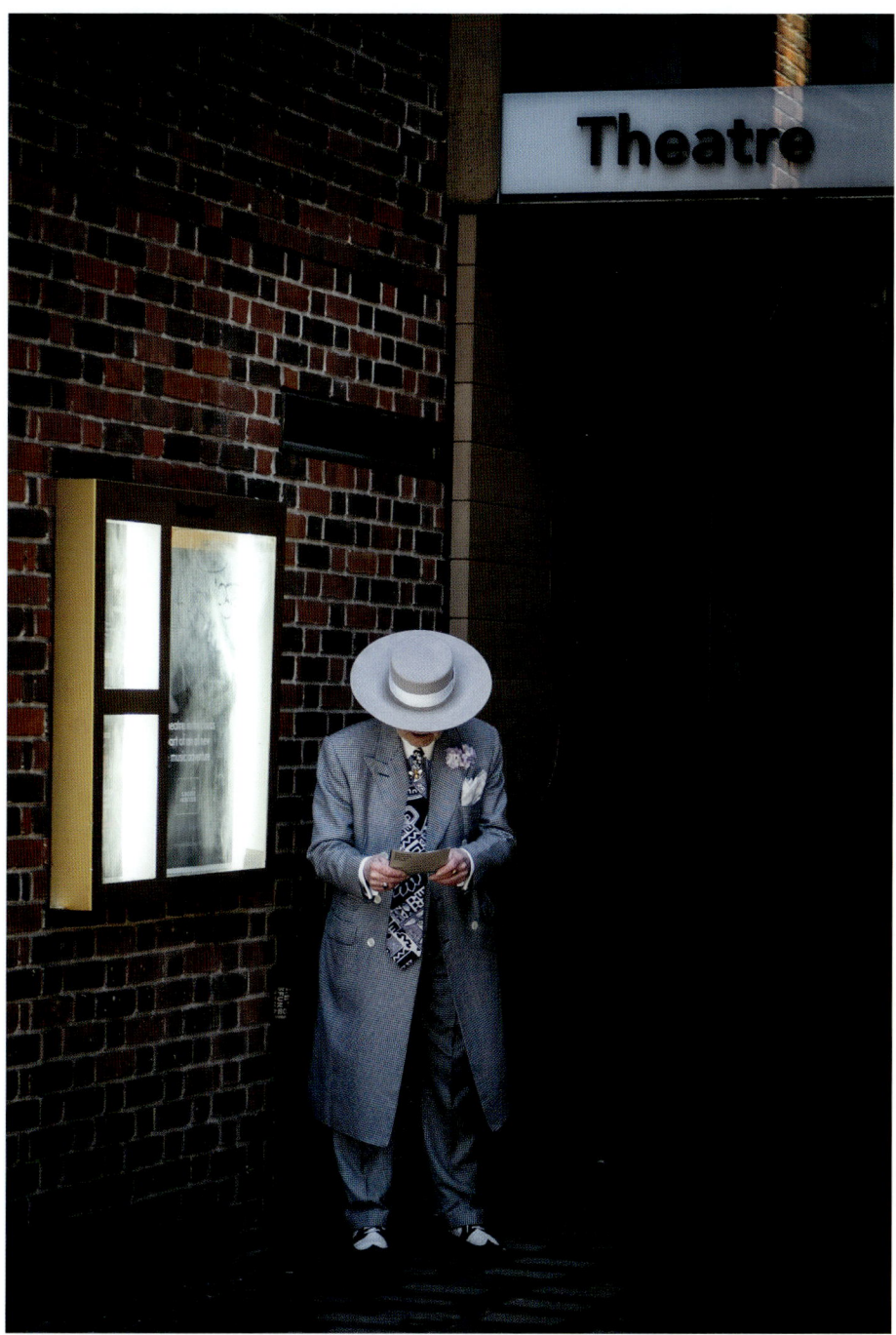

This is from my project about the elegance of days gone by, represented by scenes I come across in the twenty-first century. It's quite fun looking for these timeless images.

EXPLORE YOUR ARCHIVE

I often cast an eye over my archive in search for inspiration from pictures I have taken previously. I could be casually looking through an old hard drive and come across an image I had forgotten about, and that random single image may just give me the flicker of an idea for a project. Alternatively, I may detect patterns or trends, where I spot a cluster of similar images that I was not previously aware of.

It's a good idea to go back to the beginning and scour your archive. You'll almost certainly discover images that will spark ideas. You may even find that you already have a number of projects in the making.

STUDY WHAT OTHERS HAVE DONE

Whilst directly copying another photographer's projects is never a good idea, we can certainly take inspiration from work we admire or can relate to. Sometimes just a faint spark of inspiration from someone else's book, exhibition, or even Instagram post is all we need to ignite the fire.

Always strive to put your own spin or interpretation on that work, rather like adding your own addendum to an existing narrative. It doesn't matter that something has been done before (most things have!). Your work will reference the same conversation, but do it differently and with your own creative interpretation.

FOLLOW YOUR PERSONAL INTERESTS

Examine your interests outside street photography for inspiration. What you already know is a good starting point for a project, whether that's politics, music, art, sports, charity work, or anything else that you do in your spare time. Most of us have an interest outside of photography we are passionate about—and that passion can provide us with all the inspiration we need for a project.

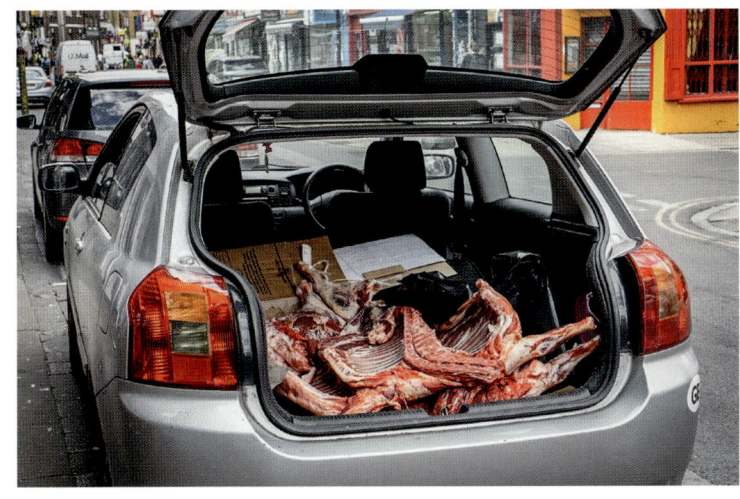

Left: I'm quite interested in cars, and another of my ongoing projects is about unusual things seen in cars, like these animal carcasses.

Below: Another of my ongoing projects is called *Polite Protest*, whereby I aim to document the sole protestor, not someone who's part of a big demonstration, but someone fighting for a cause on their own.

TELL A STORY

There is an element of the documentarian in many of us, and street photography is the perfect vehicle for telling stories. You could shoot projects based on stories about people, events, places, activities, community or political issues, locations— anything that allows a narrative to flow logically through a set of images.

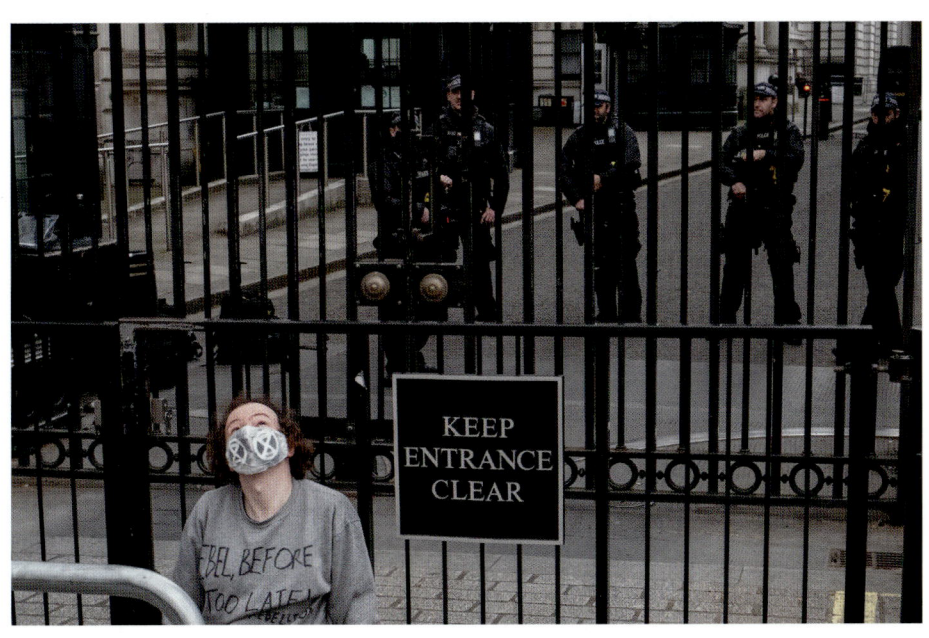

SIMPLY ART

Maybe you just want to create some art. There's nothing wrong with that! We discussed the aesthetic approach to street photography in Chapter 2, and there are plenty of successful street photographers who base their projects on the artistic merit of their images. A project of this nature could culminate in a coffee-table book, a set of prints, or even an exhibition.

Projects don't need to tell a story or contain witty moments. Sometimes they're just about visual appeal. One of my projects, now a zine, *A Essencia de Lisboa* (*The Essence of Lisbon*), is just about the lovely light, colours, and vibe from Lisbon.

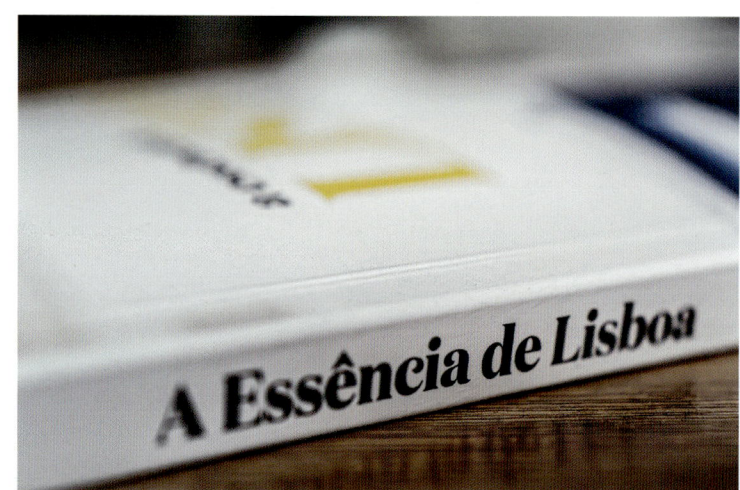

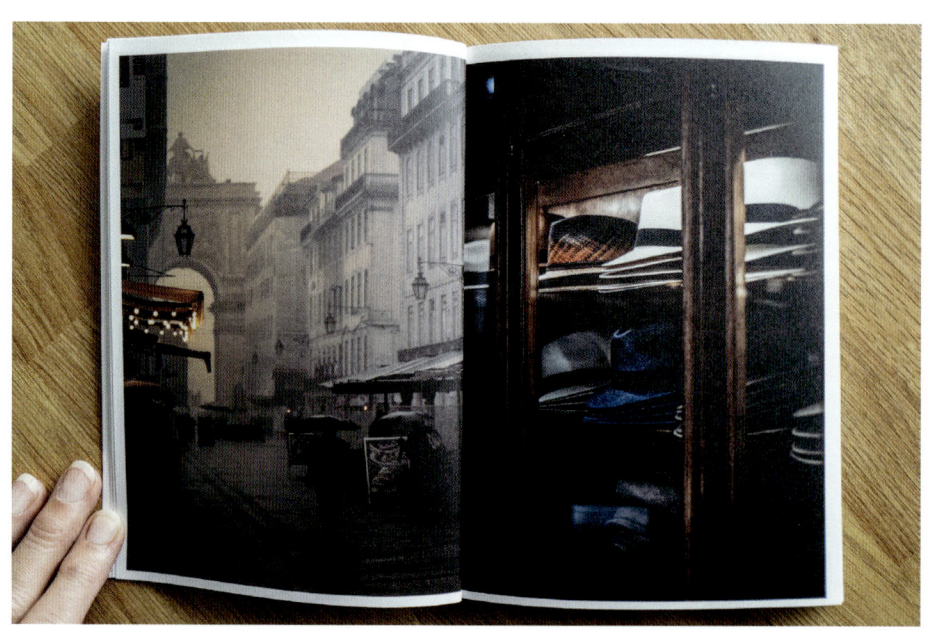

CASE STUDY: Neil Goodwin

Neil Goodwin is a street and documentary photographer based in Scotland. He has completed numerous projects over the past five years, and I asked him to share his approach with us.

Why do you use projects?

Projects allow me to explore issues of personal interest in greater depth and create a body of work of potentially lasting value. They also help in developing photographic and related skills in different contexts and environments, which is an approach I've deliberately pursued in my own work. Furthermore, whilst creating single images can be great fun and rewarding, I would argue that completing a project instills a greater sense of achievement and personal satisfaction for the photographer.

Where do your ideas for projects come from?

I enjoy social documentary-based projects, and I'm driven largely by my career in academia and UK public services, which was mainly in healthcare and social housing. So I've always been interested in social issues. When I eventually stopped work, it gave me more time for photography, and I thought I could use my photography practice, principally in street, coupled with my career experience and knowledge, to create projects. Also, I'm a results-focused person who's quite used to organizing work, both essential for creating successful projects.

How much planning and research do you do?

Planning and research is a necessary prerequisite, especially given the nature of the projects I pursue. *The Other Blackpool* project emerged from my general street photography in the town. As I explored the back streets, I could see there was another side to the town away from the glitz of the seafront and promenade, fuelled by years of economic and social deprivation.

In my subsequent research I alighted on an annual report of England's Chief Medical Officer about the public health challenges facing the country's coastal communities, including Blackpool (which is a brash seaside resort in the northwest of England). This provided a framework for the project, and I decided to combine short extracts from the report alongside the photography, which I eventually published as a documentary photobook. However, I also thought it important not to focus solely on the negative side of Blackpool, for despite its economic and social challenges, it is first and foremost a holiday and fun destination for 18 million people per year. So I decided the project should present a balanced picture by including moments of humour characteristic of England's seaside towns.

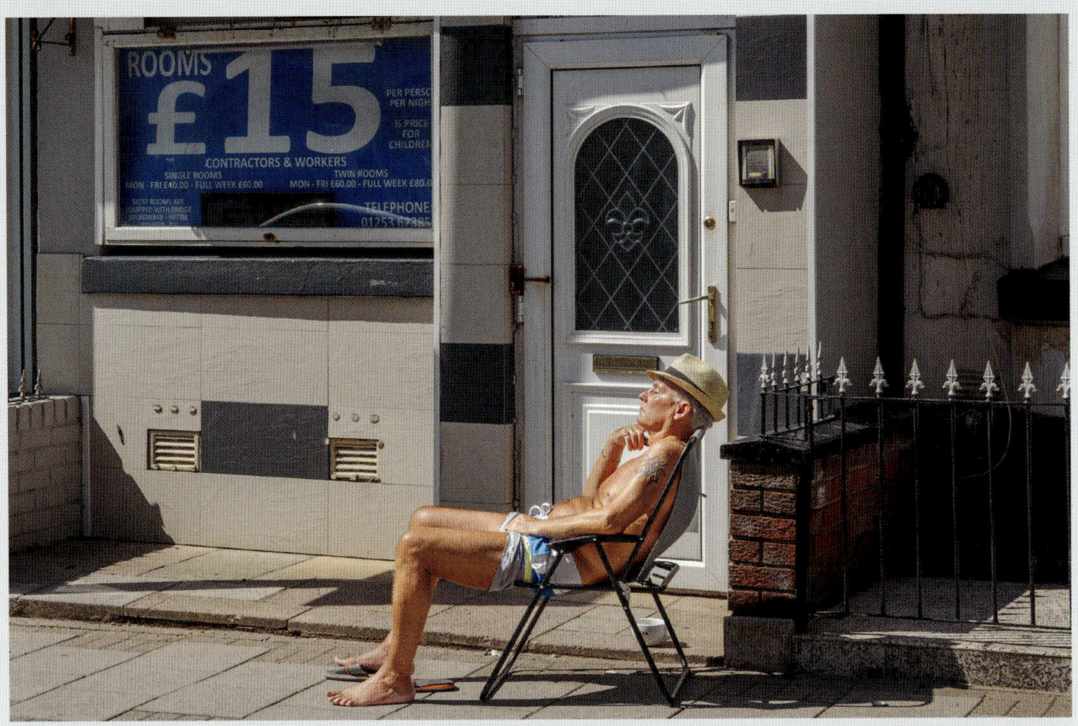

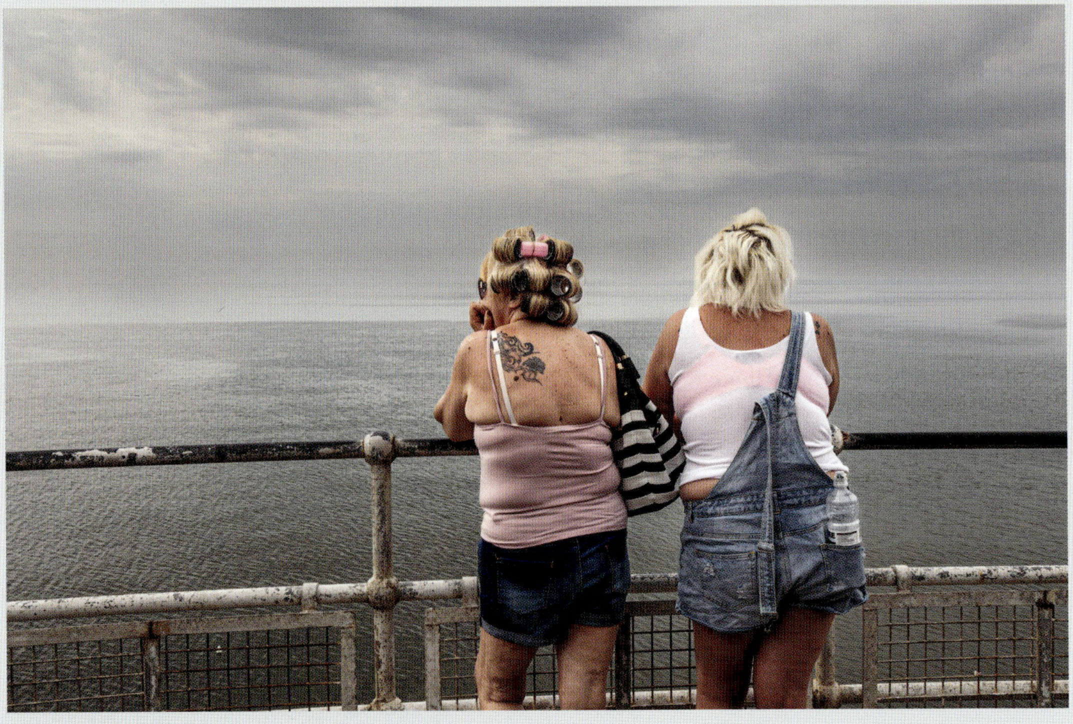

From Neil Goodwin's project, *The Other Blackpool*

Do you visualize the final output at the beginning of the project?

Never completely. At a minimum, I always aim to publicize the results on social media and photography sites I subscribe to, directing people to my own website for further information about the project. I always consider producing a documentary-style photobook, by which I mean images and text. I self-published my projects on Blackpool and living alone (*As Long As I Keep Busy*), registering them with ISBNs to help publicize the work. I've also given talks on my projects and had them featured in publications and exhibitions, for example The Centre for British Documentary Photography and Shutter Hub.

What advice would you give to others who are considering projects?

It's important to choose a subject that interests you, perhaps even one you're passionate about, in order to maintain motivation over what is likely to be a significant period of time. I believe that photographers have to bring something of themselves to projects, so it isn't quite the same as pursuing commissions for commercial work. In my case, I've focused on social documentary not only because I worked in public services and enjoy research, but also because I believe that photography can, if only in a small way, contribute to highlighting important social issues. Furthermore, projects are often a long haul because irrespective of how much research and planning you do, there's the important challenge of making the images. I have lost count of how many times I visited Blackpool to secure the compositions I was looking for.

For social documentary work in particular, I've emphasized the importance of research. In the case of *As Long As I Keep Busy*, I researched the literature on living alone, which is now an international social phenomenon with strong links to loneliness and poor physical and mental health. The research influenced my approach to creating the project in terms of the participants I looked for, the aims I wanted to achieve, and then thinking how to create the images and marry them with the supporting text. So, I sourced participants of different ages, gender, ethnicity, and background, decided to photograph them in their own homes, and supported the images with participants' summary life stories and key points from the research literature. Completing *As Long As I Keep Busy* involved travelling across England, Scotland, and Northern Ireland in my search for participants. I had a few false starts because some prospective participants changed their minds about the project. I also revisited most participants a few times for subsequent photography sessions in my desire for the compositions I was seeking.

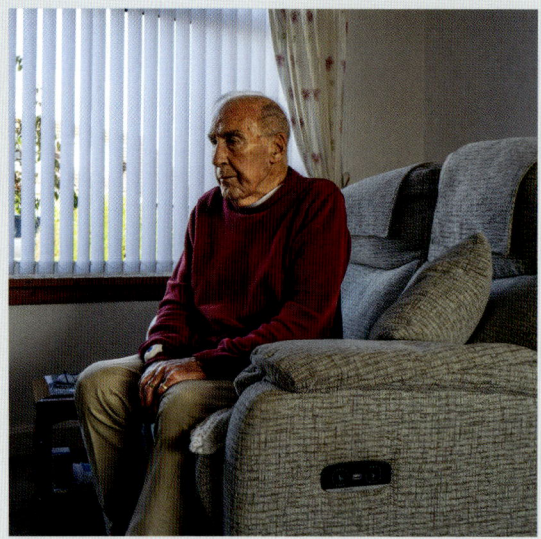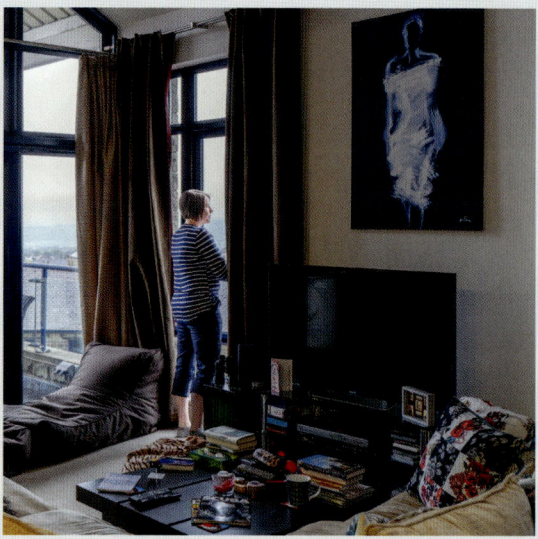

From Neil's more documentary-focused project, *As Long as I Keep Busy*

What's your next project?

I'm currently finalising a project called *Disappearing Life*, about abandoned crofts in the highlands of Scotland. Crofting, a form of agricultural small holding, started during a dark period of Scotland's history three centuries ago when landowners created large scale farms by evicting people onto small, often inhospitable pieces of land called crofts. Today, the number of empty crofts is increasing because of people not taking up their inheritance or moving to towns and cities for work. Consequently, this is resulting in a cycle of depopulation and economic decline, and crofting is now a story of abandonment and decay.

What else have you learned from undertaking projects?

I've already referred to the need for research, planning, goals, time, and motivation. What I've also learned is that projects are not solely about compositions and post-processing. Projects are very personal because we're creating our own interpretation of how we see an issue. If the project involves interacting with people, then the photography is almost incidental because first and foremost we need to establish relationships with participants. This is about developing trust without which people won't relax, affecting both the photography and the content of any accompanying text derived from discussion with participants. So having good interpersonal skills is crucial. Finally, there is something very satisfying about viewing your completed project in published form.

—Neil Goodwin (neilgoodwinphoto.com)

PROJECT PLANNING AND LOGISTICS

Every good project starts with a plan. When I get even a vague idea for a project, write it down in my projects notebook. As the idea takes shape, begin to flesh out the detail, developing that concept over a period of weeks or months. I find that making physical notes is really satisfying, though others find digital note-taking more effective. Just do what works for you—a note is a note!

Here is the plan I follow to help give my project the best possible chance of success:

- **The concept:** It all starts with a concept. I work out exactly what I want to say: the what, why, when, where, and how of the idea. The stronger the concept is, the stronger the project will be.

- **Research:** This is a critical step. For projects with a more documentary intent, for example, you'll need to become an expert in your subject, with an almost journalistic depth of understanding. In addition, figure out what resources you need to make the project work. What permissions or access will you need? Who are the gatekeepers or influencers who can open doors for you? Is there a good or bad time of year to shoot? What locations will you use? Also research any similar bodies of work that have gone before you; this will help you concentrate on doing it with your own tone of voice.

- **Set a timeframe:** Decide how long you'll work on the project. It could be a week, a month, a year, or even much longer; it really doesn't matter. You don't have to rigidly adhere to it, but I find some target setting really useful (and motivating) here.

- **Write a synopsis:** Get into the habit of writing an elevator pitch for your projects so that you have a focused understanding of what you're doing that you can articulate to others. Imagine you're in an elevator and someone else steps in; you should be able to explain your project to that person by the time the elevator reaches the top floor.

- **Test:** I always shoot some test shots to help me find the right voice or aesthetic for my project. It's sometimes worth putting together a mood board to help you get the look and feel right before you start shooting it for real (some people use Pinterest for this).

- **Visualize:** Try to visualize how the images will look. What will the tone of voice be? How will you ensure consistency? Will the images all follow the same orientation (portrait, landscape, or square), or will there be a mixture? Will the project be shot in colour or black and white? (It's generally not a good idea to mix the two.)

- **The output:** Do you see the project manifesting itself as a zine, a book, or an exhibition, perhaps? If you formulate this vision at the outset, it will help you to shape your concept.

The more time and effort you put into planning your project, the more polished the end result will be. Time invested up front is time well spent.

EDITING YOUR PROJECT

"Editing" refers to the selection and sequencing of images rather than post-production. At this stage you'll choose which images will be included in the final cut and in what order.

You will edit different projects in different ways. For example, a documentary project will need a clear narrative arc (a beginning, a middle, and an end); there will probably be transitional images along the way, which take the viewer on the journey from one part of the story to the next. There will probably be a few filler shots, maybe to add mood or a sense of place. Alternatively, a more aesthetically driven project will rely more heavily on how one image connects visually with the next (and previous) in the sequence.

Deciding which images to exclude is one of the toughest decisions we have to make when editing a project, and I always find it helpful to ask someone to provide input (they don't necessarily need to be a photographer, just someone with a good eye). We can get very attached to our own images, and it's easy to overlook obvious misfits; enlisting the help of another can bring some objectivity and clarity of thought to the process and is highly recommended. Also bear in mind the maxim "less is more:" It's better to have 32 stunning images than 72 images with lower impact.

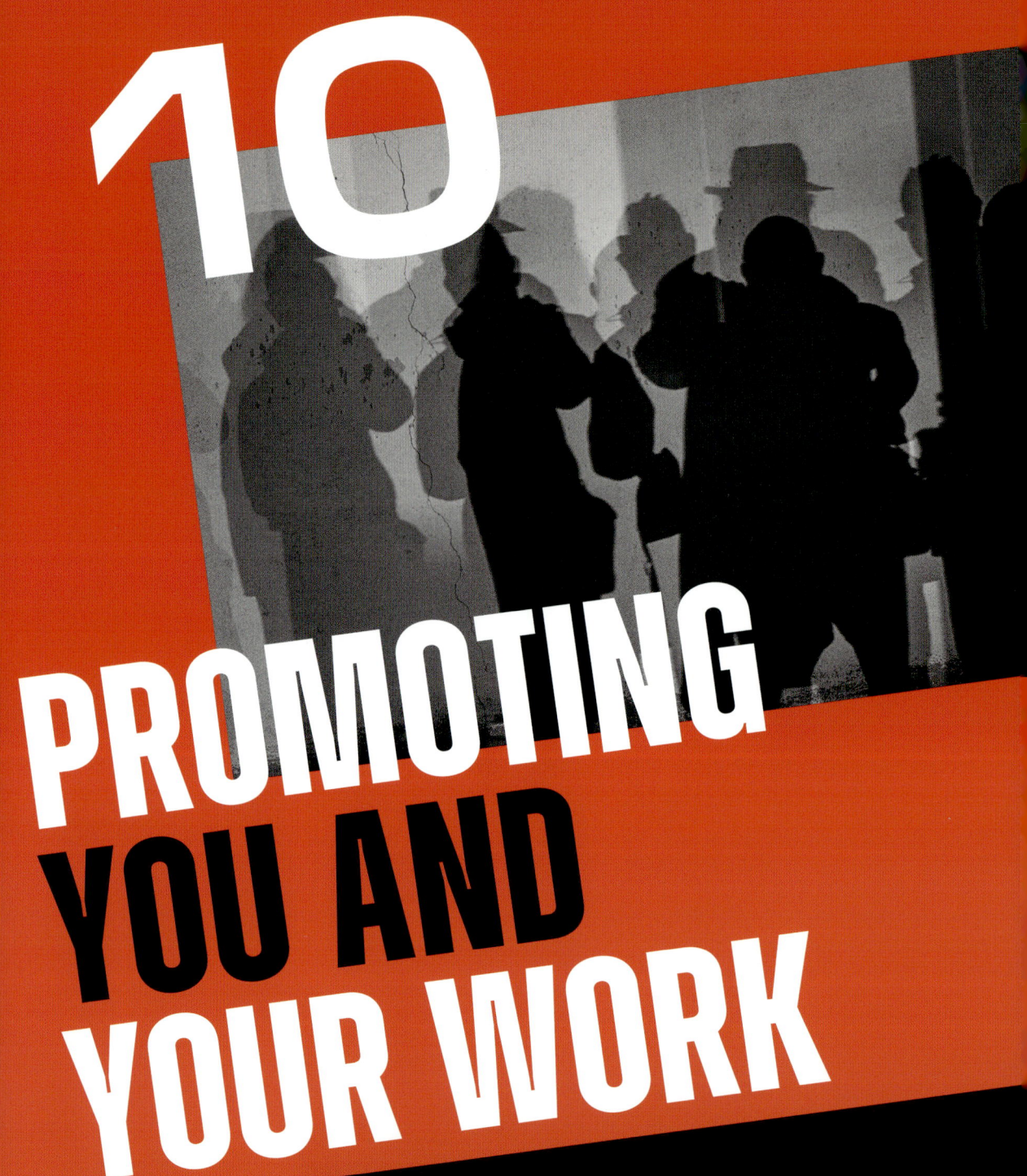

10

PROMOTING YOU AND YOUR WORK

It's worth reflecting at this point where all this is leading you. Where do you want your street photography to take you? What are your long-term goals, objectives, or aspirations?

Some people just want to make nice pictures purely for their own personal satisfaction. Of course that's fine, and hopefully this book has helped you on that journey. Others want to be part of a street photography community. These come in all shapes and sizes, in all corners of the world. Some are social, looking to foster interaction with other street photographers, and some are more competitive.

For the purposes of the rest of this chapter, let's assume that you're a serious street photographer and, to a greater or lesser degree, that you would like to make a name for yourself. Maybe that sounds a little lofty, but it's a reasonable expectation and something I encourage most people to aspire to. Do you seek peer group recognition? Do you want to make money? Win competitions? Be famous? Or, do you just want to produce nice images?

Do you want to be another anonymous photographer, or are you determined to get your work out there? It's fine either way, but if you aspire to the latter there's some hard work to do!

YOUR PERSONAL BRAND

Your personal brand is not about a logo (although you could certainly create one). It's a combination of your voice, your thinking, your approach, and your artistic vision. It's all about the way you present yourself to the world, both in terms of your work and how you approach it, online and offline. It's something unique to you, and it reflects your skills, experiences, values, and personality. It's about creating a recognizable identity that sets you apart in a cluttered world. Think of it as your reputation: How people perceive you and what they associate with you.

Too few photographers pay attention to their personal brand, thinking that an online (usually social-media-led) presence is all they need. Whilst that certainly helps, it's only a small part of the story. A strong personal brand can help you attract opportunities and collaborations, network with and be accepted by peers, connect with your audience, and establish your credibility as a street photographer.

Your personal brand could include:

- Your photographic style (such as a strong cinematic influence, a noir black-and-white style, urban landscapes, or street portraits)

- The narrative content in your work

- The platforms you use (Instagram, your books and zines, your website, exhibitions)

- Your communications with the outside world (how you talk about your work and engage with others)

- Your values (authenticity, social empathy, or humanism)

- Your approach to doing business

- The visual aspects of the brand (logo, colour schemes, and other visual style elements that form part of your physical communications)

If you want to be noticed, ignore your personal brand at your peril. Make sure you invest some serious thinking time into making this a distinctive part of you as a photographer.

HOW TO DEVELOP YOUR PERSONAL BRAND

This won't happen on its own, and it is something you need to work hard at. Don't rush it, and let the brand evolve over a period of months or even longer. Here are some cues to help set you off in the right direction.

1. Define your vision and style

What themes consistently represent your work? Do you lean toward colour, black and white, gritty, moody, or cinematic tones? What's your point of differentiation and what makes your work stand apart from that of other street photographers?

You need to craft a signature look determined in part by the subject matter, how you represent that subject matter, and how that manifests itself in the finished image (consistent editing techniques and a standardized approach to post-production).

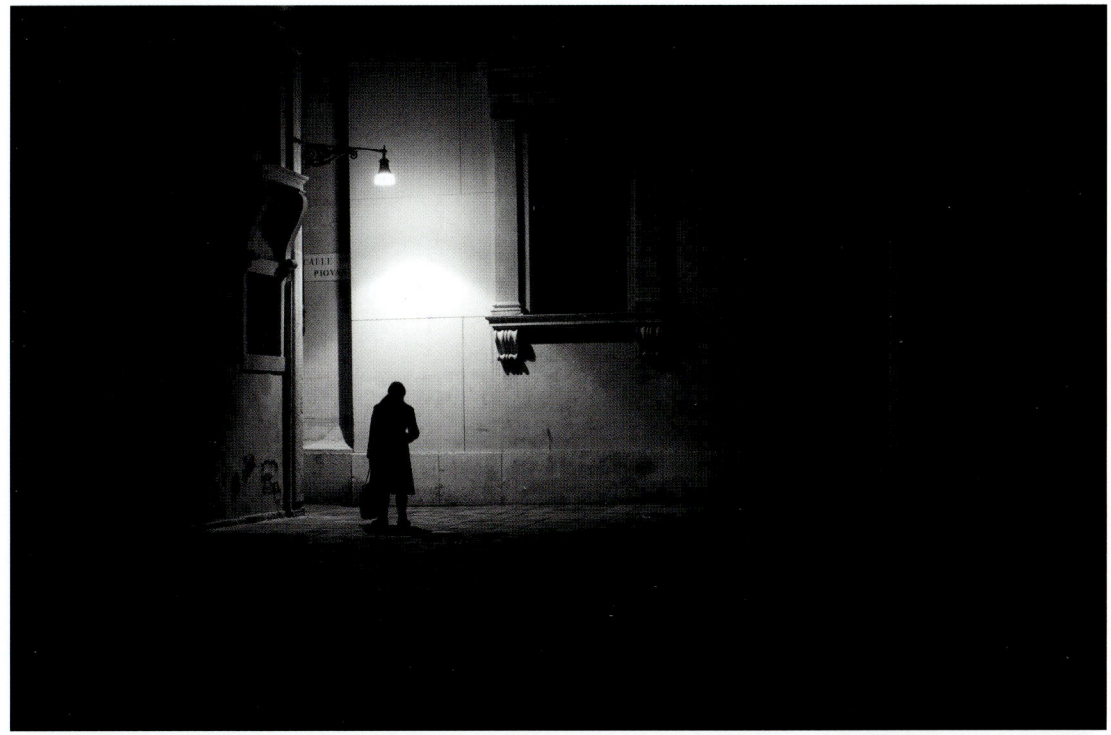

You may decide you want to base your signature look on, for example, high-contrast, minimalist monochrome scenes like this. That's fine, as long as you don't mix it up too much with other work that is the polar opposite!

2. Build an online presence

There are a number of online tools available to us and we can use them to increase our reach, expand our audience, build a community, or just to get noticed.

- **Website:** A professional looking website that shows off your portfolio to its best advantage is a must. This need not be expensive, and subscription-based platforms such as Squarespace or Format offer plenty of templates that you can infinitely tweak to create a personalized and distinctive look, all for a relatively low monthly fee.

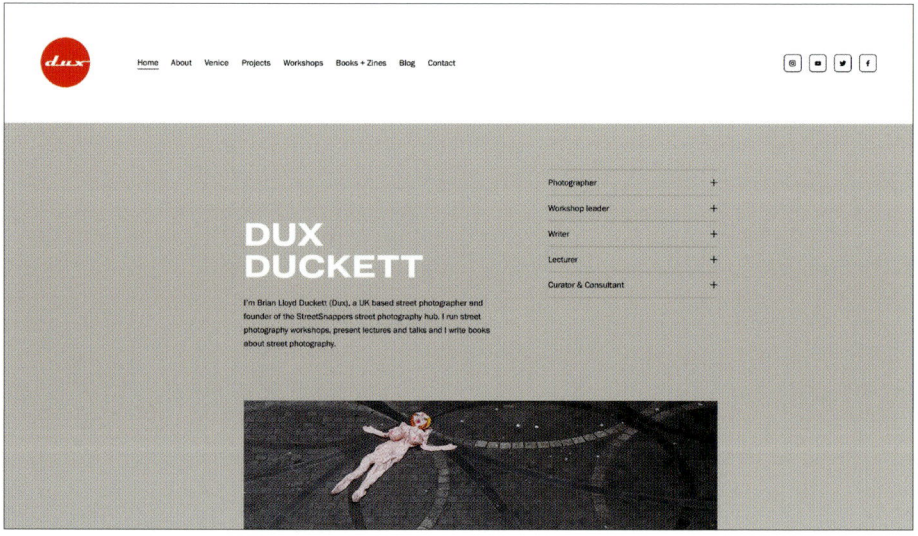

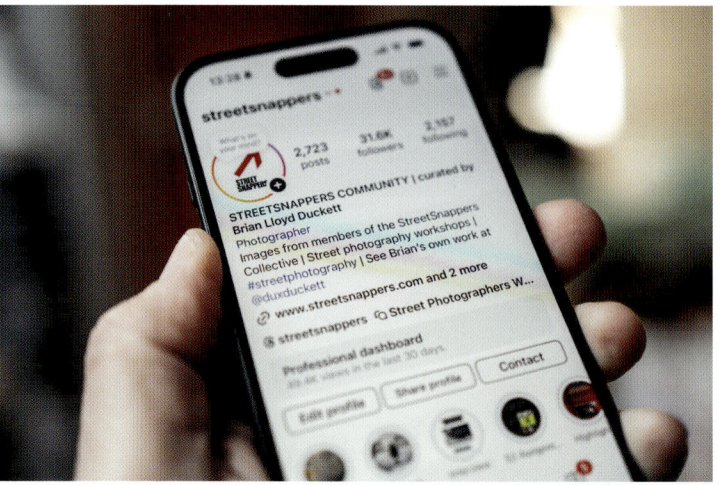

Above: A website is pretty much essential. Make sure you spend time on the design elements, not just the images, and don't be tempted to take the easy option of using stock templates.

Left: Although it tends to fade in and out of popularity with street photographers, Instagram is a great way to network and to build a community.

- **Social media:** Use whichever social media platforms best suit your needs, but use them consistently and post regularly. Instagram is still one of the most popular platforms for street photographers (see later in this chapter). Also consider using X, Threads, Vero, Flickr, and Facebook.

- **Blogging and vlogging:** It's good to share your opinions and insights in written form (with a blog either integrated into your website or hosted independently) or via YouTube.

3. Tell your story

It's good to share the *who* and *why* behind your work. Let people know who the real you is; tell them what makes you tick, how you think, and what sort of person exists on the other side of the lens. Also share insights into why you shot certain images, what techniques you used, and how those images benefited you or others. Talk about where you find inspiration, be honest about the difficulties you face, and share your aspirations. Maybe shoot behind-the-scenes imagery to humanize your brand. This personalization of your brand can really help people understand you and empathize with you. Use elements of storytelling in your image captions and on the about page on your website.

4. Network

Street photographers can be solitary, but try to avoid keeping to yourself. Collaborate on projects with other street photographers, join online communities, take part in competitions and exhibitions, and attend street photography events.

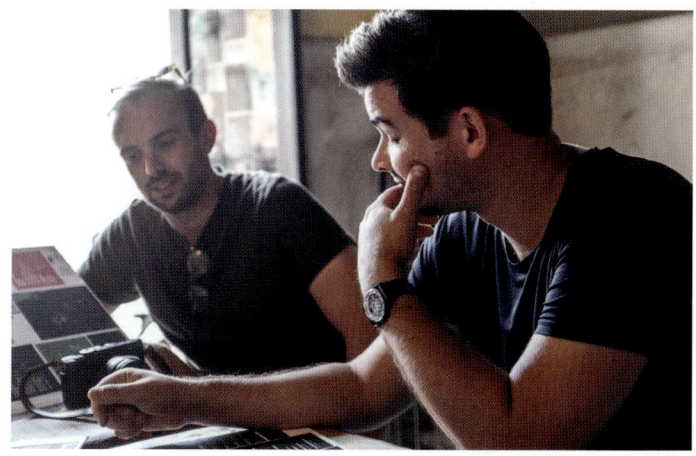

Don't plough a lonely furrow. Collaborating with other street photographers on projects can be immensely productive and fulfilling. Use your social media to network with others who may want to join you.

5. Monetize your work

It's never been easier to build your personal brand by selling prints or licensing your images. Assuming you have the requisite level of skill and the right sort of personality, consider running workshops or photo-walks. Offer to write articles for magazines and blogs and offer yourself as a talking head for podcasts and YouTube channel hosts.

6. Stay authentic and evolve

Trends change and, whilst you need to be fleet of foot to keep abreast of developments, you should ensure that your vision remains intact and distinct. When you need to change things, experiment around the edges rather than making massive leaps. The world will take you more seriously this way. Keep experimenting, but always maintain your core identity and your central beliefs.

THE INFLUENCE OF INSTAGRAM

Love it or hate it, social media has a big part to play in all this, and it can play a significant role in getting us where we want to be. Earlier in this chapter I alluded to several forms of social media but perhaps the most useful and influential platform available to us as street photographers is Instagram.

Street photographers have had a long-standing attachment to Instagram which, in its earlier days, was just for pictures taken on a phone, a way to record what you snapped, and it was relatively unsophisticated.

Then, over the years, more serious photographers got involved and it became more of a showcase for their work. Fast-forward to today, and what we have is a real mix. Yes, there's still lots of spontaneous stuff shot on mobile phones and lots of short-form video content, but we also see high-end commercial photographers marketing their portfolios and a great many serious photographers vying for a few seconds of your time. And in the middle of all that we have street photographers, and *lots* of street photography.

Street photography has become huge on Instagram. Look at the hashtag *#streetphotography*, and you'll see many thousands of images posted every day. Having said that, I do think this illustrates how hashtags can be abused or misused: A lot of what you will see is most definitely *not* street photography by any definition.

WHY USE INSTAGRAM?

As a street photographer, I'm fairly committed to Instagram, and it serves several purposes for me. Firstly, it's a showcase for my own work. I have several Instagram accounts with a combined following of around 36,000; not huge, but plenty big enough to be of benefit. So, if I post one image every day, that's hitting a pretty big audience—assuming, of course, that some of them actually look at it. I think that if at least *some* do, I'm pretty happy with that. As well as there being a commercial imperative (I sell workshops and books), this is good for my personal brand. So in that sense, Instagram works for me.

Secondly, I use it as a means to keep in touch with what other people are doing, and by that, I mean people whose work particularly interests me—maybe because they're great inspirational street photographers or perhaps they're my workshops students (it's a great way of keeping track of what everyone's up to and watching how their work is developing).

Thirdly, it can be inspirational. If you follow the right people, you'll have a constant steam of good work landing on your screen all day long. I find this inspires me. It makes me more creative in my own thinking and it sparks ideas for work, particularly projects.

Finally, it's a social network and I use it to communicate with people I know, meet new interesting people, collaborate on projects, and so on.

HOW TO MAKE INSTAGRAM WORK FOR YOU

For me, Instagram does have value. But I also think the more careful I am about who I follow, the more value it has.

Followers

Please remember this key point about followers: It's the quality that counts, not the quantity. It's far better to have 100 good followers than 10,000 who you don't know and many of whom won't care one bit about you or your work. So I would strongly advise against what is often a crazy, grabbing attempt to get followers, whether that means buying blocks of them or subscribing to one of these follow/unfollow services that are popular.

Look at it this way: Does anyone actually care about how many followers or likes you have? Do people think you're a better street photographer if you're popular? I hope not. If you're doing all the right things and producing strong images, the followers and the likes will come. You really do need to play the long game.

What to post

Post only your best work. People will quickly form an impression of you and your work, and first impressions really do count. They will often decide whether or not to follow you or engage with you on the strength of the most recent image you posted. If they like what they see, it could lead to some positive interactions. If they're not seeing your best stuff on there, the chances are they'll move on and won't come back. Remember that people's online attention span is minimal, and if you don't hit them with something interesting right away, they're gone.

Use Instagram stories as your visual notebook and journal and for any additional content, such as your behind-the-scenes material; don't clutter up your main feed with this—save that for your best work.

Don't chase likes

An often-repeated complaint about Instagram is that strong, complex images are often ignored and "Instagrammable" content with (perhaps) dramatic light, bold colours, or strong form will get lots of interaction.

And herein lies a big problem. It is very tempting to post images that fall into the latter category because we crave the gratification of likes and shares. Even if an image is off-brand and far from being our best work, the validation we get from the adulation takes over and we post more of this (often) substandard content because we assume it's "working." It isn't. People are liking it for the wrong reasons; they do it because it requires little of them. They don't have to think about the image or study it in any detail. It looks okay within the first second or two, so it gets their vote.

The point here is that this level of support for your work is fickle and meaningless. The people who like a certain type of image often do so for the wrong reasons. This leads you to believe, falsely, that you're doing everything right, and you end up with an Instagram feed that is popular but is way off-brand and it just isn't you.

Believe in your work, and, if it's good enough, it will get support from a better quality of Instagrammer.

Composing for Instagram

On Instagram, composition matters just as much as it does elsewhere. Remember that Instagram is made up of horizontal and vertical lines; it's a grid system, so get your lines straight, and take care about how one image lines up with its neighbours, not only to the sides but also above and below it.

Carefully consider how pictures work together: Will certain images jar when positioned next to each other? How they work on the page is important, and your page needs to feel *designed*. Some photographers use apps like Whitagram, which allows you to create a white border around the images (or other apps for different effects).

Consistency

Don't try to be all things to all people. For example, don't mix landscapes with street photography with still life with weddings; if you want to post images that belong in very different genres, consider setting up separate feeds. It's very easy to set up multiple accounts on Instagram. Think about how your feed reflects your voice as a photographer. Is the right tone of voice coming across, loud and clear?

Be generous

This is incredibly important if you want to grow your presence on Instagram. Remember, this is a community, a network, and we're all there because we want to engage. The best way to do that is by offering genuine praise and feedback to others (although I would usually resist offering critique on this platform unless it was specifically asked for). If people take the trouble to comment on your images, reciprocate with a few nice words. It only takes a second, and it reinforces your standing as a good person.

Optimize your profile

Have a simple, memorable username, and keep your bio succinct, simple, and relevant. Mention that you're a street photographer, and consider using the *#streetphotography* hashtag in your profile. For your profile picture, use a clean, recognizable image or logo. Use links (services such as Linktree can be helpful), and if you have a personal website, make sure you direct visitors to it.

Post regularly

Personally, I find that one post per day feels about right, but do whatever works for you. If you can only post an image every few days or once a week, that's fine, it may just take you longer to build your community. Try to be regular and consistent in your posting habits: If you normally post between 7 and 8 a.m., then try to keep with that convention.

Timing is very important. Think about when your audience is tuning in. For me, 7 to 8 a.m. and around 6 p.m. works well. This is when I get the most traction on my posts, but different times may work better for you and it's worth experimenting. I think that aiming for a time when people are having breakfast, commuting to work, having lunch, or heading home is probably a good time.

Keep it real

Leave the filters, emojis, watermarks, and overlaid text in the description box. While these things all have their place online, they can end up spoiling the look of a carefully curated street photography-based feed. Street photography is, after all, a genre typically, historically defined as capturing candid moments with much importance given to authenticity.

Play the algorithm game

Use hashtags but don't abuse them. Hashtags are important in drawing attention to your post, but just look, for example, at all the images that have the hashtag #streetphotography. So if you're posting, for example, an image of a bowl of lovely Amalfi lemons in the sunshine, don't include the *#streetphotography* hashtag, or tag one of the well-known street photography collectives. Doing so just undermines your credibility on Instagram.

Whilst you can use up to 30 hashtags, this feels like too many, and the (constantly changing) algorithm may push against it. However, a small number of carefully chosen hashtags can reel people in and will help new people discover you and your work. Also, captions are important, from both an algorithm perspective and because people like to read them (research has shown that people engage more with a captioned image).

MAKE ZINES AND BOOKS

This is something we all want to do, and we should all do it! With lots of online self-publishing tools available and plenty of printing companies wanting your business, it's never been easier to create a physical publication such as a zine or a photobook.

It's immensely satisfying to hear your doorbell ring, and open the door to the delivery driver handing you a big box containing your latest publication. There's no better way to bring your latest project to life, whether the product is just for personal use or to sell.

Many street photographers are happy to produce zines or books simply to give away to family, friends, and colleagues; the fact that there is no commercial gain doesn't diminish the sense of achievement. Alternatively, there's a huge and growing band of street photographers who do this to make money—and why not? One of the benefits of being part of a community (and that includes Instagram) is that there's a ready-made market of people who yearn to buy street photography zines and books.

ZINES

The zine (short form for magazine) is incredibly popular, and is a great way to bring your work to life, particularly if it's a well-defined body of work in the form of a project.

Zines started life as informal and often homemade booklets, used extensively by students and artists. They have become very popular (and often desirable) in the street photography world. The great news is that zine publication is within the reach of all of us.

There is always strong demand for a well-produced, attractive zine with focused content. Those from a street photographer who is a "name" will command a higher price tag.

Zines come in all shapes and sizes, from a slim 16 pages up by increments of 4 to a substantial 80 pages. The most common format is A5 (210mm x 148.5mm), in either portrait or landscape orientation. The cover is usually softback and made from slightly thicker paper than the internal pages. Paper thickness can be anything from a fine 80gsm stock to a substantial 200gsm and

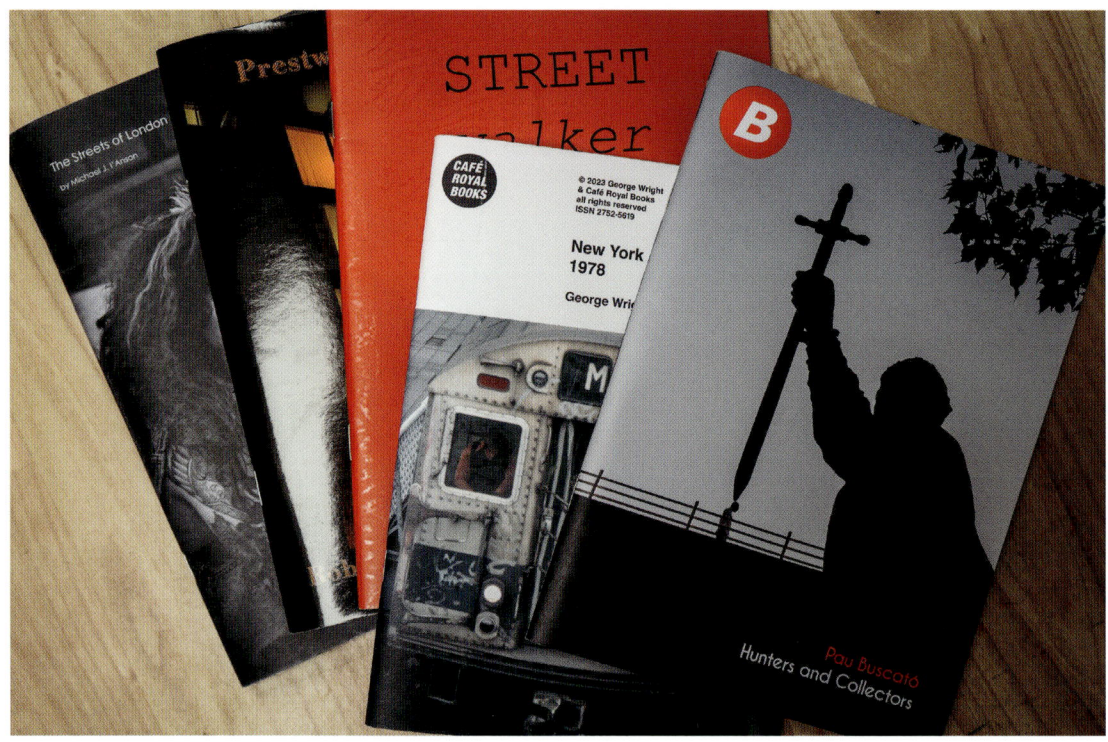

Zines are easily produced and provide the perfect vehicle for bringing a project to life.

could be glossy, silk, uncoated, or recycled. Zines are supposed to be informal and shouldn't be produced to compete with photo books.

They are cheap to produce, costing far less than photo books, and they're relatively quick and easy to create. You can usually have a zine designed, printed, and delivered within a week. Some printing companies provide templates for you to download, and some have websites with a drag-and-drop facility so that you can quickly and easily design and upload your zine online.

Many street photographers sell their zines from their website or social media platforms. If you produce something that is interesting enough, you'll be surprised at how quickly word gets around.

Produce a zine in 10 easy steps

Making a zine may seem intimidating, but don't be too overwhelmed by the thought of self-publishing to get your work into print. Here's a 10-step plan to make the process easy for you:

1. Base your zine on a clearly defined project or theme rather than a collection of random images. Try to visualize how that collection of images might look on the page, and consider the style, mood, and narrative. Is there a story, or is it a visual exploration?

2. Work out how many images you would like to use, which will give you a page count. The number of pages (sides) will go up in multiples of 4: 12, 16, 20, 24, and so on. Don't forget to allow for front and back covers and perhaps a page for some introductory text.

3. Think about the sequencing of the images in your zine. Make sure there's a logical flow from beginning to end and that pictures on facing pages work well together. Aim to take the viewer on a journey with a logical sequence of images with a nice flow.

4. Do a dry run to get the sequencing right. Make a small (postcard-size) print of each image and spread them all out on the table. Then move them around until you get the sequence you're happy with.

5. Design your zine. If you have a program such as Adobe InDesign, Affinity Publisher, or Canva, you can design it yourself and send the finished files to the printer. Alternatively, some printers have a drag-and-drop image upload facility whereby you can populate one of their templates. Don't be afraid to use white space as a design feature (I'll often have a blank page opposite one of my "hero" images to draw attention to it). Add page numbers and captions if you wish.

6. Make decisions about the finish and weight of paper used, the paper for the cover pages, the zine size (for example it could be A6, A5, or A4), and the type of binding, such as stapled or perfect bound. Stapling is usually cheapest, though perfect bound looks more like a book and very professional.

7. Choose a company to print your zine. If you don't know of any, a web search is a good starting point. They don't need to be local to you, as most will allow you to undertake the whole process online. Alternatively, you can produce it

yourself using your own photo printer; this is how zines started life, and it's a perfectly acceptable and wonderfully organic approach.

8. Follow the printing company's guidelines for image sizing, colour space, file types, and so on; most will provide detailed guidelines to make the process simple and painless for you. Then prepare your images for print according to those guidelines.

9. Decide on the print quantity. Some printers will produce as few as 10, but a print run of 50, 100, or 200 will usually be much more economical.

10. Now you need to decide what to do with them. Many people sell their zines through a local bookshop or gallery, a camera shop, or via their website or Instagram. Set a price you're happy with, ideally including a little profit. Alternatively, just do this for fun and give copies to your friends and family.

PHOTO BOOKS

Many of the principles discussed above relating to zines also apply to creating photo books. Quality coffee table books have been popular for many years, and they provide a great platform to present your best work. If you favour the self-publishing approach, there are many companies who will produce lovely coffee-table books for you, whether you order one or 1,000 copies. As with zines, many of these companies have a user-friendly image-upload portal and book-design facility, and you can often have your book uploaded, designed, and ready to go the same day.

Self-publishing is now accessible, and companies such as blurb.com and Bob Books will make the process easy and cost effective for you.

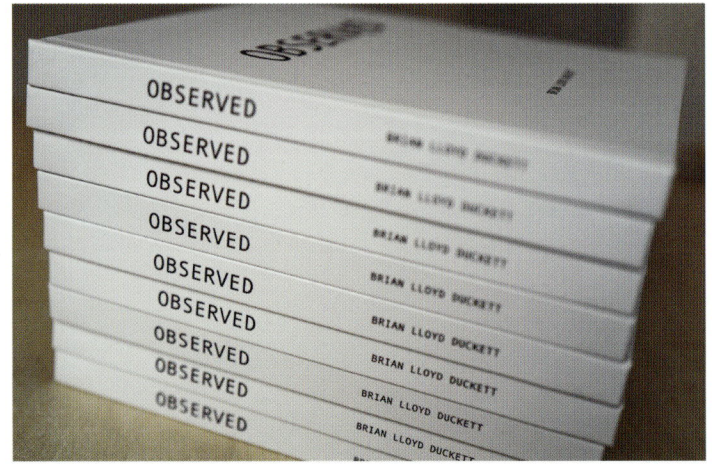

Alternatively, you could approach a mainstream publisher who may publish your book on your behalf. This is a highly competitive field, and most photographers experience much rejection before finally getting their work accepted by a publishing house. Some will expect you to pay a substantial fee to underwrite the design and production costs, and it could take a long time before you see any profit. This approach is fundamentally risky and is not for the faint-hearted.

Another option, if you have a project that you think has real sales potential, but that has not been accepted by a publisher, is to consider crowd funding. Platforms such as Kickstarter have made publication a reality for many new and aspiring photographers. This can be a viable option.

CASE STUDY: Gary Williams

London-based street photographer Gary Williams recently turned a project into his first book. He's a great example of how we can all make this work for us. Here he talks about his journey and offers advice to other would-be self-publishers.

What is Camden Passage *about?*
Camden Passage is a charming little street close to my home in London. The buildings are mostly Georgian, and although it's only a stone's throw from one of the largest train stations, it seems a world away from the bustle and modernity of the rest of the city.

Where did the idea come from?
Just before the pandemic changed everything, I was in a workshop in India with the great Martin Parr. We spent most of the time in Old Delhi, where (like every other street photographer) I photographed a lot of shopkeepers. I was drawn to these little shops and how they represented everything in the shopkeepers' lives. When I returned to London, I continued photographing shopkeepers, this time on my local high street. I knew of Camden Passage and started to photograph the shopkeepers and market traders there. I had no plan. It was just another little project and an excuse to get out and take photos.

How much planning and research did you do?
None, initially. But the more time I spent there, the more I realized that it could form the basis of a project in itself. Not just the shopkeepers, but the shoppers, diners, and passersby. At that point, I started asking some of the older traders about the history and discovered a book that had been written about the passage. I slowly learned more—especially from people there who remembered how it used to be in the decades since the '60s.

What was your experience of shooting the images?

I found the people working in the shops were almost always very open to having their photo taken. The market traders were more cautious. It took many months of me showing up week after week before they trusted me. In most cases it was weeks before I even got my camera out of the bag. I knew they were sick of street photographers snatching photos and just walking away without asking permission, truly "taking" a photo in a self-serving way. I needed to build trust and for them to understand this was a collaboration. I always ask permission. I prefer that approach. I like the interaction, the understanding, and the trust that comes from even just a short conversation. Though I love seeing the work of street photographers who purely observe, I've found it's not for me. This way I made real friends through this project and as a result, felt far more connected to my community.

There were some shopkeepers who were happy to be photographed, but only after hours, when they weren't busy serving customers. In these cases, we'd arrange a time and I'd come in, sometimes with lights, and spend maybe an hour shooting their portrait. A very different approach, but just as rewarding.

I always shared the images with the subjects and was happy for them to use them as they liked. Often, I would come back a week later and give them physical prints. This kind of open, kind, generous approach helped to gain the trust and support of the community.

One of my favourite photos is of Annie on the last day in her famous vintage shop just before she handed back the keys back to the landlord. She'd been there for years before being forced out by rent increases and changing tastes. Sitting in her chair with the shop almost empty, she looks somewhat bewildered as she contemplates the end of this chapter in her life. There is no way she would have given me access to take this picture had I not spent years building her trust.

Did you visualize the final output at the beginning of the project?

No. I was just looking for something interesting to photograph. Once the project gained momentum, I started its own Instagram (@thisiscamdenpassage) which was a simple way to showcase the work.

How did you design and print the book?

Here again, Martin Parr came into the picture. He was hosting a one-day workshop at his foundation in Bristol on bookmaking by Adrian Tyler. He encouraged us to bring along some of 6 x 4 prints of our work. From these we selected about 30 and worked on a simple sequence. By the end of the day, we had a little maquette. This was important because I was able to hold this object and flip through the pages, and for the first time I could see that this work might actually "be" something.

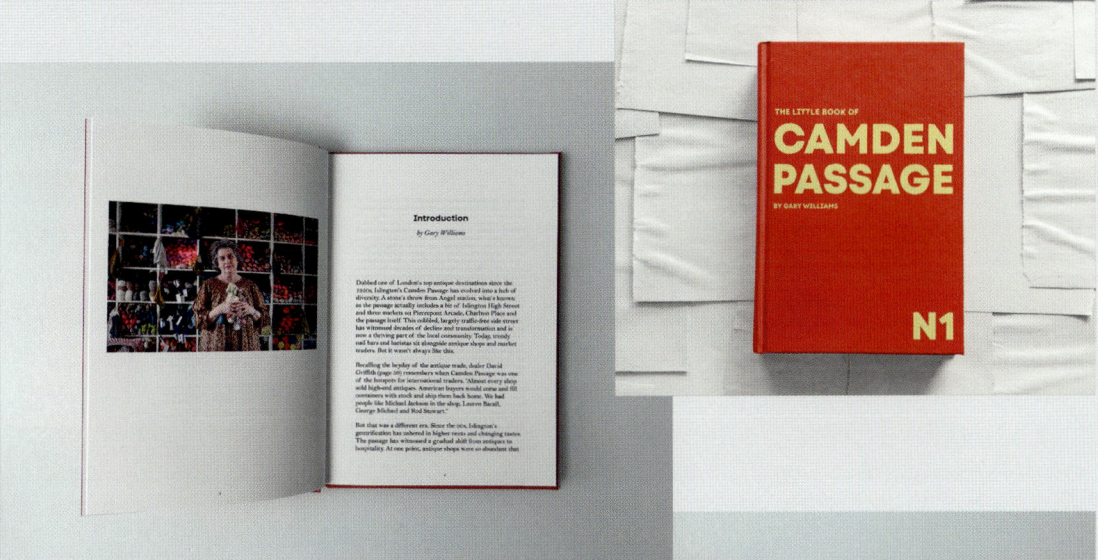

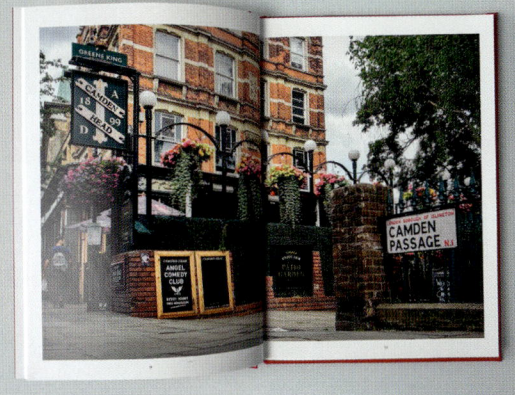

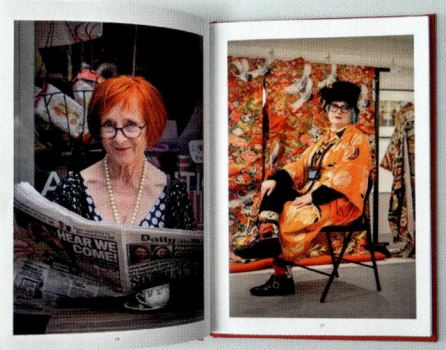

It's not too difficult to create a high-quality photo book that wouldn't look out of place on the shelves of a high street bookshop, and Gary's experience proves the point.

I then learned everything I could about sequencing and going back to all of my photo books, and studying not so much the photos, but the way they were sequenced and how they told a story. I spread about 120 6 x 4s all over the studio floor and spent weeks playing around with the sequence. From there, I eventually put together a draft book and, with the help of some very kind photographers, had the final design for the book.

What difficulties did you encounter in doing this?

Culling. There are many photos that I absolutely loved that I knew I had to cut. This was made even more difficult by the fact that many of the people that I'd photographed had become friends and had been super helpful to me in making this project happen. I felt as though I would be letting them down if I didn't include their photos in the project. In the end, I prioritised the integrity of the book, which is something I now regret. Though the book is a lovely thing, it did leave some people in the community disappointed, and in some cases upset with me. I was wrapped up in finding the perfect sequence (often motivated by subtle links that probably only other photographers would care about or notice), and the subjects just couldn't understand why their "lovely photo" wasn't included in the book. I regret this now. I should have been slightly less about the art and more about the community. It was their book as much mine, and I could have made some compromises.

What advice would you give to others who are considering creating their first book?

Find a subject you are truly passionate about. If you don't love it, you simply won't be able to maintain the motivation and energy you'll need. I spent four years and took almost 6000 pictures making this book. Why? It certainly wasn't for the money! Though you may have a book in mind, that should not be what motivates you. You have to love the journey, the process, the doing. Wherever that leads you—a book, awards, exhibitions—is just the icing on the cake. It's the journey that matters.

What's your next project?

It's called *At Home* and is simply photographs of interesting people in their homes. It's time consuming as I can't just pop out with my camera when I feel like it, but that's okay because again, I love the process. Will there be another book? Who knows. At this stage all I care about is having fun trying to take the best pictures I can.

—Gary Williams (@thisiscamdenpassage)

ENTER COMPETITIONS

As a vehicle for getting your work out there, competitions are a possibility but something of a mixed bag. Entering a street image into a mainstream photography competition (such as at a camera club or in your local newspaper) is unlikely to yield results, mainly because the genre of street photography is often misunderstood and sadly underrated by judges. If you enter a dedicated street photography competition, things should be different, with a much more knowledgeable judging panel who have substantial experience as working street photographers.

Before entering any competition, ask yourself why you're doing it. Is it to get impartial feedback of your ability? To measure progress? To get exposure? To win a prize? All are valid reasons, and the answers will probably inform your decision about which competitions to enter. Before entering, it's worth asking some questions about the validity or integrity of specific competitions:

- Who are the organizers? Are they reputable and passionate about the art of street photography, or is it just a commercial money-making exercise?

- Who are the judges? Have you heard of them? Do they have a track record as street photographers?

- Is there an overall theme and/or different categories?

- Is there an entry fee? What do you get for your money?

- Do you get any feedback or critique on the images you submit?

- Who retains copyright? Be careful not to sign away your rights, and always check the terms and conditions before submitting images.

- What are the opportunities for recognition or exposure?

Competitions can be a great way to challenge yourself and to get a measure of your skill or development as a street photographer. However, always do your homework and choose your competitions carefully—entering multiple competitions can become an expensive pursuit!

EXHIBITING

Everyone should exhibit their work at some stage, and it is perhaps the most satisfying form of exposure. Showing your pictures in a gallery or other space, particularly for the first time, may sound like a lofty ambition and even daunting. It's actually not difficult, and it should be a realistic goal. If you're new to exhibiting, start small. Ask your local cafe if you can use one of their walls to mount a small exhibition of your work. They'll probably be glad to have something interesting to display; you may even sell some prints, offering the cafe owner a commission on sales. It's also worth trying your community centre, town hall, shopping mall, or local library, particularly if your work has a local theme.

Once you have found a suitable venue, choose the right theme for your exhibition and keep it focused, ideally in the form of a project. Random, unconnected images tend not to work well as an exhibited body of work.

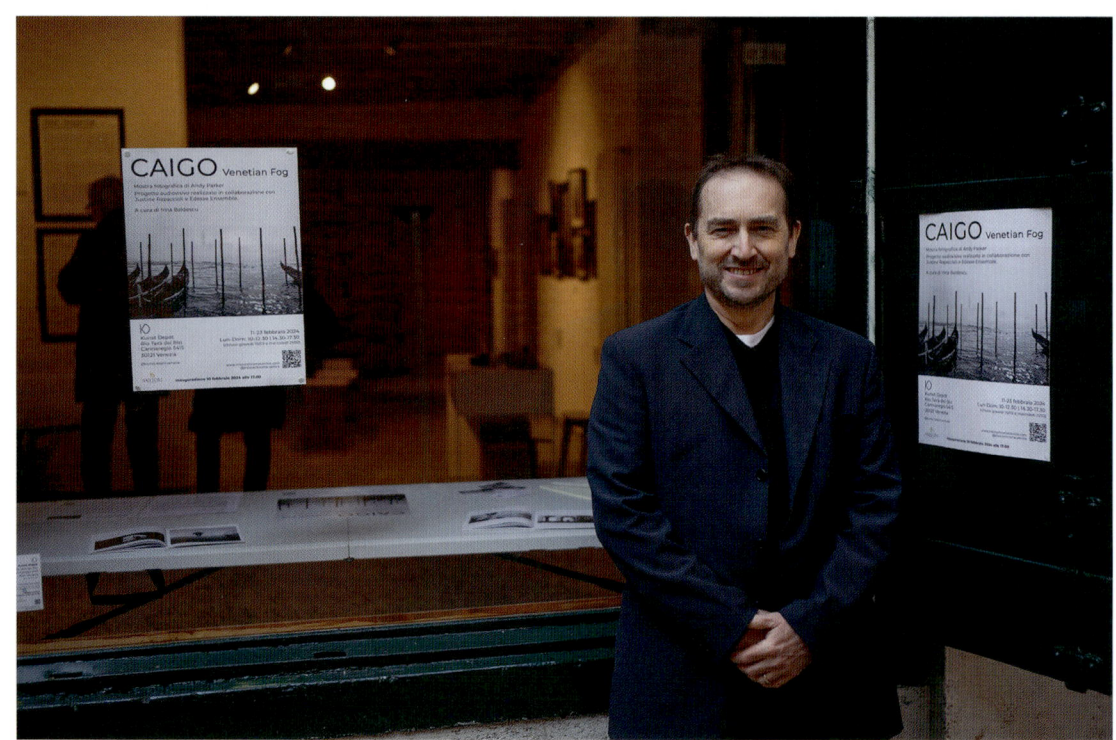

The opening day of your first exhibition can be a combination of exhilarating, terrifying, and immensely satisfying. There are plenty of small galleries who are willing to show the work of unknown street photographers—you just need to do some legwork to find them.

Pop-up gallery spaces are an increasingly viable option for street photographers. These could appear in, for example, large office buildings, outdoor spaces, or empty retail units, and they can be an effective, low-cost way to get your work seen.

Stepping up a gear, art or photography galleries may be prepared to show your work, and it's often worth approaching a gallery owner or curator and taking samples of your images to consider. Be prepared for plenty of rejection, but don't be put off by it. Eventually, someone will say yes.

Once you have a commitment to exhibit your work, you need to ensure it is gallery ready, which usually involves framing and/or mounting the images and applying the required fixing points to the back, all to the gallery's precise specification. Some galleries may apply a "make good" fee, which is usually for plastering and painting the walls to restore them to their original state.

When you do exhibit, have a clear strategy for selling your images and ensure that it is clearly communicated to visitors. Be confident of your pricing, and be clear about how and when prints will be delivered.

PRINT SALES

The market for photographic prints remains strong, from serious collectors to consumers who just want to have some nice art on their walls. However, the market for street photography is much smaller, and, unless you're a well-known photographer, the reality is that you won't make much money. This is largely because street photography has relatively limited appeal and is not usually seen as being part of the mainstream print market.

However, street photographers *can* make money from print sales, particularly those that could be considered fine art. Sales are typically transacted through the photographer's website, often via a plug-in or link, to a specialist printing lab that will handle the payment, production, and fulfilment for you, usually for a small commission. This is a very good option if you want to avoid the hassle and costs of home printmaking.

If you have an exhibition, it's a good idea to offer unframed prints for sale during the show as well as the framed exhibition prints once the show has finished. It's also possible to sell your prints in local shops, art galleries, and at art or craft fairs. In the case of fairs, smaller prints (A5 and A4) tend to be better sellers because they're easier for people to carry home with them.

You can either produce your own prints, which can be costly in terms of quality papers and inks, or you can get a lab to do them for you.

Here are a few tips to help make print sales work for you:

- **Curate your work:** Don't dilute your offering by trying to sell everything. Only offer your very best work for sale. You can test the market initially by posting a selection online to see which images get the most engagement.

- **Offer limited editions:** It's simple economics: Scarcity stimulates demand, so it pays to offer limited editions (maybe 10–50 copies per print). Number and sign each print to add value, and provide a certificate of authenticity.

- **Find the right format:** Experiment to find the optimal combination of print size, paper type, framing options, and price. Consider selling both framed and unframed prints.

- **Establish your own online store:** This is now straightforward using platforms like Shopify, Squarespace, Etsy, and others. Alternatively, partner with print-on-demand services like The Printspace or Saatchi Art if you don't want the hassle of fulfillment.

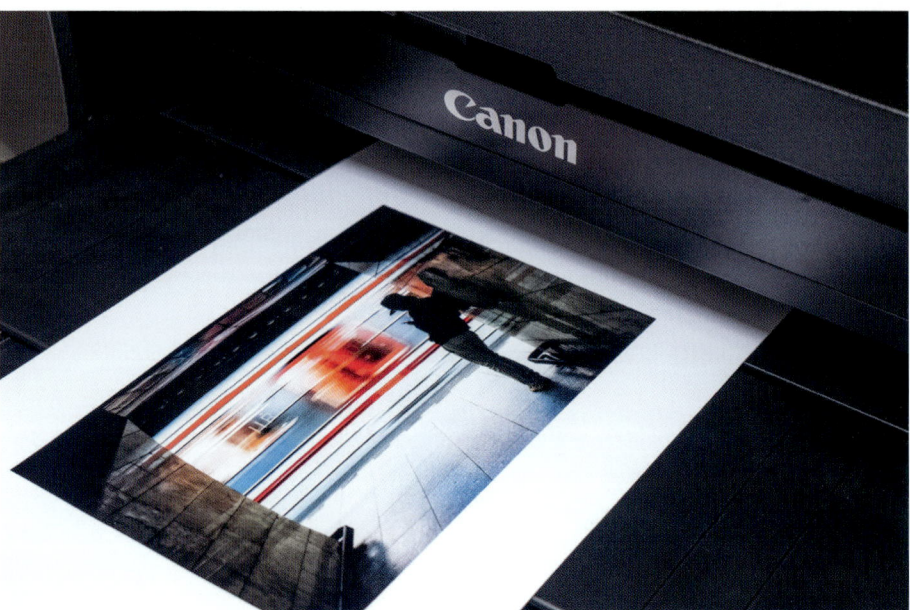

You can test the market for print sales by starting small: All you need is a capable home printer and some high-quality paper.

- **Leverage social media to stimulate sales:** Use Facebook, Instagram, and others to market your prints. Build an email list, and offer exclusive discounts or early-bird deals.

- **Sell through local galleries:** Art fairs, craft fairs, and local exhibitions can also generate in-person sales.

- **Create stories around your work:** People buy art for emotional connection, so it's good to share the story behind each image.

Finally, don't forget to make prints simply for yourself! It's hugely satisfying to see your artwork on your walls, and plenty of photographers (including me) use their home as their gallery.

START YOUR OWN COMMUNITY

It's not difficult to find others who would be keen to engage with like-minded street photographers. Whilst photographic societies and camera clubs can fulfill this function to a degree, it's unusual for street photography to figure prominently in their activities.

Sometimes, therefore, we need to take the lead and create an environment where we can indulge in our shared passion for street photography. A great starting point is to create a group on social media. Facebook groups are ideal for this. Then use that platform to arrange discussions, organize meet-ups, share knowledge, and more.

Some of the biggest and most successful street photography communities started in a small way with a group of a few people on social media.

JOIN A COLLECTIVE

Street photography collectives seem to be everywhere. They are groups of photographers who have come together to share ideas, collaborate on projects, host exhibitions, run workshops, or create books. They often have an influential voice in the sector, and their output is usually based on a specific photographic style and common ethos.

Such collectives come in all shapes and sizes and many street photographers aspire to join one. One of the best-known collectives is iN-PUBLiC, founded in 2000 by Nick Turpin. It quickly built an international presence and was known for its innovative output. Some collectives are quite general and will promote all styles of street photography, whereas some will follow a narrow approach. There are even single-issue collectives that operate within very narrow parameters. Joining a collective isn't easy, and it's usually a case of "don't call us, we'll call you." If you're a suitable candidate, they will probably already know about you.

Recent years have seen the growth of online collectives. Many of these are not collectives in the traditional artistic sense, but are businesses that exist to make money by running workshops and charging people to enter competitions.

Here's an idea for you: Why not start your own collective? Just find a few like-minded street photographers, agree to some common goals, and away you go. It really is as simple as that!

ASSIGNMENTS

1 UP CLOSE AND PERSONAL

Whilst getting very close to your subject isn't for everyone, it's a skill you should possess because, at some point, you'll probably need it.

Bruce Gilden immediately pops to mind when thinking of this style of shooting. His approach probably goes beyond what you would wish to aspire to in that it's aggressive, confrontational, and in-your-face. He often uses flash to provide bold compositions, capturing raw emotions and often reactions of shock.

Why you should do this:

- You will inevitably come across opportunities when you wish you possessed these skills.

- Becoming more comfortable at being very close will give you the confidence to shoot very close. This will give your images increased energy and intimacy.

- You may find that you enjoy this intimate distance to the action, and it then becomes part of your modus operandi.

- You'll be the envy of your peers: Most people will never experience the feelings and the results of close-quarters shooting.

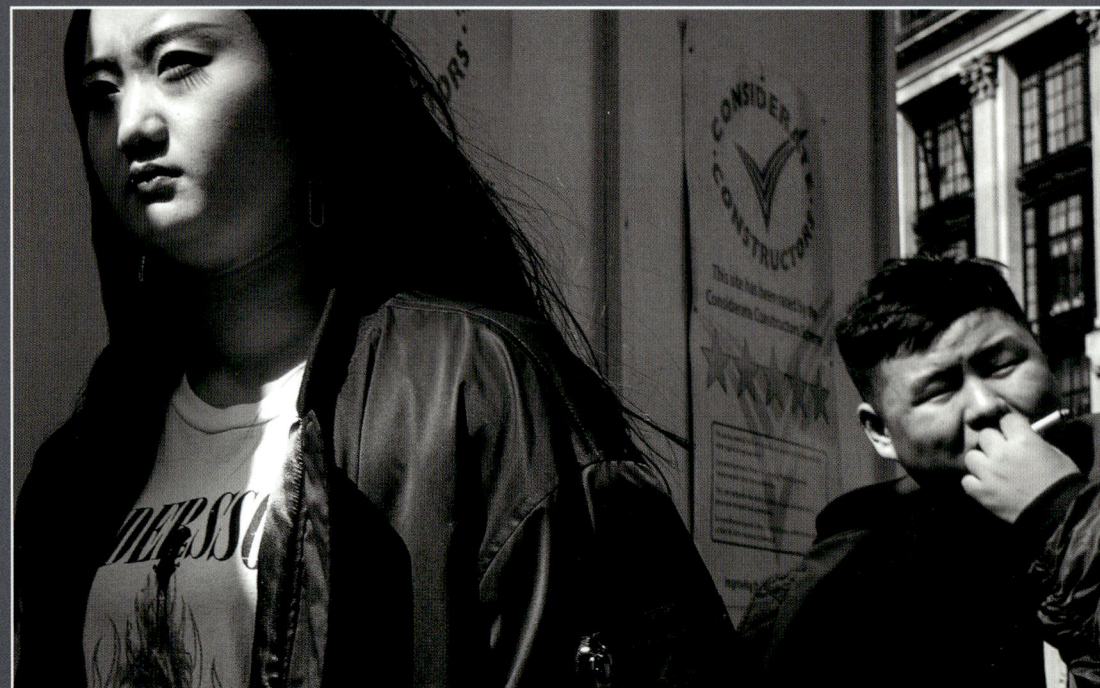

FIELD NOTES

Shoot wide to get close

Proximity is key here. You can't shoot from across the road with a 200mm lens. You need to get physically close to your subjects. Gilden usually shot just a few feet away from people, which requires bravado and confidence. Try a 24mm or 28mm lens. (If you find this too difficult at first, start with a 35mm and work backward.)

Use flash

Use an off-camera flash to create high-contrast, crisp, and dramatic images. The flash isolates your subjects, freezes the moment, and adds a stark, gritty look. This will also add separation and real punch to your images. Practice balancing flash with ambient light for the best effect.

Shoot quickly

You need to get used to working fast. Find your interesting subject, step into their path, take the shot, and move on. Avoid eye contact and just walk away.

Use the right camera settings

Use a fast shutter speed and zone focusing so you can concentrate on timing instead of fiddling with settings. Pre-set your focus to a distance of 3–5 feet, use a small aperture (ideally f/8 or f/11), and let your flash calculate the right exposure.

Build a narrative

This is not just about shock value. These images can capture the human condition, often focusing on the vulnerability or individuality of subjects. Consider the story you're telling with your images and how they connect to the world around you.

Shoot in busy locations

Avoid quiet streets, and head for busy shopping areas or large squares or markets. Focus on areas where people are likely to pause or interact, such as pedestrian crossings.

Learn to deal with reactions

This approach sometimes provokes strong reactions, and you never quite know how people will respond to you. Be prepared for some questioning and even confrontation or anger. Your best response is to relax, stay calm, smile, and be polite.

Practice

The up-close-and-personal style is not for the timid. Practice building your confidence by starting in less intimidating environments or by shooting with a slightly longer lens and gradually working your way into busier or more challenging areas. Engage with your subjects when necessary, but try to get into the habit of taking the shot and walking away.

For inspiration

Bruce Gilden, Mark Cohen, Weegee (Arthur Fellig), Richard Sandler, and Jeff Mermelstein

Opposite: If close-up shooting is too uncomfortable, you could always try shooting from the hip to start.

"I want to go into the soul of a person and express that soul in one frame."

BRUCE GILDEN

2 SHOOT STREET STILL LIFE

Shooting still-life street photography is a creative way to find beauty in the small, overlooked details of urban life. You're looking for beauty in the mundane, usually overlooked everyday objects, signs or textures, often in places where you wouldn't expect to find them—maybe it's something abandoned in the gutter, left on a wall, or written on a window. This is street photography without people, though these images will often imply or suggest a human presence.

Why you should do this:

- It's a great way to help develop your powers of observation.

- You can relieve the tedium of nonproductive areas by looking out for these opportunities (when walking from one location to another, for example).

- It's a good way to inject humour into your street photography.

- It can make great material for a fun project.

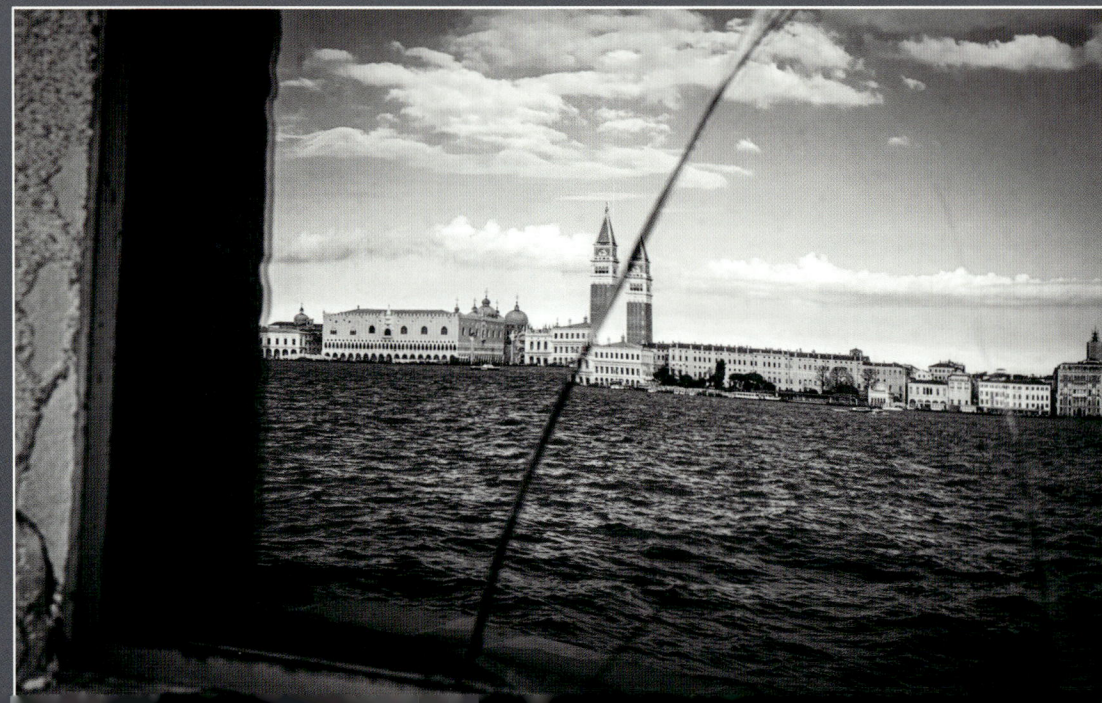

FIELD NOTES

Create stories in objects

There are objects everywhere: abandoned items, forgotten things, discarded things, all of which could have an interesting story to tell. You don't need to actually tell that story, just leave the viewer to construct their own narrative.

Embrace minimalism

Simplicity is usually required here. Focus on a single object or detail within a busy scene and remove distractions from the frame to help the subject stand out.

Compose carefully

There's usually no need to rush these shots, and you have plenty of time to think about the composition and get it right. Consider the best angle, the effect of the light, and the foreground and background. You may have to wait, while people passing through the background move out of the scene, for example.

Use a wide aperture

Draw attention to the subject by isolating it and minimizing distractions in the foreground or background. Bear in mind that if you're shooting at close range, some of the subject may not be in focus.

Experiment with colour

Look for vibrant colours, which will stand out in an otherwise muted scene. Alternatively, shoot in black and white to emphasize form, lines, shadows, and textures.

Always be ready

You never know when an opportunity will present itself; they happen at the least expected times! Always have a camera with you (even if it's only your phone), and always be prepared.

Make a project

Whilst you may get the occasional stunning single shot, this exercise is more likely to be fulfilling over a longer period if you shoot street still life as part of an ongoing project. Be prepared for the long haul. I found that projects like these often take years rather than months.

For inspiration

André Kertész, Fred Herzog, Saul Leiter, Joel Meyerowitz, and William Eggleston

Opposite: This shot is from my ongoing project *The Death of Venice*, which is about the vulnerability, viability, and future of the city in the face of over-tourism.

"You should be looking all the time. The act of looking is a form of meditation."

— JOEL MEYEROWITZ

3 A LEITER APPROACH

For this assignment, you'll step into the shoes of the great Saul Leiter, embracing a poetic, painterly approach to street photography. If you're drawn to a more aesthetic vision, this style may be for you. His work is known for its layers, warm colours, reflections, obstructions, and an intimate, almost abstract composition that transforms everyday street scenes into dreamlike images.

Why you should do this:

- Be inspired! This isn't about copying Leiter's work, it's more about taking inspiration from his approach and incorporating it into your own work.

- Try something new. For example, if you're normally an observational street photographer, this more poetic style will add a new, artistic dimension to your work.

- It's relaxing! This is slow street photography, and you'll find yourself getting into an almost Zen-like state while you're waiting for compositions to evolve.

- It's nonconfrontational. You'll be shooting from farther away with a longer lens and people probably won't even notice you.

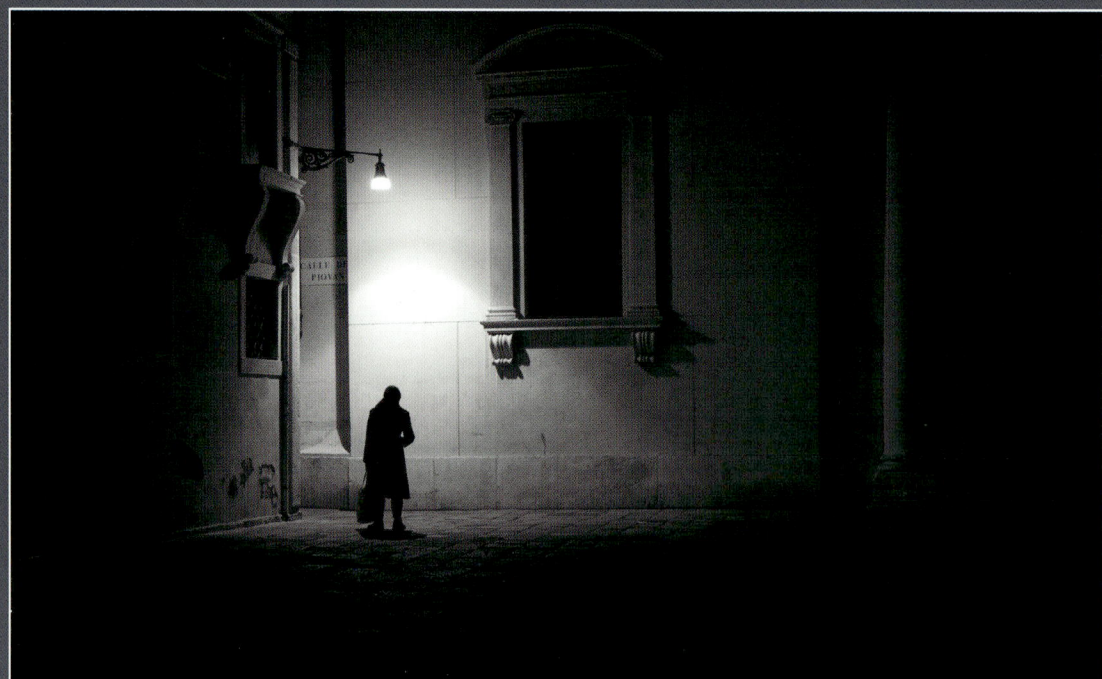

FIELD NOTES

Go back in time

Imagine yourself shooting in the 1950s, '60s, or '70s, and try to eliminate any traces of the twenty-first century from your compositions. It's not easy, but it's fun, and the results can be strikingly stylish.

Adopt a warm colour palette

Leiter favoured the softer, warmer colours, particularly yellows, oranges, and reds; look out for these hues on the street, and allow them to dominate.

Use mainly vertical framing

The majority of Leiter's images were shot in portrait orientation.

Shoot through layers

Put something between you and the subject: A misted-up, dirty, or raindrop covered window is ideal. Also, use reflections on windows, on other reflective surfaces, and in puddles.

Shoot long and wide open

Shoot with a focal length between 85mm and 135mm for a compressed perspective, to isolate subjects, and for a sense of voyeurism and detachment. Open up your aperture to its widest setting to concentrate the viewer's attention.

Find your motifs

Leiter had his favourite motifs, which he would try to bring into a composition. These included umbrellas, taxis, shoes, leather bags, gloved hands—very ordinary but often stylish things. Use similar motifs, or, ideally, create your own list of desirable artifacts.

Underexpose

Generally err on the side of darkness. Leiter's images were rarely bright, so let shadows be deep and don't overcorrect colours, embracing a slightly faded or muted palette. (Leiter often used expired film, which created unpredictable but often soft results.)

Use obstructions and negative space

Obscure part of your subject behind cars, window frames, poles, doors, or passing people. Don't be afraid to allow a significant portion of the frame be out of focus or empty to guide the eye subtly.

Find a dirty foreground

By placing a large, out-of-focus obstruction in the foreground, you can add lots of volume and depth to your image.

For inspiration

Saul Leiter (of course!), Ernst Haas, Fred Herzog, and Harry Gruyaert

Opposite: It's worth investing some time in studying Leiter's work to try to understand his approach; there are plenty of excellent books and some documentary films that should give you lots of inspiration.

"I like it when one is not certain of what one sees. When we do not know why we are looking at it, all of a sudden we discover something that we start seeing. I like this confusion."

— SAUL LEITER

Assignment

4 DOCUMENT YOUR NEIGHBOURHOOD

A photo documentary of your neighbourhood presents you with the ideal opportunity to ease your way into a documentary style of street photography. It's a great way to tell a story, capture the essence of where you live, and create a compelling visual narrative. The character of a neighborhood is derived from the people, the architecture, the light, the social activities—almost anything. It's too easy to overlook the potential when it's so close to home.

Why you should do this:

- It will allow you to connect with your community in new and engaging ways. You'll talk to the people you would normally pass by, getting to know their stories and their lifestyles. You'll probably even make new friends.
- This will give you a real sense of purpose and a great reason to get out and about with your camera.
- You'll be creating a historical account of where you live for the benefit of future generations.

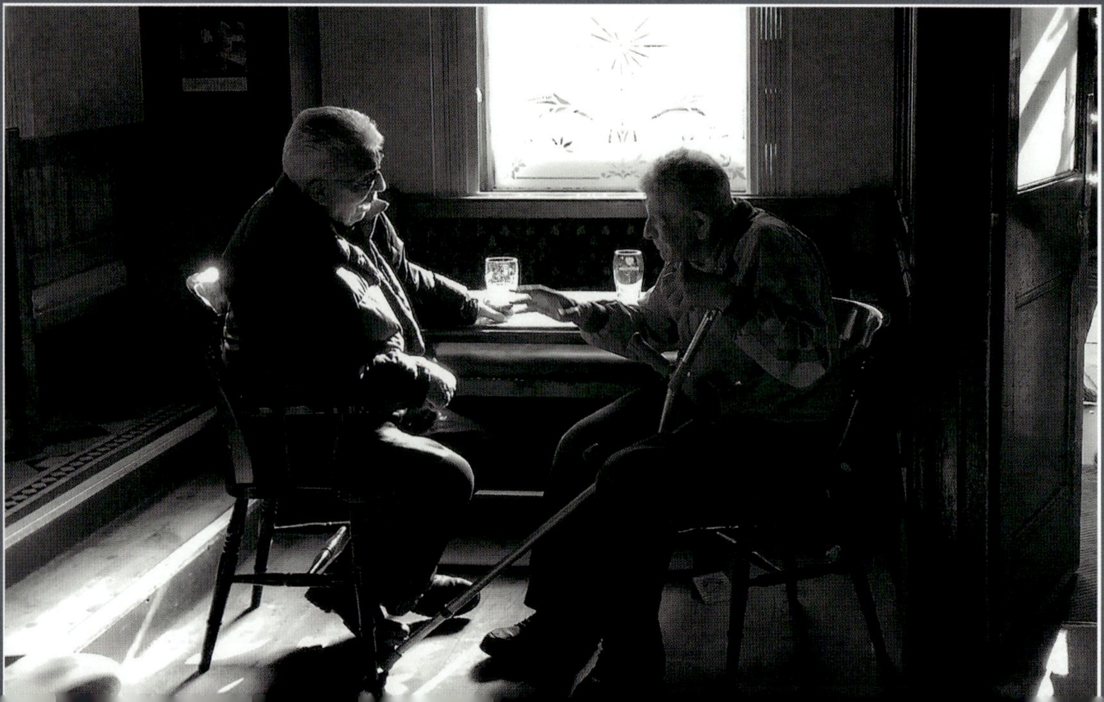

FIELD NOTES

Define your concept

It all starts with a story—a good idea—so work on your angle or theme before you start. For example, your project could be about everyday life in the area, about local people and their habits or routines, the architecture, the history, or the social or cultural aspects of life.

Spend time observing

Walk around the area at different times of the day and night. Study the light, watch the people, notice details; make notes to help inform your concept. Maybe use your phone camera to create a visual notebook of ideas.

Create your aesthetic

Will it be shot in colour or black and white? Will the people involved be shot candidly or posed? Will the lighting be bright or muted? Natural or artificial light? Which lens(es) will you use to create a consistent aesthetic?

Capture a mixture of shots

This will keep the project fresh and engaging, and you will benefit from creating a variety of shot types, such as establishing shots (wide or scene-setting), portraits, detail shots, street still life, and so on. All this needs to be thought out at the planning stage.

Create a narrative arc

As with any story, you should have a beginning, a middle, and an end. Take the viewer on a logical, pre-planned journey.

Collaborate

Join forces with others. Find like-minded street photographers, and invite them to join your project to share ideas, inspiration, and motivation.

Get the project out there

Don't let it languish on your hard drive! Make a zine or book, produce a set of prints, host a small exhibition, or create an online presence for your story. Get some publicity for it in the local paper. Ask your local coffee bar if they will hang some of your work on that empty wall: a mini exhibition. Speak to local museums and galleries—again, you'll find that if you start to get yourself known, this becomes a whole lot easier.

For inspiration

Chris Killip, Fred Herzog, and Don McCullin

Opposite: The local bar is often a great place to capture life's local characters.

"A good photograph is one that communicates a fact, touches the heart, and leaves the viewer a changed person for having seen it."

— IRVING PENN

5 GO NIGHT SHOOTING

Some great street photography can be shot during the hours of darkness, and night shooting is something we should all try; it's almost a rite of passage. Think neon lights, shop windows, reflections, car lights, bars, restaurants, people having fun— there is plenty of material to explore.

You can shoot this assignment in any town or city where there are good light sources, and this works just as well in small towns as it does in big cities like London or New York. There's no reason that shooting in the dark should be any more difficult than daylight shooting, but as well as the aesthetic issues, there are some different technical and practical considerations to take into account.

Why you should do this:

- You'll experience a different kind of energy; cities come alive in a different way after dark, with nightlife, lots of lights, and quiet streets. You'll also find different stories and characters that don't exist in the daytime.

- Master your low-light skills. Shooting at night pushes you to better understand how ISO, aperture, and shutter speed work together, and it will help refine your ability to work with minimal light and available sources.

- You can develop a cinematic and noir aesthetic, with a film-like quality and moody, mysterious, or perhaps storytelling-style photography.

"The city at night has a completely different face. The lights, the shadows, the people—it all changes. There is an ambiguity that I find fascinating."

DAIDO MORIYAMA

Opposite: Look for bold shapes at night, and aim to create an air of mystery or intrigue.

FIELD NOTES

Use the right gear and settings

I recommend using a fast prime lens of between 35mm–85mm. Shoot at the widest aperture and set an auto ISO range of 400 to 6,400. Shoot in RAW and set the white balance to auto.

Use exposure compensation

If you're taking pictures at night, they need to look as though they've been taken at night. I nearly always deliberately underexpose at night, using an EV of –1 to –2 to induce a moody, atmospheric look.

Find good light

Identify a good light source first, then build a composition around it. Seek out light sources that give depth to your image. You need good contrast, with well-defined areas of light and dark. Use this light creatively to frame your subject or create contrast and silhouettes. Be like a moth, seeking out lights and being drawn to them all the time.

Slow down

To really absorb and become part of night-time street life, you should slow down, stopping frequently to take in your surroundings, watching the light and waiting for the scene to evolve. Fishing is great for night shooting.

Use windows and reflections to create layered images

Use shop or cafe windows, which reflect the lights outside or have moisture on them. Rain can also help by creating puddles that cause reflections on roads. Also look out for strong shapes, such as big hats or umbrellas.

Stay safe

Be aware of your surroundings, and be mindful of your environment; always have an exit route.

For inspiration

Daido Moriyama, Brassaï, Anders Petersen, and Weegee

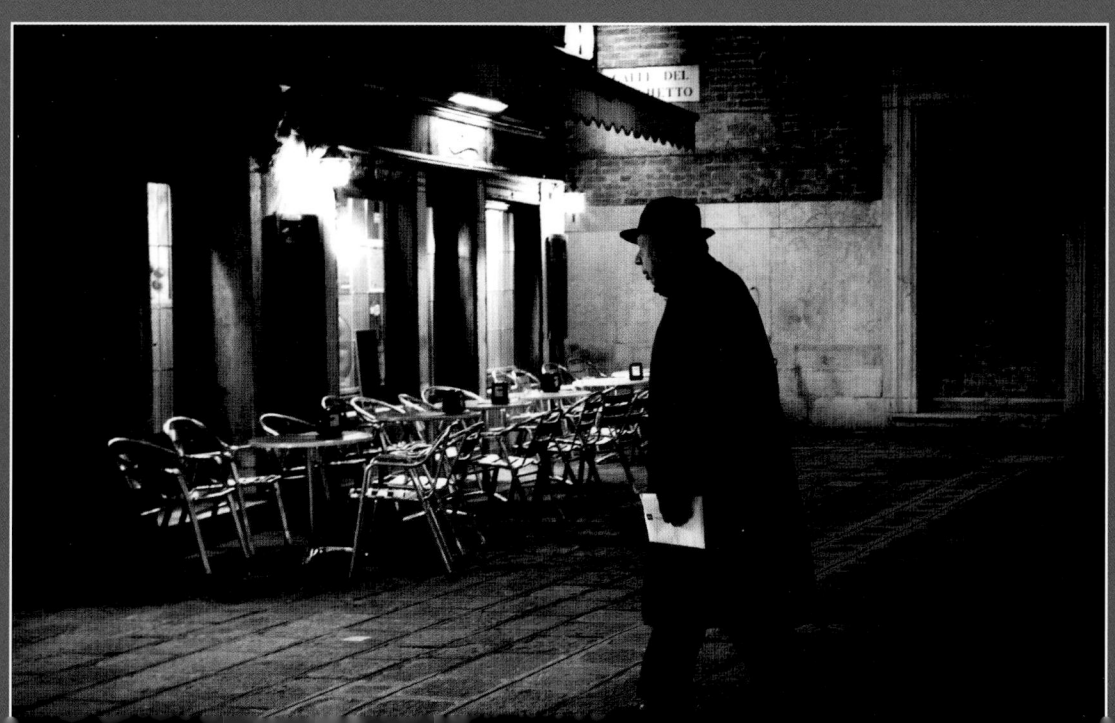

6 SHOOT STREET PORTRAITS

How many times, when you're walking the streets, do you see someone who looks really interesting and think *"I'd love to ask them for a picture,"* but then back out? Many of us find this awkward, difficult, or even intimidating. But what is a street portrait? We usually think of street photography as being mainly candid shooting, but a street portrait is shot with the knowledge and usually also the consent of the subject. I know some people will argue that this isn't strictly street photography but in my view it is—albeit in the margins of the genre.

Why you should do this:

- Approaching strangers for a portrait takes courage. Doing this regularly improves your ability to connect with people and builds confidence in your wider street photography pursuits.

- You'll build connections with people you might never have spoken to otherwise. Every person has a story, and even a brief interaction can be meaningful.

- You'll be documenting humanity. In a world of fast-moving digital content, a strong street portrait slows people down and reminds us of the beauty, struggles, and depth of everyday life. It can be a grounding experience.

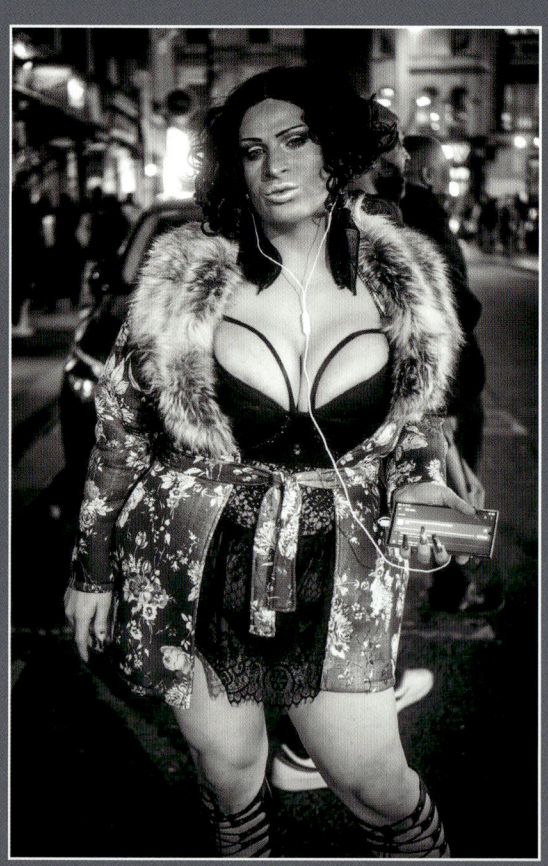

People who look interesting, stylish, or outrageous are probably attention-seekers, and they're most likely to agree to a portrait.

FIELD NOTES

Set some objectives

For example, do a project using a particular type of person or a specific location. For some great inspiration, look at the *Humans of New York* project by Brandon Stanton.

Develop a style and make it yours

For example, do you want people to pose to your direction, or will you just snap away while you're chatting to them? Will the background be in or out of focus? Will it be an environmental portrait where the background plays a crucial role? Will the shots be close-up, half-length, or full-length? Will they be looking to camera or off camera? If this is going to be a project, this consistency of style becomes super important.

Focus on the attention seekers

People who look good or who have made an effort will usually say yes. It could be fabulous clothes, great hair, an unusual hat, lots of tattoos—whatever it is, they're likely to be proud of it. And that usually means they want to show it off and will happily pose for you.

Get your approach right

Know what you're going to say and how you're going to introduce yourself. Work out a patter, and be prepared to explain what you're doing. And remember, a bit of flattery works wonders. Keep it short, snappy, and confident. This isn't the time for your life story. And approach people from the front or side, not from the back, which could appear threatening.

Good light and background

Make an effort to get your subject in the best possible light and to find the most suitable backdrop.

Relax

Make sure you approach people in a warm, relaxed manner with a smile on your face. If you seem relaxed, they'll relax; if you seem nervous and shifty, they'll be starting to have doubts. Smiling is infectious, and this initial warmth will go a long way to getting a successful portrait.

Take your time and don't rush it

Take anything upward of 2 minutes, and in that time take a 10–12 (or more) shots. Sometimes you'll get the vibe that your subject is enjoying the experience, and they'd be happy to spend longer—and this is great.

Be generous

Offer to send the subject a copy of the image. It's a nice *quid pro quo* for their efforts.

Homeless or vulnerable people

Please don't ask them for portraits. They're having a tough enough time as it is, and someone sticking an expensive camera in their face isn't going to make their day any better.

Have some cards made

This will not only make you feel more authentic, but it's also a demonstration of your legitimacy as a photographer. The card can make the difference between acceptance and rejection.

For inspiration

Brandon Stanton, Joel Meyerowitz, and Bruce Gilden

7

SHOOT FILM

Despite the explosive advances in digital technology, film is making a big comeback, and there are plenty of compelling reasons why you should shoot film. Almost everyone who tries this finds it an enriching experience.

Shooting film is great fun, and it need not be expensive. For this assignment, all you need is an analogue camera (even an old one from a charity shop) and a few rolls of film. Aesthetically, film has a distinct look with rich tones, organic grain, and dynamic contrast that digital cameras often try to replicate, but can never quite match. Each film stock has its own personality, giving your street shots a signature feel.

Why you should do this:

- It slows you down and makes you think much more about what you're shooting. You will pay more attention to the composition, exposure, and focusing. You get a real sense that you're creating something just a little bit more special every time you press that button.

- If you shoot *only* film, your images will take on a consistent look. Film shooters tend to find one type of film they like and then stick with it.

- You will be more thoughtful when shooting, more conscious of your surroundings, and more in the zone. You'll also be more discerning about what to shoot, and will become more self-critical.

- Rather like learning theory in music, analogue photography will help you better understand the technical aspects of your camera. If you understand how emulsion reacts to light and how a darkroom works, if you get to grips with the nuances of different film stocks and speeds—all this will help your development as a photographer and pay dividends in your digital life.

"The negative is the equivalent of the composer's score, and the print the performance."
ANSEL ADAMS

Opposite: You don't need expensive equipment to do this. In many ways, the more basic the gear is, the better.

FIELD NOTES

Choose the right camera for you

Whether you spend $30 or $3,000, a whole new world will open up for you. Start small and, if you enjoy the experience, upgrade later. It doesn't matter whether you start with a compact camera, a rangefinder, an SLR, medium format, or even large format; the organic experience will be similar.

Experiment with different film stock

Try lots of different types of film to find out what works best for you. They produce widely varying results, and you'll probably gravitate towards a particular look. Personally, I like Kodak Tri-X for black and white (giving a contrasty, gritty look) and Portra 400 for colour (lovely, soft, natural, and warm tones).

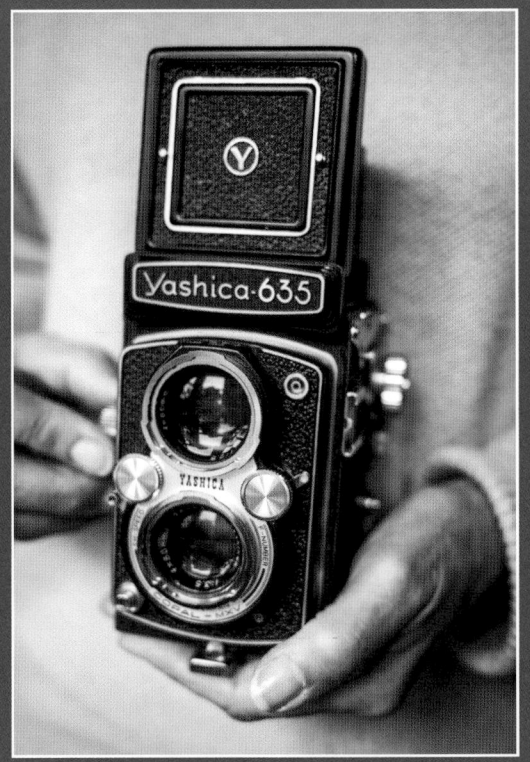

Learn how to meter the light

Whether you use the camera's built-in meter, a handheld meter, or just guesswork, just thinking about it will help you appreciate and understand how the light works and how it effects the emulsion.

Learn to focus quickly

This is an essential skill. Many people use zone focusing (preset your focus distance and aperture) for quick, sharp shots.

Work on your timing and anticipation

You should get used to pre-focusing and anticipating. Find an interesting scene, focus, then wait for the subject to enter the frame.

Developing, scanning, and printing

There are now many labs that will do this for you. However, many street photographers develop their own film (minimal kit needed), then scan the negative and make prints using a standard home printer. This way you still get many of the benefits of shooting film but without some of the drawbacks.

Enjoy the process

Analogue photography is about intentionality. Accept the delay, and relish the surprises and the serendipity that come your way. You'll make every frame count, thus making each shot more meaningful.

For inspiration

Garry Winogrand, Helen Levitt, Elliott Erwitt, Henri Cartier-Bresson, Saul Leiter, and Joel Meyerowitz

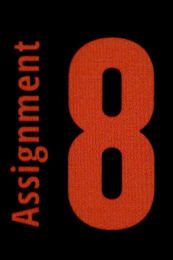
WITH A LITTLE HELP FROM GESTALT

Concerned that your photos look dull or uninspiring? It may be due to your brain failing to interpret content. Perhaps there is too much visual clutter, the colours don't work well together, or the subject isn't prominent enough. One way to solve these problems is by incorporating Gestalt theory into your compositional repertoire. Gestalt principles explain how visual perception works and why some images have more impact than others. Using Gestalt principles when taking a picture will create an easier-to-digest image. For this assignment, you need to learn the Gestalt principles and actively incorporate them into your images. Take two or three pictures that demonstrate the use of the principles below.

Why you should do this:

- You will create simpler and more impactful pictures because they are easier to understand.

- They will captivate and draw the viewer in, engaging them for longer (we should always strive for more dwell time).

- Images with layers are more complex and sophisticated.

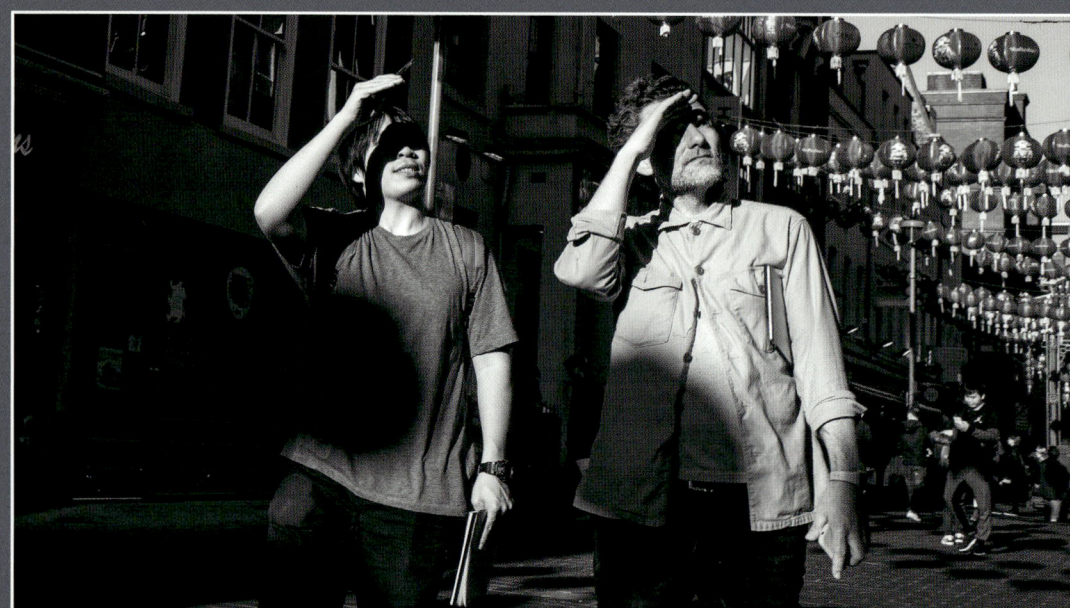

FIELD NOTES

Here are five relevant Gestalt principles to try:

Simplicity

Our brain tries to reduce an image to its simplest form. The law of simplicity says that it's important to simplify an image for the brain to feel comfortable interpreting the presented meaning. So, when you're looking at a scene, look for its simplest explanation to make it easy for the mind to digest. After a while, the mind will work harder to realize more complex meaning in the image.

Figure-to-ground ratio

This simply refers to the relationship between the subject (figure) and the background (ground). Sometimes you want to draw attention to your main subject, but the viewer can't see it clearly because the subject blends too easily into the background. The figure-to-ground principle helps explain which element will be perceived as the subject and which element will be the background. This principle is particularly effective when you are shooting in busy places like big cities, when it's difficult to isolate your subject from all the background noise. You can create a strong figure-to-ground ratio through the use of focus, contrast, or differences in colour.

Proximity

Elements close to each other are perceived as a group, so you can deliberately capture groups of people or objects arranged in a way that suggests relationships or interactions. So, if you want to consciously create a connection between two or more elements in an image, you can place them in close proximity to each other.

Common fate

The principle of common fate explains that visual elements that are moving together in the same direction will be perceived as part of a united group, and the other elements will be considered outsiders.

Similarity (or repetition)

We tend to perceive elements as belonging to the same group if they look alike. You can apply the principle of similarity using form, colour, size, texture, tone, or any other attribute. By using this principle, you can more easily make connections between unconnected elements.

For inspiration

Alex Webb, Harry Gruyaert, Constantine Manos, and the @streetrepeat Instagram account

Opposite: Street photographers love the concept of repetition, particularly when it relates to activity.

"Seeing is more than a physiological phenomenon. We see not only with our eyes but with our brains."

— DOROTHEA LANGE

9 EXPERIMENT WITH LAYERS

"Layers" refers to a compositional technique deployed at the picture-taking stage, not a post-production editing method. Alex Webb uses this technique, and many of his iconic images feature a strong foreground, middle ground, and background—each layer making an important contribution to the overall image. Embrace the concept of layers, and you'll find your images have greater complexity and depth, and they engage viewers longer.

Why you should do this:

- Layers add depth, volume, and complexity to your compositions.

- They will captivate and draw the viewer in, engaging them for longer (we should always strive for more dwell time).

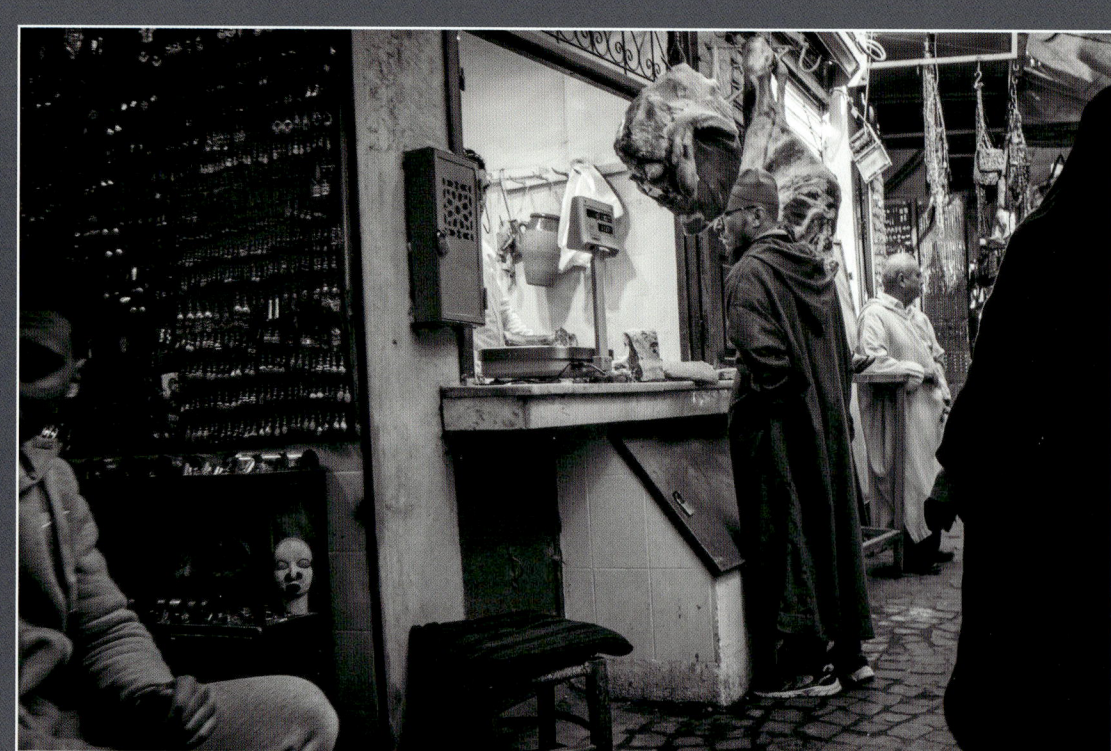

FIELD NOTES

Start with a foreground, middle ground, and background

The foreground could be in or out of focus and could contain objects such as people, cars, or something else close to you, all of which help frame your subject or add context. Place your primary subject in the middle ground—it's the main focal point of the image. The background could include elements that complement the story, such as buildings, distant figures, or walls.

Shoot wide

A wide-angle lens (between 24mm and 35mm) will capture more of the scene, allowing you to include multiple elements at different depths. Get closer to your foreground subject to exaggerate the sense of depth.

Choose the right aperture

Use a small aperture (f/8 or f/11) to keep all the layers in focus; if you want to isolate your subject, open up the aperture to blur the foreground and background whilst keeping the middle ground sharp (like Alex Webb).

Experiment with overlapping elements

Arrange different subjects in various parts of the frame to create a sense of interaction or juxtaposition. Avoid clutter by ensuring the layers don't blend into each other. Try to avoid overlapping people.

Use reflections

Puddles, shop windows, and even cars can create interesting secondary layers. (Sometimes it's best to use manual focusing when shooting reflections if the camera can't decide what to focus on.)

Experiment with light and shadow

Use light patterns to create layers, like sunlight filtering through gaps in buildings. Silhouettes in the foreground or background can add a dramatic layer.

Shoot through obstacles

Use foliage, brick walls, doorways, or windows to create framing and depth; such obstacles can act as a natural foreground layer.

For inspiration

Alex Webb, Harry Gruyaert, and Constantine Manos

Opposite: Crowded places like street markets offer good opportunities to create layers.

10 MAKE A ZINE

A zine (shortform for "magazine") is a booklet, often A5 size (but can be bigger or smaller) and usually containing between 18 and 48 pages. Zines are easy to make and cost-effective to have printed, and, as I've said elsewhere in this book, they are a great way to bring a project to life.

Zines have never been more popular, and if you haven't produced one before, now's your chance to jump right in! Whilst it's relatively straightforward to make a zine yourself (all you need is a decent printer and a sharp knife), I suggest you find a printing company in your area and have your first one professionally printed (you should be able to have them made for a few dollars each, depending on size and quantity ordered).

Why you should do this:

- Zines provide a physical showcase for your project. In the digital era, having a tangible version of your work makes it more impactful and your images take on a life beyond screens, allowing people to engage with them in a more intimate way.

- They provide an affordable and accessible output. Compared to photo-books, zines are cheaper to produce, easier to sell, and can reach a wider audience. You can sell it, trade it, or just give it away as a creative calling card.

- Zines will get your work out there, building exposure and getting your work in front of people. You might even make some money from it.

- You have complete creative freedom. Unlike Instagram, for example, a zine lets you curate a sequence of images, experiment with layouts, and tell a cohesive story without algorithms dictating visibility.

"A book forces you to be ruthless. You can't include everything— you have to shape a story, and that's the challenge."

MARTIN PARR

FIELD NOTES

Choose your project

It doesn't matter what it is or how many images it contains (but probably no more than 50–60), it just needs to be a cohesive body of work.

Curate and sequence

Select what you consider to be your best images, and don't be tempted to use filler. Less is more! Aim for a smooth visual flow throughout the zine. The sequence should be logical and should keep the viewer engaged.

Layout and design

Some zine printers have a drag-and-drop facility, making layout easy. If you're a little more design savvy, it's better to use something like Affinity Publisher or Adobe InDesign. Alternatively, you should be able to hire a local designer by the hour to get this absolutely spot-on. Ensure you have a striking cover image. Pages should be divisible by 4.

Decide on the format

The majority of photographers choose A5 (210 x 148mm), which can be either portrait or landscape orientation. It's perfectly reasonable to stray outside this common format, perhaps use A6, A4, or square.

Print and bind

Will you do this yourself at home of use a printing company? Popular choices for the latter include Blurb, Mixam, and The Newspaper Club.

There's nothing quite so satisfying as taking delivery of your first zine!

Distribution and promotion

Will you sell it or give it away? Many street photographers sell their zines from their Instagram page or website; others give them away to friends. You could also sell at camera club events, exhibitions, art fairs, and through your local bookshop. Set a price which covers your costs and which encourages purchases.

For inspiration

Zines from Café Royal Books, who have used the identical format for many years and who have produced hundreds of editions.

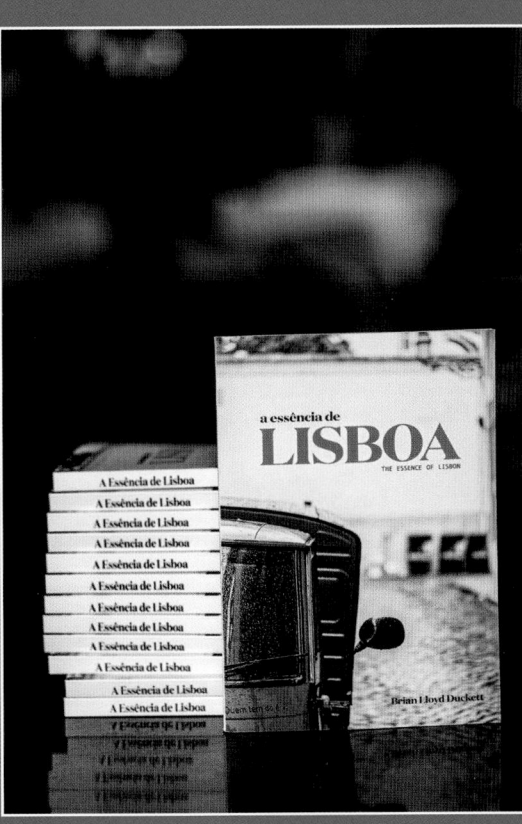

INDEX

200mm lens, 205
24mm lens, 205
28mm lens, 68–69, 205
35mm lens, 64–65
50mmn lens, 65, 125

A

accidental moment, 153
Adams, Ansel, 216
Adobe Lightroom, 5
aesthetics approach, 27, 208
AI, 11
algorithm, 188
Americans, The, 8, 24, 163
anticipation, 52, 85, 90, 217
Arbus, Diane, 8, 36
architectural photography, 109
archives, 42, 168
As Long as I Keep Busy, 173–174
assignments, 204–223
Atget, Eugène, 7
atmosphere, 18
authenticity, 14, 158, 180, 184

B

background, 131, 146, 221
Basketball Awareness Test, 82–83
Beckett, Samuel, 139
black and white, 132
books, 180, 189, 192–196
brand, 180–181
Brassaï, 8, 153, 213
Burn My Eye, 11
Buscató, Pau, 154

C

Camden Passage, 193–196
camera, 53, 58
camera, choosing a, 66–67
    articulating screen, 66–67
    battery life, 67
    durability, 67
    ergonomics, 66
    focusing options, 66
    image quality, 67
    lens options, 66

low–light, 67
operation speed, 66
portability, 66
stealth, 67
weather resistance, 67
weight, 66
camera bag, 69
camera settings, 72
candid, 12, 26, 95
Capa, Robert, 68, 124
Cartier–Bresson, Henri, 8, 20–21,
    25, 32, 36, 86, 89, 217
Case Study, 33–35, 171–174,
    193–196
cliché, 130
Cohen, Mark, 22, 40, 205
coincidence, 155
collective, 201–202
colour matching, 131
colours, 18
commentary, cultural and social,
    26, 100
common fears, see *fears*
communication, 180
compact camera, 60
competitions, 197
composition, 18, 29, 52, 125, 143
concentration, 127
confidence, 53
confrontation, 22, 103–104,
    117–118
connections, 93, 154
consent, 11, 99
content, 5, 7
contrast, 18, 28, 150

D

Davidson, Bruce, 10, 18
Death of Venice, The, 207
*Decisive Moment, The (Images à la
    Sauvette)*, 20
decisive moment, the, 8, 152
definition, street photography,
    5, 11
depth of field, 76–77
details, 91, 132

develop, 217
digital revolution, 10
diversification, 10
documentary photography, 9, 12,
    25, 210
Doisneau, Robert, 25
DSLR, 59–60

E

easy target, 107–109
editing, 126, 176
education, street photography, 3
Eggleston, William, 207
emotion, 18, 25
empathy, 95, 180
Erwitt, Elliott, 18, 21, 25, 32, 86,
    90, 137, 161, 217
ethics, 11, 22, 99
Evans, Walker, 36
everyday life, 48
evolution, 184
exhibitions, 180, 198–199
expectations, 53, 136
experimentation, 8, 32
exploitation, 9, 100
exposure settings, 72–76, 125
extrovert, 36

F

Facebook, 183
fears, 104–106
feedback, 32
Fellig, Arthur, 205
figure–to–ground ratio, 148, 219
film, 43, 61–62, 216
filters, 70
fishing, 27, 87, 89, 110, 117
flâneur, 7
flash, 70
Flickr, 10, 183
focus, 76–77, 125
followers, 185
foreground, 146, 221
framing, 52, 143, 209
Frank, Robert, 8, 24–25, 32, 163
Friedlander, Lee, 9, 36

G

gear, 69, 71, 139
geometric style, 30–31
    human interest, 31
    light and shadow, 31
    lines, 31
    negative space, 31
    patterns, 31
    perspective, 31
    reflections, 31
    shapes, 31
Gestalt principles, 147–148, 218
getting close, see *proximity to subject*
Gilden, Bruce, 10, 18, 20, 22, 36, 40, 70, 106, 161, 204–205, 215
globalization, 10
golden hour, 152
Goldin, Nan, 10
Goodwin, Neil, 171–174
Gruyaert, Harry, 13, 18, 28, 40, 161, 209, 219, 221
guidance, 3

H

Haas, 13, 109, 209
herd mentality, 126
Herzog, Fred, 207, 209, 211
hesitation, 128
high–contrast style, 18, 28, 150
Ho, Fan, 30, 32, 89, 109
homeless people, 131, 215
hotspot, 96–97
humanism, 8, 25, 180
humour, 21
hunting, 9, 87–88

I

Images à la Sauvette (The Decisive Moment), 20
iN–PUBLiC, 11, 202
inspiration, 40, 46, 165
Instagram, 5, 10, 180, 183–188
intention, 18
introvert, 36

J

JPEG, 75–76, 126
Johanson, Neil, 33–35
Jorgensen, Nils, 154
juxtaposition, 22, 154–155

K

Kar–wai, Wong, 40
Kertész, André, 7, 30, 207
Killip, Chris, 211
Klein, William, 8, 18, 20, 36, 95, 144
Koudelka, Josef, 8
Kubrick, Stanley, 40

L

Lange, Dorthea, 219
laws, 99–100, 119
layers, 145–146, 209, 220
leading lines, 143
Leica, 7, 10–11
Leiter, Saul, 13,18, 20, 27, 29, 32, 40, 42, 107, 207–209, 217
lenses, 63
    200mm lens, 205
    24mm lens, 205
    28mm lens, 68–69, 205
    35mm lens, 64–65
    50mm lens, 65, 125
    nifty fifty, 65
    prime lens, 63–64, 114,
    zoom lens, 63–64, 114
Levitt, Helen, 8, 86, 217
Light, 18, 28–29, 136
    dramatic contrast, 18, 28, 150
    low light, 18
    natural light, 18
    shadows, 18
    silhouettes, 18, 28–29, 84, 130, 150
light and shadow, 30–31, 84, 149, 221
Lightroom, see *Adobe Lightroom*
likes, 5
limited editions, 200
low-light shooting, 18
Lynch, David, 40

M

Maier, Vivian, 8, 32, 36, 161
Manos, Constantine, 28, 219, 221
McCullin, Don, 95, 211
medium format camera, 61
memory cards, 62, 76
Mermelstein, Jeff, 205
    metaphor, 29
metering, 75, 217
Meyerowitz, Joel, 9, 11, 21, 32, 36, 50, 83, 89, 115, 161, 207, 215, 217
    middleground, 146, 221
mindset, 81
mirrorless DSLR style, 59–60
mirrorless rangefinder camera, 58–59
mistakes, 123
monetization, 184
mood, 18, 29
Moriyama, Daido, 13, 18, 28, 95, 212–213, 144
motivation, 46–47

N

narrative, 24, 48, 164, 169, 180, 205
natural light, 18
neck strap, 70, 114
negative space, 30–31, 209
network, 183
nifty fifty, 65
night shooting, 212

O

observation, skills of, 52, 82–86, 206
observational approach, 20, 24
obstructions, 209, 221
On The Night Bus, 127
ordinary life, 13, 18, 29
Other Blackpool, The, 171–172

P

Paris After Dark, 8
Parke, Trent, 10, 18, 36
Parr, Martin, 10, 70, 222
Penn, Irving, 211
perfection, 95
peripheral vision, 84
personality type, 36, 106
perspective, 137
Petersen, Anders, 213
photo–potential zone, 90
photojournalism, 25
poetic style, 29
portraits, 12, 156–157, 214
post–production, 18, 28
practice, 120
presets, 5
prime lens, 63–64, 114
print sales, 199–200
printing, 217
privacy, 11, 100, 119
projects, 48, 161–176
    concept, 175
    editing, 176
    output, 176
    research, 175
    timeframe, 175
    synopsis, 175
    visualize, 176
proximity to subject, 124–125,
    204–205, 219

R

RAW, 75–76
reflections, 29, 31, 84, 213, 221
repetition, 155, 219
representation, 11, 100
rule of thirds, 143

S

Sandler, Richard, 205
scanning, 217
shadows, 18
shoot from the hip, 116, 137
shoot wide open, 125, 209
shutter speed, 125
silhouettes, 18, 28–29, 84,
    130, 150
similarity, 155, 219
simplicity, 147, 219
smartphones, 10, 63
    Smith, W. Eugene, 8
social media, 10, 180, 183,
    186, 201
spotlight effect, 150
Stanton, Brandon, 215
    stealthy, 114, 129
still life, street, 23, 206
strap, 70, 114
street performers, 130
street photography workshops,
    44–47
street portraits, see portraits
street still life 23, 206
Stuart, Matt, 154
style, 180–181
sunny days, 28
symbolism, 29
Szarkowski, John, 9

T

technical issues, 125
Threads, 183
timing, 52
tourist, 110
travel, 40–41
tropes, 130
Turpin, Nick, 109, 127, 202

U

umbrellas, 130
underexpose, 28, 152, 209
unplanned, 13
urban landscape, 109
urbanization, 8

V

Vero, 183
visualization, 85
Vohra, Vineet, 154
voice, 17–19, 31
voyeurism, 9

W

Wallace, Dougie, 36, 70
weather, 29
Webb, Alex, 10, 18, 28, 146, 162,
    220–221, 219
website, 180, 182
Weegee, 18, 36, 205, 213
windows, 213
Williams, Gary, 193–196
Winogrand, Garry, 9, 21–22, 32,
    58, 88, 161, 217
work ethic, 50
workshops, street photography,
    44–47
wrist strap, 70, 114

X

X, 183

Y

YouTube, 6, 183

Z

zines, 180, 189–192, 222–223
zone focusing, 77
zoom lens, 63–64, 114